International and Cross-Cultural
Management Research

SAGE SERIES IN MANAGEMENT RESEARCH

SERIES EDITORS

RICHARD THORPE
Department of Management
Manchester Metropolitan University

MARK EASTERBY-SMITH
Centre for the Study of Management Learning
The Management School, Lancaster University

The *Sage Series in Management Research* contains concise and accessible texts, written by internationally respected authors, on the theory and practice of management and organizational research. Each volume addresses a particular methodological approach or set of issues, providing the reader with more detailed discussion and analysis than can be found in most general management research texts. These books will be indispensable for academics, research students and managers undertaking research.

International and Cross-Cultural Management Research

Jean-Claude Usunier

SAGE Publications
London • Thousand Oaks • New Delhi

First published 1998

SAGE Publications Ltd
6 Bonhill Street
London EC2A 4PU

SAGE Publications Inc.
2455 Teller Road
Thousand Oaks, California 91320

SAGE Publications India Pvt Ltd
32, M-Block Market
Greater Kailash – I
New Delhi 110 048

British Library Cataloguing in Publication data

A catalogue record for this book is available from the British Library

ISBN 0 7619 5280 2
ISBN 0 7619 5281 0 (pbk)

Library of Congress catalog card number 98–60953

Typeset by M Rules
Printed in Great Britain by Biddles Ltd, Guildford, Surrey

Contents

List of figures and tables

Figures

Tables

Preface

This book covers the topics that are relevant to cross-cultural management research. It is aimed at management researchers who undertake projects with comparative and international designs involving culture as a key input for explanation. It is built on the view that language matters considerably, both English as it is the worldwide language of business, and foreign languages because they uniquely express culturally specific patterns in context-embedded situations, such as consumption or work relationships.

An underlying assumption of this book is that the final aim of cross-cultural research in business is not to find universals, in a fairly dichotomous way whether universal or culturally specific. The real world is more subtle: a lot is shared, especially since there is a dominant normative model for business activities worldwide. Cross-cultural research progressively increases our understanding of the influence of culture on management theories and practices and, consequently, helps define the kinds of compromises which can be negotiated and implemented when behavioural standards and management styles are obviously conflicting.

Although a consistent topic for the last twenty years, cross-cultural management research is still in its infancy. A possible reason is that researchers worldwide still do not adequately manage the cross-cultural dialogue which is acutely necessary for generating in-depth insights in the field. This dialogue implies full respect for the others' languages and cultures, be they informants or co-researchers. Despite the best intentions, this full-fledged dialogue remains difficult for those, including myself, whose native culture is near to the dominant values and practices of global business and management research. In this sense the process of cross-cultural research, which is most often limited to the contexts studied, should extend to the researchers themselves. It is only by a reflexive attitude vis-à-vis their own cultures that management researchers will be able to search for cross-cultural equivalence and uncover true areas of non-equivalence.

Another underlying assumption of this book is that, to increase the significance of findings in cross-cultural business research, we have to free ourselves as much as possible of the enduring, and obviously meaningful, opposition between the scientific cultures of 'number crunchers' and 'word lovers'. Generating meaning by both words and numbers is necessary, even though both approaches may at times be difficult to reconcile. That is why this book will not appear to most readers as clearly favouring a particular avenue for scientific inquiry. In my view, methodological pluralism makes much sense for cross-cultural business studies.

Chapter 1 offers a general view of international management research and progressively explains the methodological choices that can be made when cross-national comparisons are the privileged way of investigation; it offers insights on how culture can be defined and used in such research undertakings. Chapter 2 deals mostly with the researcher's own position vis-à-vis her terrain and topic, elaborating on ethnocentrism, prejudices, stereotypes, intellectual styles and the influence of language on cross-cultural research. Chapter 3 describes how cross-cultural management research should be designed, given the inherent complexity of such research undertakings: the necessary trade-offs involve research questions as well as substantive paradigms and data collection issues. Chapter 4 is entirely dedicated to the search for equivalence across cultural contexts with regard to concepts and theories used, measurement instruments and data collection procedures. The final chapter proposes some advice for increasing the relevance of cross-cultural research in terms of meaning. The whole book views the increase in shared meaning (commonly and similarly understood) across cultures as the strongest criteria of the significance of cross-cultural findings.

1
Introduction

Management has long remained ignorant of its roots. The universality of managerial theories and practices was unquestioned. Progressively, however, the diversity in management styles and decisional contexts has been affirmed, as well as the diverse paths to effectiveness which are evidenced by differences in the implementation of managerial decisions and the diversity in management styles (Laurent, 1983). The economic breakthrough of Asian countries has been a formidable engine for cross-cultural studies. In the mid-1960s, there was extensive pessimism about the future of Asia, considered as overpopulated and unable to achieve proper development. A book published in 1968 by Gunnar Myrdal, a Nobel Prize winner, was entitled *Asian Drama, an Enquiry into the Poverty of Nations*. This pessimistic view has been largely denied by facts. The different nature of Asian motivation and organization systems has drawn the attention to other recipes for success than those traditionally taught in the main American business schools.

In the words of Earley and Singh, the first research question for the international management researcher is often: 'How do they do things out there?' (1995, p. 327). Curiosity is a starting motive. Questions result from looking at how people do better: who are the more effective in production and/or sales; how do they manage to create more satisfaction for employees; how do they define and/or implement more adequate strategies, etc.? It also stems from problems specific to international business activities, in the area of foreign direct investment, export management, or expatriation, to name but a few. Fierce international competition has led to a search for the best practices worldwide. Initially, this quest was somewhat naive and more in-depth issues have been quickly addressed, such as the search for reasons for Japanese global success, the rationale for some nations performing better in particular industries, the issue of quality and quality management, or the criteria for best practices and the conditions for their transfer in different cultural contexts.

The complex implementation process of international management decisions has also been a driving force for the increasing literature in the field. Difficulties in constructing turnkey projects, negotiations with host country authorities, the management of joint ventures when partners belong to two different cultural settings, among other issues, have led to the following question: do differences in values, relational systems and attitudes towards individual and collective action make partially inappropriate the use of standard managerial practices, often imitated from a culturally dominant partner? This has led to addressing the issue of whether management science follows universal rules (Aharoni and Burton, 1994) and, consequently, whether or not culture is a determinant of management style.

This chapter starts with an overview of research in international management, describing the major issues addressed, and how they have changed over time, as well as the regional or national origin of the people involved, as researchers or informants. The second section offers a typology of research designs in international management and provides some basic insights into the role that culture may play. This leads to an examination of what kind of theories and paradigms serve for international and cross-cultural management research: a major choice in this book is to insist on the comparative research paradigm which underlies cross-cultural management research rather than on the substantive paradigms which are used as central explanation and most often borrowed from management or other major disciplines. The next step is to try and define culture by providing the reader with definitions of culture, highlighting the process and its significant components. How the construct of culture can be used in international research in management is then addressed. The last section of this chapter reviews some key empirical studies, based on ethnographic work or on survey data and gives a basic description of the most widely used empirical dimensions in cross-cultural management research, those of Hofstede (1980a, 1991, 1994b).

International research in management: an overview

International research in management has progressively developed over the last thirty years. A leading publication, *Journal of International Business Studies*, celebrated its twenty-fifth anniversary in 1994. Among the early topics, one of the most significant was the phenomenon of the internationalization of companies, especially export activities, foreign direct investment and the progressive emergence of multinational corporations. A large Harvard research project in the 1960s was dedicated to the study of multinational companies and led to some breakthrough articles such as Raymond Vernon's (1966) 'International Investment and International Trade in the Product Life Cycle'. As the title suggests, international management has largely come from international economics, and especially from the theory of international trade and investment, just as Eve came from Adam's rib. The paradigmatic focus has long been on why companies internationalize; why they choose such and such locations and/or modes of foreign operations, production and/or sales; and what are the steps in the gradual internationalization of businesses. John Dunning has been a major contributor with his 'eclectic paradigm' of international production (Dunning, 1980, 1988).

However, with a growing body of knowledge explaining why firms internationalize, there has been a need to investigate deeper into 'how' they do (or should do) it, with increased focus on tactical rather than strategic issues, functions rather than operations, and implementation rather than merely decision-oriented issues. A variety of research tracks has been elaborated by giving the international dimensions to existing research in the functional areas of business studies (accounting, finance, marketing, human resources management, operations and logistics), often by the means of replications in foreign contexts of published American research. Those who had originated the early bases of international business have been pleading for a more interdisciplinary approach (Dunning, 1989). This has resulted in

- a large diversity of topics covered, research in international business also being to a large extent the result of the internationalization of research in the various domains of management studies (see Table 1.1);
- an even greater diversity in the academic journals where research in international management is published (see Table 3.1).

International business issues have progressively expanded from the theory of internationalization of firms and foreign direct investment to, *inter alia*, export management (especially for medium and small firms), the relationships with host countries, and international business negotiations. More specialized topics have also been developed, some of which are quite typical of the international arena such as countertrade. The international dimension of functional areas has developed following the globalization of businesses and markets. Research in finance, for instance, has adopted a strong international dimension which is in line with the worldwide nature of financial markets, the global reach of telecommunications

Table 1.1 *Research issues addressed by* JIBS *articles over a 25 year-period*

Subdiscipline covered by *JIBS* articles over 25 years (1970–94)	Number
Theory of foreign direct investment and the multinational enterprise	98
Business strategy	90
International marketing management and strategy	80
Export/import: foreign entry modes	67
Cross-cultural management	65
International financial markets	61
International trade	60
Global competition and markets	60
International product/promotion/pricing/distribution strategy	57
Comparative management	54
Business/government interaction	53
Foreign exchange management	51
Inter-firm organizations (Joint ventures, alliances, networks)	41
Human resources (including personnel) management	41
Industrial organization	40
Decision-making structures, headquarters–subsidiary relationships	38
Foreign direct investment policy	38
Cost of capital and financial structure	37
Cross-national consumer and industrial behaviour	35
Management of risk	33
Investment appraisal	31
Economic development	30
Management and information systems (planning, strategy, control, information)	30
Research methodology in international business	30

Source: Inkpen and Beamish, 1994, pp. 711–12

technologies and the progressive deregulation of national stock markets. However, even when making international comparisons, research in finance never addresses the issue from a cultural perspective (see, for instance, Rajan and Zingales, 1995, comparing capital structure cross-nationally). Marketing has also strongly developed an international dimension, with typical research topics such as the issue of whether to standardize the marketing mix worldwide or to customize for local markets, or the influence of the country of origin on product and brand images.

Areas such as organization studies have been compelled to internationalize their research by the increased need to understand headquarters–subsidiary relationships and organizational issues in the multinational corporation. Human resources management and accounting are fields which depend quite largely on national legislation. Thus they have been somewhat slower to internationalize, although some typically international research issues have been the subject of much investigation (for example, in human resources management, the expatriation and management of overseas personnel; for a review, see Black et al., 1991). Until recently, accounting research was not very internationally oriented since accounting was almost purely based on national rules; it has now adopted an increasing international focus as a consequence of the international standardization of accounting. There is a consequent flow of research in comparative accounting (see for instance, Baydoun and Willett, 1995; Doupnik and Salter, 1995; Kantor et al., 1995).

Where does research in international business emanate from? It is overwhelmingly of North American origin which comes as no surprise. Because the *Journal of International Business Studies (JIBS)* covers all topics, it is a good indicator of what is researched by whom in international management. Table 1.2, building on data presented in the twenty-fifth anniversary special issue (Thomas et al., 1994) shows that 90.9 per cent of the authors for the twenty-four year period are North American. There is only slight change over time: North American authors average 93.5 per cent for the period 1970–73, and 88.5 per cent for the period 1986–93; Europeans count for 11.5 over the whole twenty-five year period while Asians account for 5.6 per cent. The journal is linked to an international academic association, the Academy of International Business which, although originally American, now has a worldwide readership. The reason for the relatively poor presence – as authors – of non-North Americans is surely not to be found in some sort of structural, ethnocentric prejudice of the journal against foreign authors. Several facts are probably revealed:

- the predominance of US universities in management research;
- the relative lack of international orientation of university research systems in many other countries;
- the relative under-investment in higher education and research in many countries in comparison to North America (a country like France invests in higher education – as a percentage of GNP – three times less than the USA);
- the language problems encountered by researchers from non-English-speaking countries when they have to write and publish their research in English.

Over time there has been slightly more diversity in the areas studied and relatively little change in the regions of origin of researchers. The single striking change concerns the rise of Asia, both as an area of study and as a place of origin for authors. The shift in the areas studied is very clear in relation to Asia (from 13.8 per cent to 32.8

per cent over the twenty-year period). Over the last twenty years Asian researchers have moved from a position of minimal input to occupy a significant place. This is evidence of the internationalization of management research. If one adds two other journals with an international management research orientation, *Management International Review* (a European publication) and *Columbia Journal of World Business*, the geographic distribution of authors and areas studied is in fact quite similar (Thomas et al., 1994, p. 683).

Table 1.2 *Areas studied and origin of authors for the 25-year period of the* JIBS

Continent	1970–73		1986–93		1970–93	
	Studied	Authors	Studied	Authors	Studied	Authors
North America	54.5	93.5	54.0	88.5	51.7	90.9
Europe	22.8	8.1	25.5	14.0	24.8	11.5
Asia	13.8	0.0	32.8	8.9	24.9	5.6
South America	12.2	0.0	8.1	1.7	8.3	1.0
Oceania	4.1	0.0	4.7	0.9	4.5	0.7
Africa	5.7	0.0	5.1	0.0	6.0	0.3

Source: Thomas et al., 1994, p. 682

An important fact about international management research is its diversity. The range of interested parties is quite disparate, for instance, compared to finance. Those interested in research results include companies, ranging from the large MNEs to highly specialized and internationalized SMEs, public authorities in charge of export trade promotion, or faculty members and higher education institutions that are striving to internationalize their curricula. International management research is not a unified body of knowledge. This is evidenced by the large number of academic associations and related journals where relevant international management research can be found (see, for instance, the citation of academic journals in *JIBS*; Chandy and Williams, 1994, p. 721; Table 3.1). Most of the international management research can be found in the general management literature; it does not remain the privilege of specialized 'international management scholars' who are generally not very territorial. However, they share a common field of investigation and the variety of research designs is not infinite.

Research designs: from international to cross-cultural management research

I have combined various typologies of international and/or cross-cultural management studies (Adler, 1983a, 1983b; Neghandi, 1983;

Adler and Doktor, 1989; Boyacigiller and Adler, 1991; Earley and Singh, 1995; Boyacigiller et al., 1996) with my own views to compose Table 1.3. The criteria are neither fully separated from each other, nor exhaustive; nor do they ensure the absence of overlap between categories. Most actual international management research uses mixed designs, if judged in terms of the categories outlined in Table 1.3. A first element of the distinctiveness of international and cross-cultural management research, compared to general management research, is that it systematically takes a broader view, considering different countries and their economic and social systems and extending the analysis further to cultural variables.

Table 1.3 *Main aspects of international management research designs*

Criteria	Type of international/cross-cultural management research studies
Type of issues	National versus international
Geographical focus	Country descriptive, foreign, cross-border, international, multinational
Researcher's orientation	Parochial, ethnocentric, polycentric, comparative, geocentric, culturally synergistic
Basic type of design	Comparative (cross-national/cross cultural) vs. interactive
Basic underlying model	Context/environment versus built-in/behavioural
Culture in the design	National versus cultural vs. 'multiple culture perspective'

The first criterion is whether the issue addressed by the researcher(s) is national versus international. A typically 'national' type of issue is pay and compensation systems and their influence on employees' motivation. This can further be studied at the comparative levels whether cross-nationally or cross-culturally. An example of a 'national' issue studied in a comparative way is offered by Kanungo and Wright (1983), who have studied managerial job attitudes in four countries (Canada, France, Japan and the UK), looking at the types of job outcomes sought by managers and finding finally that the preferred outcomes differed significantly across the countries surveyed. On the other hand, a typically 'international' issue in human resources management (HRM) is expatriate personnel or, for marketing, the choice of distribution channels in foreign countries and the management of relationships with foreign agents. Most accounting issues are national ones (for example, goodwill accounting), but some are typically international, such as the consolidation of accounts when a multinational company has hundreds of subsidiaries worldwide, or the reporting systems from foreign subsidiaries to headquarters.

Another significant factor of differentiation for international management research is whether the design describes a specific country (generally, that of the researcher), a 'foreign' country (generally foreign to the researcher), or if it is a cross-border, international or multinational study. Country-descriptive studies are centred on a specific country (often with a typically international focus), such as a study of the relationship between firm size and export intensity based on a large survey of Italian manufacturing firms (Bonnacorsi, 1992). A large number of these country specific studies are devoted to the special case of Japanese management (fifteen articles solely in the *JIBS*, for the period 1970–94). Country-centred research presents an implicit comparative design because the researcher tries to 'translate' a unique culture and its idiosyncratic management concept and practices for outside observers. Export management is of the second type, that is, foreign oriented. The exporter's country is the focus (subject) whereas the target countries are objects, and as such are denominated 'foreign'. Cross-border designs comprise two or more countries which do not necessarily share a common border, when none of them is considered foreign. Many studies have such a two-country design, comparing or describing an interaction such as the study of US–Japanese business negotiations . This type of design is facilitated when the two countries are geographically near and/or co-operation prone (US–Canada, France–Germany, etc.). International studies consider many countries but are generally limited to one major regional area such as intra-European research. Finally, multinational research includes quite a large number of countries taken from different areas of the world and the major cultural and geographic areas are represented.

A second element of distinctiveness of international and cross-cultural management research is that research has a 'home country', generally that of the researcher, who, as we will show in subsequent chapters, plays a central role in the design of international management research. The origin of the theories used as well as the context to which they apply are also key determinants of the research design. These three criteria can be combined in the (hypothetical) example of a Japanese management researcher applying US theories to an African country. Adler (1983a) has produced a typology of management studies which, although intended for describing cross-cultural management research, applies in fact to all international management research. Her typology stresses the researcher's own orientation towards reality and interpretive frames and the degree of openness to foreign fields of experience, theories and interpretations. According to Adler (1983a, pp. 31–2), parochial studies are based in the USA and conducted by Americans. This concept of parochialism in research extends naturally to any country with a fairly large population and a significant economic and intellectual base (for example, Britain, France, Germany, Italy, Japan). Researchers from smaller countries cannot indulge so easily in parochialism because their 'parish' would be too small. In Adler's second category, 'ethnocentric studies', researchers attempt to replicate American management research in foreign countries. Polycentric studies focus on describing, explaining and interpreting the patterns of management in foreign countries. Comparative management tries to identify similarities and differences in organizations and management across cultures. The fifth type, geocentric studies, focuses on studying organizations that work in more than one culture and tries to identify similarities which will allow multinational companies to unify their management systems for worldwide operations. The last approach, and according to Adler the least common, culturally synergistic studies, focuses on cross-cultural interaction and tries to build on both cultural similarities and differences to create organizational processes which offer worldwide relevance and can be tailored to local specificity.

An important aspect of the design is whether the research focuses on comparing or on observing interactions between people or organizations from differing cultures. The term 'cross-cultural' is often used as a general category for both. However, it makes considerable sense to distinguish between 'cross-cultural' and 'intercultural' approaches to management research. A cross-cultural approach proceeds by comparing national management systems and local business customs in various countries. It aims to emphasize what is country specific and what is universal. Such an approach is essential for the preparation and implementation of management decisions in different national contexts. An intercultural approach is centred on the study of interaction between business people, organizations, buyers and sellers, employees and managers, who have different national/cultural backgrounds. In the words addressed by Adler et al. to cross-cultural management researchers: 'Interaction, not merely comparison, is the essence of most managerial action' (quoted in Boyacigiller et al. 1996, p. 169). Interactive research can be viewed as between or within individuals. Razzouk and Masters (1985) for instance study cultural marginality in the Arab world, that is, the fact of belonging to two cultures, the Arab culture and the culture of a former colonial power, generally France or England, without being able to identify oneself completely with either, which is a within-individual, intercultural issue. These authors also outline the implications of Arab cultural marginality for western marketers who sell and negotiate in Arab countries, that is, a between-individuals, intercultural interaction.

The question of whether a research design is comparative or interactive is not as simple as it may originally appear. First, the comparative dimension is always present, even if implicit. In an early study about international business research Nehrt et al. (1970) exclude from their scope studies of business activities in given foreign countries. They take the example of a study of marketing channels in Turkey and argue that, whether it is carried out by an American, French or Turkish professor, it is still a study about domestic business in Turkey. However, the study done by the American or French researchers will always be comparative, because they will refer spontaneously to their own context and experience, if not explicitly at least implicitly. When undertaken by a researcher, foreign to the context studied, the study obviously belongs to international management research. Second, the interactive dimension can be located at various levels. If not located at the individual level (negotiations), it can involve organizations from different cultures, or a firm and the host country authorities. Interactions can be also thought of as one-way (as in the literature on technology transfer) or as a reciprocal process. The transfer of management knowledge is an example where interaction can be thought of as unidirectional or multidirectional. As emphasized by Neghandi (1983, p. 23): 'We need to conceive the transfer process [of management knowledge] in multiple directions – from the U.S. to other developed countries and vice-versa, from the U.S. to Japan and Japan to the U.S., and from developed countries to developing countries and vice-versa.'

Another important difference in international management research designs is whether they see the variations across national contexts as being constructed mostly in different environments (economic, social, political) or as built into people's and organizations' behaviour. In an early text on the construct of comparative marketing research Boddewyn (1966, p. 149), stresses that the 'marketing environment has various physical, economic, political, social and cultural dimensions, that interact with marketing's actors, processes, structures and functions in many direct and indirect ways', and remarks that 'while comparative studies are somewhat precariously balanced between marketing itself and its environment, one must be careful not to throw out the marketing "baby" with the environmental "bath", or smother it in a "blanket" of social context'. Whether to assign variables and their differences across nations to context/environment or to behaviour/people and organizations, is an important choice in international management research. A typical contrast between context versus behaviour orientation would be rendered by such alternative hypothetical titles as 'consumer market environment in the Middle East' versus 'the Middle Eastern consumer'.

The last distinction in Table 1.3 deals with how culture is integrated in the research design, which is often by a simple assimilation of countries to culture. The expression 'cross-cultural' is used instead of 'cross-national' because countries, USA, Japan, Germany, etc., are treated as surrogates of cultures. The cross-cultural perspective tries to give culture its full significance. While generally using national culture as its main explanatory variable, it avoids equating countries to cultures. The approach where other sources of culture may intervene (stemming from industry, education, and so on) has been termed the 'multiple culture perspective' by Boyacigiller et al.:

> Researchers holding this conceptual perspective believe that any and all of these types of cultural groupings may exist and coexist within an organizational setting. That is, organizations and the people who compose them, do not carry one specific culture (e.g. national culture); instead they are embedded in a pluralistic culture context . . . This precludes, then, the strong and purposeful focus on national culture as the cultural grouping of *certain relevance* to the organization (as assumed in cross-national intercultural interaction research) and as a culture of *permanent identity* for the individual (as assumed in cross-national comparative research). (Boyacigiller et al., 1996, pp. 183–4)

Theories and paradigms underlying international and cross-cultural management research

There are two kinds of paradigm used by management research: substantive and research paradigms. While substantive paradigms are broad explanatory frameworks which privilege a certain way of seeing the issue, the research paradigm deals with how research should be conducted on this precise issue. There are obviously some linkages between both. That the earth is flat or that the sun revolves around the earth are substantive paradigms; similarly for management, that products go through a life cycle leading to their decline and death is a substantive paradigm. We will start with substantive paradigms and then describe some research paradigms.

Substantive paradigms
Most of the paradigms used in international management research are borrowed from other fields of management and from general

disciplines such as economics, organization theory, psychology, etc. For instance, when Kanungo and Wright (1983) compared managerial job attitudes in Canada, France, Japan and the UK they used the framework of Lawler (1973) which divides job outcomes into two broad categories, intrinsic and extrinsic job outcomes. The first outcomes comprise internally mediated rewards such as responsibility, autonomy, a sense of achievement and the interesting nature of the manager's job. Extrinsic outcomes are more tangible and external, comprising salary, fringe benefits, job security, status, and so on. An international management researcher who privileges a cross-cultural perspective will typically wonder whether this intrinsic/extrinsic model of job outcomes is applicable to Japan, and to Confucianist countries in general(see Kawabuko, 1987).

There are also paradigms specific to the field of international management such as the theories of internationalization of the firm, for instance, the international product life cycle theory (Vernon, 1966) or the eclectic theory of international production (Dunning, 1980, 1988). These dominant paradigms are at some moment challenged by alternative paradigms such as that which describes internationalization as a knowledge development process (Johanson and Vahlne, 1977) rather than as a resource allocation process as in traditional paradigms. Some areas have specific theories which are ad hoc conceptualizations, for instance, the U-curve describing the modalities of the expatriate's adjustment to the host country over time. This is globally supported by empirical studies, but without all the results being in clear favour of it (Black and Mendenhall, 1991). This curve plots the degree of adjustment against the duration of stay. The expatriate typically starts at a somewhat misleading stage called 'honeymoon' which corresponds to the pleasant discovery of new places, new people, with amazement at experiencing an exotic culture. Then comes a phase where the discovery of the new culture leads to culture shock; the perceived degree of adjustment will diminish. Finally, in the third phase the expatriate gradually adjusts.

Compared to other fields of management or disciplines like law or economics, international management has really few specific substantive paradigms. Paradigms non-specific to the field are used in most areas, especially in functional areas such as international finance or international marketing. Quite often, existing theoretical frameworks that have been developed from a domestic context, generally the USA, are applied to other countries and contexts. Theories which are popular among international management researchers include agency theory, property rights, transaction costs theory. Finally, a number of studies have no specific paradigm and propose multifaceted research that shares the international markets as common focus, for example, research about the efficiency of export trade promotion systems.

The cross-cultural approach as a key research paradigm
A Delphi survey organized by Nehrt et al. (1970) cited cross-cultural organization studies as only one avenue among thirty-two main tracks for future research in international business. In fact, a new paradigm has emerged during the 1970s and 1980s which questions the transferability of management systems across cultural contexts. Haire et al. (1966), in their cross-national study of managerial thinking, and Hofstede (1980a, 1980b) were among the first to address the issue with full explicitness. The cross-cultural research track is both a substantive paradigm, because it presupposes that culture is a major explanatory variable for values, organizational behaviour and practices, and a research paradigm because it entails a definite form of questioning which will be expounded throughout this book. Cross-cultural researchers put into perspective the research issues, theories and instruments with the researcher and researched being part of the process. The only research paradigm which is distinctively specific to the international domain is the comparative/cross-cultural one, because it seeks to build on the comparative study of in-depth differences across nations and cultures in order to generate new conceptual insights and to broaden concepts.

However, cross-cultural management research is a significant but minority track among international management researchers. In Adler's (1983b) study of management literature from 1971 to 1980 she identifies only 4.2 per cent of cross-cultural management articles out of 11,219 articles in twenty-four journals. This relative weakness of cross-cultural studies in management has remained true from 1980 to now as shown in the tables above. Among the most cited *JIBS* articles for the period from 1984 to 1993, only three cross-cultural articles appear (Chandy and Williams, 1994, pp. 725–6) among the thirty-six most cited articles; furthermore, they pertain to a special issue of the journal dedicated to cross-cultural management.

The cross-cultural approach is a branch of comparative management which takes culture as its prominent explanatory variable, making it a distinct avenue in management research. The cross-cultural branch of comparative management has grown so quickly over the last twenty years that it now tends to overshadow it. The broad question is the same: why are there such differences in economic efficiency and level of development across countries? The initial response to this question was basically economic. Harbison and Myers (1959) have argued that each society changes progressively from agrarian–feudal towards an industrial and democratic society. For them, a specific management philosophy is associated with each of the successive steps of development and all societies converge towards a participative philosophy of management (that is, McGregor's, 1960, theory Y as opposed to theory X). This universalist vision of management emphasizes the inevitable application, in the long run, of the same management methods to all organizations in all cultures. It is underlain by a strong cultural convergence assumption. Farmer and Richman (1965) have proposed to take other factors into account and to consider that managerial effectiveness was a function of external factors such as the sociocultural, political and legal environment, economic as well as educational systems. This approach privileged external explanatory variables and largely ignored those related to the internal working of organizations. Empirical testing of this track proved unsatisfactory (Nath, 1988).

Little by little the universalist vision of management has been challenged. The Farmer–Richman model identified culture as a dependent variable, whereas the Neghandi–Prasad model (1971) identified culture as an independent variable; alongside environmental factors, Neghandi and Prasad view culture as being a key determinant of managerial practices and effectiveness. Kelley and Worthley (1981) have tested both theories with American and Japanese subjects, using Caucasian Americans, Japanese Americans and Japanese managers, each of these groups sharing either sociopolitical environment or culture. Their findings support the role of culture in the formation of managerial attitudes. In a further empirical study involving a five-culture design (Japanese, Chinese, Mexican, Hispanic-American and Anglo-American managers) Kelley et al. (1987) conclude that 'this study suggests that the question is not whether management attitudes are a function of culture, but rather which attitudes correspond with which culture' (p. 29). A behavioural approach to cross-cultural management research has consequently developed, with less macroscopic focus, which is centred on the study of individuals and organizations, on attitudes, beliefs and value systems. During the process the comparative management track went away from the economic or socio-political paradigms and focused more and more explicitly on the cultural variable, emphasizing national culture, but without ignoring the existence of corporate culture (Derr and Laurent, 1989). Haire et al. (1966) produced one of the founding studies of the cross-national/cross-cultural management track, which evidences significant cross-national differences in attitudes and perceptions of managers towards key concepts and activities of management. Other significant studies are reported in Bhagat et al. (1990) and Punnett and Shenkar (1996).

The intercultural approach is both an outlet for and a complement to the cross-cultural perspective: comparison across cultures helps to calibrate one's values against those of others, and finally to negotiate a common solution. Such situations are quite frequent in the real world of international business and add relevance to research undertakings such as the study of the relationships between subsidiaries and headquarters within culturally diverse multinational companies or business negotiations between people from different cultures where intercultural interactions can be somewhat problematic (Ghauri and Usunier, 1996).

This books centres particularly on comparative/interactive research designs in international management, based on culture. Most research in international management does not take into account cross-national/cross-cultural differences and shall be considered as research in management which has the international dimension but should be treated from a methodological point of view as it is in the original domain (finance, organization, etc.). The next step is to define culture and its place in cross-cultural management research.

Defining culture for international management research

Culture can be defined in various ways, as a 'collective mental programme' (Hofstede, 1980b), a shared system of representations and meaning (Goodenough, 1971; Geertz, 1983), or as basic assumptions or value orientations (Kluckhohn and Strodtbeck, 1961) on the nature of man's relationships to nature and to other human beings (for a review of the definitions of culture, see Usunier, 1996). When researchers speak about cultures they often relate it to countries or to a significant group of countries (western countries, Latin countries, Arabic countries). The latent confusion between cross-national and cross-cultural may lead to research confusion, to which we will return. The reality is fortunately more complex: certain countries comprise diverse cultures, while corporate and other sources of culture such as education, religion and language contribute to build the full cultural background of each individual.

Culture can be considered as learned and forgotten norms and behavioural patterns. Sometimes, culture has a reputation for being rather vague, for being a somewhat 'blurred' concept. The Swedish writer Selma Lagerlöf (Petit, 1960, p. 100) defines culture as 'what remains when that which has been learned is entirely forgotten'. Depicted thus, culture may appear as a 'synthesis variable', serving when more precise concepts or theories have either proved unsuccessful or need to be linked together. It would also serve as an explanatory variable for residuals, when other more operative explanations have proved unsuccessful. Nevertheless, Lagerlöf's definition does have the important merit of identifying two basic elements of cultural dynamics (at the individual level, because individuals are the carriers of culture): (a) it is learned; (b) it is forgotten, in the sense that people are largely unconscious of its existence as learned behaviour. For example, being modest and self-effacing is a cultural norm in most Asian cultures, but Asian people forget about this and are easily shocked by what they consider as overly assertive and apparently boastful behaviour in other cultures. Although largely forgotten, culture is present throughout our daily individual and collective actions. It is oriented towards adaptation to reality, both as constraints and opportunities. Since culture is 'forgotten', it is mostly unconsciously embedded in individual and collective behaviour, in situations and institutions. Individuals find within their cultural group pre-set and agreed upon solutions which indicate how properly to articulate their behaviour and actions with members of the same cultural grouping.

Culture can also be defined as a system of meaning shared by individuals. Thus, Goffman (1974, p. 14) indicated that: 'Culture concerns systems of meaning, ideas and patterns of thought. It represents more a model *for* the behaviour of members of a given group than a model *of* their behaviour' (quoted by Van Maanen and Laurent, 1992, p. 276). Culture has been defined extensively because it is somewhat all-encompassing. Having assessed its nature as learned and forgotten, we need to provide some additional definitions of culture. Ralph Linton (1945, p. 21), for instance, stressed that it is shared and transmitted: 'A culture is the configuration of learned behaviour and results of behaviour whose component elements are shared and transmitted by the members of a particular society.' However, we should not go too far in considering the individual as simply programmed by culture. At a previous point in his landmark book, *The Cultural Background of Personality*, Linton had clearly indicated the limits of the cultural programming which a society can impose on an individual: 'No matter how carefully the individual has been trained or how successful his conditioning has been, he remains a distinct organism with his own needs and with capacities for independent thought, feeling and action. Moreover he retains a considerable degree of individuality' (1945, pp. 14–15).

Culture can be viewed as a set of beliefs or standards, shared by a group of people, which help the individual to decide what is, what can be, how one feels about it, what to do, and how to go about doing it (Goodenough, 1971). On the basis of this operational definition of culture, there is no longer any reason why it should be equated with the whole of one particular society. It may be more related to activities that are shared by a definite group of people. Consequently, individuals may share different cultures with several different groups – a corporate culture with colleagues at work, an educational culture with other MBA graduates, an ethnic culture with people of the same ethnic origin. When in a particular situation, they will switch into the culture that is operational. In this context the term 'operational' implies that a culture must be shared with those with whom there must be co-operation, and that it must be suitable for the task. This is, of course, subject to the overriding condition that this culture has been correctly internalized during past experiences, that it is so well learned that it can be forgotten. The operational culture approach, very much akin to a 'multiple culture perspective' (Boyacigiller et al., 1996), does have the advantage of clearly highlighting the multicultural nature of many individuals in today's societies, including binationals, multilingual people and those who have an international professional culture or are influenced as employees by the corporate culture of a multinational company.

Significant components of culture

Baligh (1994) defines culture as a set of components, concept of truth, basic beliefs and values, and argues for a fit between culture and the organizational structure, based on a logical connection between these components and the chosen structure. Some large cultural categories, neither fully exclusive nor completely exhaustive, can be found in the literature (see, for instance, Triandis, 1994); they cover most of the elements of cultural differentiation. The following are some significant components of culture that have an impact on international management research which are illustrated by examples throughout the book.

Relationships (relational patterns) These concern how the individual relates to the group(s); what the dominant family and kinship patterns are; and how relationships are framed (individualism/collectivism, patronage relationships). In anthropological research, relational patterns make sense because they are related to territoriality, kinship, etc. (Chapman, 1992). Relational patterns affect international cross-cultural management research through the style of interaction between people, their decision-making process, and the way in which they mix human relationships and business matters. Contrasts between the more organic societies (collectivistic) and the more independent and atomized societies (individualistic) can be used for studying such diverse topics as influence processes in buyer–seller relationships, bribery, industrial marketing, relationships with host government, or importing agents (Kale and McIntyre, 1991).

Language and communication   How people communicate (that is, both emit and receive messages) and the influence of their native language on their world views and attitudes directly affect international business. The implementation of business requires that partners write contracts in a foreign language, use interpreters, try to express ideas and concepts which may be unique in a particular language, etc. (Glenn, 1981). They have to communicate despite different native languages and communication styles   such as high context versus low context (Hall, 1959, 1976), or diffuse or specific communication styles (Trompenaars, 1993). Language is especially important for interactive cultural research. It can be seen as influencing the whole research process, including the researcher, the researched field, and the ways in which to address issues and to collect data. Its place in the research process is examined in Chapters 2, 4, and 5. Language may be a negligible or an important element of the research paradigm, according to whether one considers it simply as a 'technical' issue, involving the mere search for translation equivalence, or as shaping the individual and collective world views of those who speak a particular language, in which case it becomes a key concern in the research process.

Institutional and legal systems   Differences in legal systems, contractual formalism and recourse to litigation, express contrasts in how societies are organized in terms of rules and decision-making systems, to what extent they accept display conflicts, and the ways and means to solve them. The modalities of contract enforcement, for instance, vary across culture (Choi, 1994). The level of formality in addressing public and private issues in any kind of negotiated intercultural partnership, including the discussion of joint-venture contracts, the registration of subsidiaries and sensitive issues with the public authorities of the host country, reflects different conceptions of institutional and legal systems. For instance, Kantor et al. (1995) studied financial reporting practices in Egypt, Saudi Arabia and the United Arab Emirates, and showed that Arab countries tend to follow the French rather than the Anglo-Saxon model, that is, with much less accounting information being publicly disclosed. This is due to an early adoption by Egypt of the Napoleonic code and the transfer of corresponding practices to neighbouring countries.

Values and value systems   The prevailing values in a particular society and the extent to which they are respected in the everyday behaviour of individuals, are important because they may impinge on the willingness to take risks, on leadership styles, and on the relationships between superiors and subordinates. Numerous studies in the cross-cultural management literature have been based on values, basic assumptions or value orientations. For instance, the influence of religious assumptions on the degree of fatalism is worth examination because it conditions the inclination to retain control over one's environment, together with attitudes towards managerial action (see the literature on Arab and Muslim entrepreneurs and managers, for example, Baligh, 1991; Ali, 1993, 1995; Ali and Wahabi, 1995; Bakhtari, 1995; and for other cultural areas, Berger, 1991). Values have also been studied cross-culturally by international replication of well-known American lists of values, such as the Rokeach values, the list of values inventory of Kahle (LOV), or the VALS values and lifestyles scale (Grunert et al., 1993). Certain values have been derived from multinational studies such as Hofstede's (1980a, 1980b) classical study of work-related values, which was further extended by taking into account Confucianist values (Hofstede and Bond, 1984, 1988; Chinese Culture Connection, 1987).

Time orientations   Time is a prominent variable in management, for planning, strategy, for synchronizing people at work, etc. Cultural attitudes towards time shape the way in which people structure their actions. This pervasive influence is reflected in punctuality in everyday management behaviour which probably appears as the most visible consequence. Yet differences in time orientation, especially toward the future, are more important as they affect long-range issues such as the strategic framework of decision-making or the trade-offs made by organizations between long-term company value and short-term profitability. Differences in the patterning of time include the dominant model of time (linear versus cyclical), the nature and degree of temporal orientations to the past, present and future (Hay and Usunier, 1993), and the way to schedule activities according to time and people (monochronism versus polychronism; Hall, 1983). Cross-cultural studies are increasingly carried out to understand how cultural concepts of time impact upon a variety of management behaviours (Bluedorn and Denhardt, 1988; Usunier, 1991).

Mindsets   These are mental maps and structures which correspond to a certain type of world view (*Weltanschauung*), linked in particular to the language structure, a facet of culture generally neglected by both international and cross-cultural management researchers. Whether called 'mindsets' (Fisher, 1988) or 'intellectual styles' (Galtung, 1981), they reflect major contrasts in the way people address issues, according to whether they prefer to rely on data, ideas, speech, or a combination, and how they relate words to emotions and actions. Mindsets influence ways of addressing issues, collecting information, choosing the relevant pieces of information and assessing their 'truthfulness', so that finally they influence organizational processes, decisions and their implementation. The differential emphasis across cultures, on the left brain (personal, diffuse, affective, intuitive, synthetic) versus the right brain (impersonal, specific, neutral, rational, analytical), has been developed as a broad contrast hypothesis that would serve to explain why organizations are managed quite differently (Trompenaars, 1981, 1993; Hampden-Turner, 1991.

The construct of culture in cross-cultural management research

How the construct of culture is used in international management research is both a question of research philosophy and a practical and operational issue. A key assumption is whether knowledge is universal or relative. A related assumption is whether management practices and knowledge are context embedded or context free. If the researcher's view is that management knowledge is universal and context free, then the use of culture in international management research designs makes little sense. If she thinks in relative and contingent terms of a local knowledge, embedded in local ways of doing things, it is still not enough to justify the use of the culture construct. The researcher has still to decide, even implicitly, about the issue of whether cultures converge or not, and at which pace. The cross-cultural study of management and marketing issues assumes that convergence will be slow so that research findings can hold true for a long period of time. The profound impact of technology on culture cannot be ignored, and many new facets of the world's cultures are the products of social adaptation to new technologies. Many cultural assumptions can be termed 'modern', such as the master of destiny orientation or individualism. Conversely, their contrast, fatalism and collectivism, would naturally be meant as 'traditional' value orientations. The real world is more sophisticated: individualism is globally 'modern', but collectivism is not 'traditional' or even 'conservative'. Many collectivist nations, especially in Asia, have been brilliant achievers over the last twenty years. 'Modern culture' is predominantly based on western values, those held by philosophers, scientists and politicians in England, France and other European countries, during the period when they experienced industrial revolution and colonized other people, and later by the USA, as the dominant political and cultural actor on the twentieth-century world scene. The influence of a cultural assumption being considered as 'modern' is that it is more legitimate, sometimes to the extent that it is officially considered as the only possible belief. Thus other assumptions tend to be repressed, leading to complex situations where people finally imitate behaviour which does not correspond to the assumptions really prevailing in their culture.

Viewing culture as marked by times, rather than simply as a marker of spatially distributed groups, is natural. Migrations, ethnic minorities and assimilation processes have led to a complex world, where the borders of culture often cross the individuals themselves. Ethnic subcultures are based on shared belief and habits and the sense of belonging to a specific group of people, different from the society at large. Ingroup orientation is central in ethnicity, but to a large extent the sense of belonging to the subcultural community is thwarted by the necessary and difficult identification with the values and behaviour of the dominant ingroup. Ethnicity is a matter of shared belief about a common descent but since ethnic belonging in the immigration country is cut off from the territory and people where the culture really originated, people often maintain the subculture by the means of ethnic stereotyping. Assimilation takes place when the relative influence of the culture of origin diminishes while immigrants hold faster to the values and behaviours of the country of residence. The process of assimilation, a lengthy one which may require several generations to be fully accomplished, is evidenced in the areas of consumption patterns, employment, marriage with people originating from the host culture, participation in the political process as a candidate, acquaintances outside the ethnic community. Despite some assimilation there is a resurgence of ethnicity as a claim for identity; as Bouchet (1995) explains, ethnicity has much to do with the evolution of identity in general, rather than with the origin of one's historical identity. Ethnicity and individualization in present societies have led to the emergence of a postmodern culture, where the movement of globalization is paradoxically accompanied by fragmentation and singularization, especially in the area of consumption (Firat, 1995).

Thus, culture can be considered and used in many different ways by cross-cultural management researchers. Van Maanen and Laurent (1992), distinguish between culture seen as a process or as a product. The first view, that of a process, is derived from anthropology and sociology. It sees culture as codes of conduct embedded in or constitutive of the social life of a given group; researchers who follow this paradigm will speak of the culture of a nation, a tribe, a corporation, etc. On the other hand, culture can be seen as a product, an approach familiar to the humanities and literary criticism which see culture as the result of individual or group activities that carry distinct symbolic properties (ibid., p. 277), thus looking, with various interpretive approaches, at how culturally coded signs appear in the products of the media, advertising, fashion, movies, etc. Most approaches of culture in the cross-cultural management literature consider it as a process.

The important question is not so much what culture is, or what cultures are, than why is it important and what does it impact on. The definition of culture leads to significant methodological choices. The first option is to see culture as nothing: most of the international management research literature considers culture as irrelevant because management theories and practices are assumed universal and context free, which in some cases makes sense. A second option is to consider culture as a residual explanation when (almost) all possible explanatory tracks have been used. In a third option, culture can also be viewed as a programme: every individual in the same cultural grouping is supposed to be influenced in the same way. It leads to the study of groups as mean individuals who are supposed to display on average the modal characteristic of a given culture because they have been programmed in the same way (Hofstede, 1980b, 1991). Rather than a complete programme, culture can be seen as shared meaning on quite specific segments. As suggested by McCracken (1991, p. 5), in the case of consumer behaviour: 'We may see consumer goods as the vehicles of cultural meanings . . . consumers themselves as more or less sophisticated choosers and users of these cultural meanings.' Consumers buy meanings and marketers communicate meanings through products and advertisements. Many of these meanings are culture based, they are intersubjectively shared by a social group (D'Andrade,

1987). Intersubjective sharing of meanings implies that each person in the group knows that everyone else is aware of the cognitive schema. Therefore, in the process of exchange through superior–subordinate interactions or buyer–seller relations, marketing communications or product consumption, interpretations are made spontaneously, as if they were obvious facts of the world, and a great deal of information in the process of exchange and communication need not be made explicit. Culture may be considered in this fourth option as a *metalanguage* which is central in a business process viewed as exchange and communication. It works as a kind of *game rule*, a role play, indicating how people will interact in an exchange relationship, their constraints and their leeway for behaviour and decisions.

Several choices can be made simultaneously. As already discussed in the framework of Table 1.3, culture can be considered as influencing the researched field only; part of the cross-cultural literature considers 'foreign' informants as the sole carriers of culture. A different position is to wonder whether the researcher is influenced by her culture, and part of the cross-cultural management literature now extends the cultural questioning to the researcher herself. The search for cross-cultural equivalence described in Chapter 4 and the self-questioning orientation described in Chapters 2 and 4 correspond to this choice.

Figure 1.1 presents some basic ways to 'stage' culture in an international management research design. The first, from upper-left corner, is the toolkit approach, very widely used, comparative in nature, targeting individuals as basic informants and looking for values and traits of a modal personality. There is much experimental social psychology in this approach. The second has a stronger mapping orientation and defines culture in structural terms, as a way to adapt to environmental conditions. The key information comprises more factual elements and less psychometric data based on respondents' self-reports; it leads easily to a cross-national rather than cross-cultural view. The third puts the emphasis on the transmission and sharing of the cultural background, a little bit in the vein of Linton, that is, deep-seated beliefs passed through history, embedded in long-enduring institutions (see, for example, how Lessem and Neubauer, 1994, explain the formation of different management systems and organizational practices in Europe). The fourth is the strongest in its emphasis on both interaction and individuals. Typically it results in observing directly the interactions between business people or employees and their managers in different cultures as actors playing on a stage.

These approaches, though presented in Figure 1.1 as different, are combined by most researchers. For example, Hofstede discovered with research associates in Asia a 'fifth dimension', especially because the correlation between individualism and GNP/capita was progressively challenged by the rise of Asian countries (Hofstede and Bond, 1984; Chinese Culture Connection, 1987). Research on the Confucian tradition and its impact on ways of doing business in Asia can be done in the four different ways quoted above, either by studying the values of people in Asian countries based on Confucianism (toolkit); or by studying a group of countries which have a predominantly Confucianist ethic (map); by looking at what was the original teaching of Confucius and how it was transmitted to modern organizational practices in Asian countries (heritage); finally, a fourth possibility is to look at interactions between people in natural settings (business relationships, employer–employee, superior–subordinate) and try to understand how the Confucian script translates in the play of social actors (theatre). Key words in such choices are: individual versus collective, comparative versus interactive, long period/history versus short term, structural versus organic, past/primitive/archaic versus future/modern.

	Individuals	
Toolkit		**Theatre play**
Operational cultures (set of values and beliefs that guide persons and groups) Values/modal personality Social psychology/psychometry/ survey research	Theatre play/roles/interactions/ scenarios Language/communication Shared meaning and interpretations Critical incidents/direct observation or participation	
Comparative		*Interactive*
Structure/individual map/countries as cultures Adaptation to climate and geography Functionalist approach/groups of people and territorial aspects Secondary data/meta-analysis	Empowering heritage Emphasis on deep-seated sources of culture (for example, religion/ transmission/lineage and kinship) Historical and anthropological approaches	
Map	*Groups*	**Heritage**

Figure 1.1   *Staging culture in international management research*

Key empirical studies where culture construct is operationalized

Study of national cultures
For a long time social scientists have been looking at cultural differences as they pertain to national groups. The concept of national culture has been widely used, although it may seem dangerous as it sums up a complex and multiform reality at the risk of cliché and stereotype. One may wonder:

1   Is this concept coherent and substantial enough to constitute an explanatory variable in the scientific sense?
2   Should one speak of national character or national culture?

The answer to the first question is that the concept of national culture suffers a systematic lack of coherence. It is an 'intersection' of concepts, a merger of the culture concept, mostly derived from anthropology and the nation-state, belonging to the political sciences. Cultures often do not correspond to nation-states but to linguistic, ethnic, religious or even organizational entities. In modern times, the most frequent mode of political organization has been the nation-state, hence the emergence of this 'intersection' concept of national culture. The vagueness of this concept probably explains why it has been systematically underestimated, especially in international trade and international business theories. Theory-builders who generally seek to construct formally convincing theoretical explanations tend to remove such vague variables from their models, even if they have explanatory power. However, the fact that a construct is not easily measurable is no justification for ignoring it. Despite its limitations, the concept of national culture is an interesting Pandora's box.

The second question merits consideration: Some researchers favour the idea that culture directly shapes the psychological characteristics of individuals, that is, the average individual in a particular culture scores significantly higher (or lower) on certain personality traits than individuals belonging to another culture. This corresponds to the idea of national character or more precisely the concept of modal personality, which has been developed in greater detail by Inkeles and Levinson (1969). Their literature review is certainly the most exhaustive available. It might appear somewhat dated, but since national character changes over decades and centuries, their review remains largely up to date. This approach largely grew out of enquiries, stemming from World War II, which now seem to have lost some of their relevance: why are certain people more violent, more aggressive, more domineering, collectively more prone to declare war on other nations or to organize and implement genocide? Numerous empirical studies have been undertaken, particularly during the 1950s and 1960s, taking as a starting point the formation process of national character (where there could be a divergence between nations): rearing practices, early childhood, education systems, the socialization process of children, etc. Generally the results neither prove nor disprove the existence of national character.

Culture can be seen as related to the working of the social system in which the individuals live. Individual personality traits are largely free from the influence of culture as expressed by Linton (1945, pp. 14–15): 'His [the individual's] integration into society and culture goes no deeper than his learned responses, and although in the adult the greater part of what we call the personality, there is still a good deal of the individual left over.' The question of whether personality is modal (culture bound) or culture free, is not just academic. In Linton's view, individuals may have personalities quite separate from their cultural background. From a 'national character' perspective, one would expect to meet people with an average personality which reflects their culture.

The 'value orientations' of anthropologists Kluckhohn and Strodtbeck (1961) belong to those who view culture as superimposed over personality. Their framework is often cited – an indication of its analytical power at least as perceived by the social scientists. Kluckhohn and Strodtbeck have derived their value orientation theory from a comparative study of five very distinct cultural communities, each one comprised of American citizens living in close proximity to each other in the south-western part of the USA, in similar natural environments:

> Two of the populations are American Indian; one an off-reservation settlement of Navaho Indians . . . the other the Pueblo Indian community of Zuni. The third is a Spanish American village which we have named Atrisco. A Mormon village and a recently established farming village of Texan and Oklahoman homesteaders . . . are the two other communities. (Kluckhohn and Stradtbeck, 1961, p. 49)

Cultural assumptions are basic responses, expressed in a rather dichotomous manner, to fundamental human problems. They provide the members of a particular cultural community with a basic framework for the evaluation of solutions to these problems, combining a cognitive dimension (people think it works that way), an affective dimension (people like it that way) and a directive dimension (people will do it that way). Kluckhohn and Strodtbeck

(1961, pp. 11–12) have collected these common human problems under six main categories:

1   What is the character of innate human nature (human-nature orientation): good or evil, neutral, or a mix of good and evil? Is this state of human nature mutable or immutable?
2   What is the relation of humans to nature and supernature (nature orientation): subjugation to nature, harmony with nature or mastery over nature?
3   What is the temporal focus of human life (time orientation): past, present or future?
4   What is the modality of human activity (activity orientation): should people be (being), should people do (doing) or should they do in order to be (being in becoming)?
5   What is the modality of the relationship between humans (relational orientation): linearity, collaterality or pure individuality?
6   What is the conception of space? Is it considered predominantly private, public, or a mix of both?

Naturally these modalities can be found in any society: people are and do, they all display temporal orientations to the past, present and future. But different assumptions result in variation as to the kind of response which is dominant in a particular society. Other approaches of the dimensions of the cultural process have been described by other authors (Hall, 1959, 1966, 1976, 1983; Hofstede, 1980a; Triandis, 1983, 1994; Trompenaars, 1993). All of them highlight common problems across cultures, depict the most important solutions and explain the dominant contrasts.

Large-scale empirical studies using survey data
These studies lie somewhere in between maps and toolkits. They can bear some consequences for the interactive aspects but these are generally inferred from the comparative results rather than directly observed from intercultural interactions. The most famous study is Hofstede (1980a) on national cultures and the relativity of managerial practices: 834 citations of Hoftsede's works were listed in the Social Science Citation Index from 1980 to the end of 1994 (Hofstede, 1995, p. 209). Some years ago, the cover page of an issue of *Fortune* magazine accurately featured the difficult question of the transposability of management styles: it shows an American with slanting eyes eating (or, more probably, trying to eat) a hamburger with chopsticks. Hofstede was one of the first researchers to question explicitly the adaptability of US management theories and practices to other cultural contexts. Empirical studies for Hofstede's work

were undertaken between 1967 and 1973 within a large multinational company, in 66 of its national subsidiaries. The database contained more than 116,000 questionnaires: all categories of personnel were interviewed, from ordinary workers to general managers. Out of 150 questions, 60 deal with the values and beliefs of the respondents on issues related to motivation, hierarchy, leadership, well-being in the organization, etc. The questionnaire was administered in two successive stages (1967–9 and 1971–3) in order to verify validity by replication. Versions of the questionnaire were drafted in 20 different languages. Not all subsidiaries are included in the final analysis; depending on the data under review, 40–55 countries are finally comparable. The results drawn from these data were further validated by a systematic comparison with the results of thirteen other studies (Hofstede, 1980b, 1983).

Interviewees all belonged to the same multinational corporation, IBM, which has a strong corporate culture shared among its employees. Consequently there was no variance on this dimension across the sample. Each national sample allowed for a similar representation of age groups, gender and categories of personnel, thereby avoiding a potential source of variance across national subsidiaries' results. Finally, the only source of variance was the difference in national cultures and mentalities. By means of factor analysis of the respondents' scores, Hofstede was able to derive four main conceptual dimensions on which national cultures exhibit significant differences.

One of these four dimensions is *individualism/collectivism*. In collectivist countries there is a close-knit social structure, where people neatly distinguish between members of the ingroup and members of the outgroup. They expect their group to care for them in exchange for unwavering loyalty. In individualistic societies, social fabric is much looser: people are basically supposed to care for themselves and their immediate family. The second dimension, *power distance*, measures to what extent a society and its individual members tolerate an unequal distribution of power in organizations and in society as a whole. It is evidenced as much by the behavioural values of superiors who display their power and exercise it, as by the behavioural values of subordinates who wait for their superiors to show their status and power. The third dimension, *masculinity/femininity*, roughly corresponds to male/assertive versus female/nurturing roles. Masculine societies favour assertiveness, earning money, showing off possessions and caring little for others. Conversely, feminine societies favour nurturing roles, interdependence between people and caring for others (who are seen as worth caring for, because they are temporarily weak). This dimension has been so named because, on average, men tended to score high on one extreme and women on the other, whatever the society/country. The fourth dimension, *uncertainty avoidance*, features different responses to the common problem faced by people in any society of dealing with uncertainty. This dimension measures the extent to which people in a society tend to feel threatened by uncertain, ambiguous, risky or undefined situations. Where uncertainty avoidance is high, organizations promote stable careers, produce rules and procedures, etc., but they are also characterized by a higher level of anxiety and aggressiveness that creates, among other things, a strong inner urge to work hard (Hofstede, 1980b). Hofstede outlines that 'uncertainty avoidance should not be confused with risk avoidance . . . even more than reducing risk, uncertainty avoidance leads to a reduction of *ambiguity*' (1991, p. 116).

Cultural relativity of management theories
A final element which makes cross-cultural management research distinct from other branches of management research is that it considers management theories as relative to national culture. Management research, on the other hand, has integrated corporate culture in its analyses of organizational phenomena but rarely questioned the universality of management theories. Table 1.4 shows national scores of selected countries and regions for the four dimensions. Hofstede's main tenet concerns the cultural relativity of management theories, which are rooted in the cultural context where they were developed. Therefore any simple direct transposition is difficult. For instance, Hofstede shows the linkage between US-based motivation theories and the culture. Maslow's 'hierarchy of needs' and McClelland's theory of the achievement motives are directly related to two dimensions of US culture: its strong masculinity and its individualism. People are seen as being motivated in an overtly conscious manner by the expectancy of some kind of results from their acts: they are basically motivated by extrinsic reasons and rewards. In contrast, Freudian theory, which has not been greatly applied by US management theorists, represents the individual as being pushed by internal forces, often unconsciously, the id and super-ego interacting with the ego. According to Hofstede, Austria, where Freud was born and where he drafted his theories, scores significantly higher than the USA on uncertainty avoidance and lower on individualism. This may explain why motivation is more related to interiorized social values. 'Freud's superego acts naturally as an inner uncertainty-absorbing device, an internalized boss' (Hofstede, 1980b, p. 58). Numerous replications have been

undertaken (Hofstede and Bond, 1984; Sondergaard, 1994) which prove that the conceptual dimensions evidenced by Hofstede's empirical study are fairly stable over time and samples.

Table 1.4   *Hofstede's four cultural indexes for selected countries*

| | Cultural dimensions | | | |
	Power distance	Uncertainty avoidance	Individualism	Masculinity
Arab countries*	80	68	38	53
Argentina	49	86	46	56
Brazil	69	76	38	49
Canada	39	48	80	52
Denmark	18	23	74	16
East Africa**	64	52	27	41
France	68	86	71	43
Germany	35	65	67	66
India	77	40	48	56
Italy	50	75	76	70
Japan	54	92	46	95
Malaysia	104	36	26	50
Mexico	81	82	30	69
Netherlands	38	53	80	14
Pakistan	55	70	14	50
South Korea	60	85	18	39
Spain	57	86	51	42
Sweden	31	29	71	5
UK	35	35	89	66
USA	40	46	91	62
World mean	57	65	43	49

*Saudi Arabia, Egypt, United Arab Emirates, Iraq, Kuwait, Lebanon and Libya
**Ethiopia, Kenya, Tanzania and Zambia
Sources: Hofstede (1980a, 1991)

2

The role of language and intellectual styles in cross-cultural comparisons

Many management theories are ethnocentric in that they take the cultural environment of the theorist for granted (Hofstede, 1980, 1983; Adler, 1983a, 1983b). The argument of this chapter is that international research is by its very nature comparative for the simple reason that the researcher has a different cultural background to the 'researched' field and informants. Therefore, basic differences in cross-national research designs must be made clear as early as possible during the research process. The questions to be asked are simple. They are presented in the first part of this chapter which highlights the underlying assumptions of comparative international research designs: What is compared? Across which units? Who compares? What is the cultural origin of theories used? What is the reference point of the comparison process, that is, to what is something compared?

The following two parts of this chapter focus on a central actor in the process, that is, the researcher herself: emphasizing her background as a central element in the comparative setting; and the diversity of intellectual styles across cultures when defining what is appropriate research, how it should be conducted and its results evaluated. Although it is often kept in the background of the research process, language plays a key role in cross-cultural management research. Management itself has a dominant language, English, in which most of the research literature is published. Language differences may be seen simply as a major impediment for implementing research. Informants may not speak the researcher's language, questionnaires may need to be translated, and people in multilingual research teams may have a hard time understanding each other. However, the influence of language goes much beyond this: it is a significant component of culture, as argued in the previous chapter, and conveys meanings which may be unique to a cultural community. Moreover, our native language frames our way of looking at real world phenomena and interpreting them. Consequently, this book stresses the importance of language in cross-cultural management research, both in this chapter and in Chapters 4 and 5. This chapter then deals with the issue of language in the comparison process: translation, although possible, is an undertaking which tends to hide most of the culturally relevant materials; *traduttore traditore* as the Italian saying goes (translator, betrayer). The final part exemplifies the language bias by taking the example of cross-cultural literature in international marketing.

Underlying assumptions of cross-cultural comparisons

A typical research is the 'replication' in a 'foreign' context of a published study, which often works without the underlying assumptions even being explained, understood or explicitly assessed. This results in decontextualized, out of context rather than context free research. In order to expose her implicit assumptions, the researcher has to answer the following questions at the start of the process:

1 Why compare: am I looking for similarities or differences?
2 If any, what kinds of differences are sought? Are they variations in degree (along common conceptual dimensions), or differences in nature (concepts are incommensurable)?
3 To whom do I/we speak? About what, whom and why? That is, who are the 'clients' of the comparative research and who/what are the observed units?

What does 'to compare' mean?
The Collins dictionary (1990, p. 195) gives the following definitions of the verb 'compare': '1. To regard as similar; 2. To examine in order to observe resemblance or differences; 3. To be the same or similar.' Similarities are obviously central in the comparison process as well as differences, but one may wonder what are the basic, often implicit, assumptions underlying the comparison process. An example of researchers obviously looking from the outset for similar traits across cultures is given by McGrath and MacMillan (1992) who research on entrepreneurship. The title of their research says a lot about their search for similarities – 'More Like Each Other than Anyone Else? A Cross-cultural Study of Entrepreneurial Perceptions'. Their set of hypothetical propositions evidences very clearly a search for similarities:

1 There is a basic set of beliefs that entrepreneurs hold about themselves.
2 This set of beliefs transcends culture.

3   The perceived differences with others create a tension in the minds of entrepreneurs which is the seeds of entrepreneurial activity.

That entrepreneurs cross-culturally share some common characteristics, as individuals, is an idea which makes sense; their survey of 700 entrepreneurs in nine culturally different countries evidences a common set of beliefs. An opposite example is given by a study investigating the perceived approaches to productivity improvement between domestic-owned and western-owned companies in Singapore (Foo, 1992). The empirical data is based on a survey of employees' perceptions administered to participants of a productivity management course. At first sight, the findings are totally unsupportive of differences between western and local companies: out of thirty individual items concerning technology, planning, personnel, and productivity variables there is not one significant difference in mean score between the two subsamples, while the means for only three items out of eight concerning strategy and structural variables appear as significantly different. This should normally support the culture-free thesis. However, studying the correlation across items for the two subsamples while differentiating hierarchical levels, Foo evidences significant differences between indigenous and foreign firms and concludes finally that 'in seeking to improve productivity, Western management tends to integrate training more strongly, while Eastern management seems to relate training more to organizational planning and personnel systems' (1992, p. 604). The researcher was obviously looking for differences, but his first empirical findings were disappointing. He finally uncovers the expected differences by refining calculations and by interpreting these findings. The paper finishes with an ideal-type contrast between western and eastern models of organizational structure related to productivity improvement which is clear evidence of the researcher's quest for differences.

Most of the researchers will argue that they look for both. However, in the real world they tend to have a preconception of what they will (or even 'want' to) find at the end of the process. Those who emphasize similarities will favour the traditional search for 'cross-cultural equivalence' (described in Chapter 4), while those looking for differences will favour open inquiry and act deliberately as 'meaning explorers' (Chapter 5). Consequently, those who search for differences and unknowingly use research strategies that favour the discovery of similarities will be deeply disappointed and discuss their findings in great detail to highlight their cherished differences. In any case, the researcher must be aware of what she is predominantly looking for because it will influence the research design, favouring the discovery of similarities or the emergence of differences. The divide in pictures of the world is partly located in the observer's eye.

A classic distinction, Emic versus Etic cross-cultural research, was originated by Sapir (1929) and further developed by Pike (1966). The Emic approach holds that attitudinal or behavioural phenomena are expressed in a unique way in each culture. Taken to its extreme, this approach states that no comparisons are possible. The Etic approach, on the other hand, is primarily concerned with identifying universals. The difference arises from linguistics where phon*etic* is universal and depicts universal sounds which are common to several languages, and phon*emic* stresses unique sound patterns in languages. In general, research approaches and instruments adapted to each national culture (the Emic approach) provide data with greater internal validity than tests applicable to several cultures (the Etic approach, or 'culture-free tests'). But it is at the expense of cross-national comparability and external validity: results are not transposable to other cultural contexts. This is why many researchers try to establish cross-national or cross-cultural equivalence in a way which is inspired by the Etic rather than the Emic perspective.

Table 2.1 takes the example of consumer behaviour in a cross-cultural perspective, when one considers the universal/specific aspect of both the subject (the researcher, her theories), and the object being studied (the field, consumers as informants, the country/culture being studied). Perspective (1) consists in looking to world markets with the 'same eyes', meaning that theories, underlying models, concepts and views of consumers, their motives and how they behave are assumed as universal. In perspective (2) the researcher travels to foreign consumption contexts with the same eyes and no glasses; there is obviously a risk of myopia. In perspective (3) one adds glasses to the same eyes so that part of what was previously invisible comes into light. Perspective (4) requires 'looking with other eyes', that is changing the very instrument of vision; the metaphor suggests the hardship of the process.

Table 2.1   *Consumer behaviour in a cross-cultural perspective*

| Informants/field | Underlying theories | |
	Universal	Specific
Universal	(1) Global perspective	(3) Ethnic perspective
Specific	(2) Foreign/imported perspective	(4) Cultural meaning perspective

Table 2.1 should not be interpreted with the view that a particular cell corresponds to a better perspective than another. However, they display strong contrasts. The first perspective, in its purest form, is now rarely found except in the article on globalization of markets by Levitt (1983) and more generally when consumers are viewed as truly global. It may make sense for particular classes of consumers, such as business people travelling worldwide with their families ('the global nomads'). Kotler's *Marketing Management* (8th edn, 1994) is a universal success which started from position (1) and has steadily shifted to position (2) by being adapted in many languages and to various national contexts. The imported perspective may sometimes unveil minor differences across countries and cultures, but does not enable the researcher to generate deep insights into the way local consumers see their world and attribute meaning to consumption. As stated by Van Raaij (1978, p. 699): 'We should encourage researchers in other cultures to study their own reality rather than to replicate American studies.' Perspective (3) is the starting point of Hirschmann (1985) when she describes the ideological base of American consumer behaviour research as promoting conceptualizations and conjectures in a definite framework, where individuals who actively seek information make personal decisions which lead to pragmatic goals. She challenges these assumptions by looking at primitive aspects of consumption in definite US ethnic groups (Black, Italians, Wasps, Jews). Perspective (4) corresponds to the view that underlying theories and concepts have to be actively challenged.

The Emic/Etic divide is, however, a simplified perspective. Most Etic-oriented researchers are still looking for differences, but these differences are of degree, while Emic researchers look for differences in nature. Typical questions for Etic-oriented researchers are: Is it scalable? Can the constructs be operationalized? Are the differences across countries/cultures measurable on common conceptual dimensions? Researchers who emphasize the completely different nature of a specific concept are also drawn to some implicit reference point. A good case is the work by Hayashi (1988) which describes unique aspects of the Japanese management system. Although originally written in Japanese, there are references to western observers of the Japanese reality and to western concepts. For example, when commenting on the Japanese *makimono* pattern of time, he states: 'In a Western book or personal letter, the writer often treats the past, present, and future, separately; each time period is given a different chapter or paragraph. But in old Japanese books and letters, events in the past, descriptions of the contemporary scene, and speculations about what would probably happen in the future were often depicted in one long, continuous *makimono'* (1988, p. 10).

Differences can be in 'nature', for example, one might argue that what is called 'decision-making' is a fully different concept (incommensurable), since the word does not exist in Japanese (Lazer et al., 1985). Differences can also be in degree. The dimension of uncertainty avoidance in Hofstede's study, for example, assumes that national cultures can be scored on a common scaling instrument expressing the degree of tolerance of ambiguity. The researcher's practical question for such concepts is whether they are scalable, ordinally (rankings of countries/cultures) or cardinally (scores by countries/cultures). However, uncertainty avoidance has been shown to be the least robust in replications (Sondergaard, 1994), with national scores varying across studies, and is also the most difficult to define conceptually. Therefore, the search for differences in degree does not preclude at some moments a shift for differences in nature (nominal).

Cross-national studies generally assume a nominal difference. Countries are assigned codes, treated nominally as cultures and differences are observed, but neither explained nor interpreted; the causes behind observed differences remain largely unaddressed. The aim of the research is to highlight differences across countries, if any, not to explain them. For instance, differences in relative risk aversion around the world have been studied by Szpiro (1986) and Szpiro and Outreville (1988) based on demand for insurance as a function of GNP, the object of the research being exclusively to assess differences in degree of risk aversion across nations, not to explain them.

Often purportedly cross-cultural research designs use nationality as a surrogate variable of culture. Many such designs are in fact not cross-cultural, although they claim to be; they are simple cross-national designs, providing little if no theoretical indication of how culture causes such differences (Lachman et al., 1994). Comparative studies emphasizing comparison across cultures are more content oriented, describing values as components of culture, while interactive designs, emphasizing interaction between managers or organizations from different cultures, such as expatriation, culture shock or intercultural business negotiations issues, tend to explain more about the process. There is an obvious complementarity between both types of designs. However, comparative studies are more easily seen as 'scientific', because they have clearer theoretical underpinnings and are easier to implement.

Table 2.2 contrasts research perspective, with the same column headings but with different items in lines as Table 2.1; the lines feature whether the researcher is looking for similarities or differences.

Quadrant 1 corresponds to research undertakings where underlying theories are assumed universal and the author looks for similarities, such as in the example given above of relative risk aversion around the world. In large Etic research projects such as Furnham et al. (1994), who have studied attitudes towards competitiveness, money and work among young people from 41 nations, the universality of attitudes is assumed. The concepts under study are measured by using items which represent classical dimensions: work ethic as Weber's classic concept of moral commitment to work, McClellands's achievement motivation, mastery over problems and events, achievement through conformity, money beliefs and attitudes to savings. The addition of possible differences in conceptual dimensions would compromise the feasibility of a research design which is already complex in terms of countries covered. As we will see in Chapter 3, complexity is the major limitation of cross-cultural research designs. Therefore, large Etic projects look in fact for differences in degree, in the style of perspective (2).

Perspective (3) is that of Geert Hofstede. The dominant theories are questioned but the researcher looks for similarities; he strives for progressive convergence in the nature of the conceptual dimensions across nations/cultures while assessing differences in degree, since countries have different scores on the same conceptual dimensions. This type of universality emerges from successive research undertakings. Perspective (4) is predominantly Emic in style and tries to stage unique ways, unique concepts and practices. Leadership, for instance, can be treated as unique to a particular culture (for example, Ichikawa, 1993, in the case of leadership in Japan) or a phenomenon which shares cross-culturally some common traits (for example, Dorfman and Howell, 1988; Smith and Peterson, 1988) or somewhere in between (for example, Kozan, 1993, in the case of Turkey; Misumi and Peterson, 1985, in the case of Japan; Dorfman, 1996, more generally).

Table 2.2 *Comparative research strategies*

Expected picture	Underlying theories	
	Universal	Specific
Similarity	Assumed universality (1)	Emergent universality (3) (Hofstede)
Differences	Etic with differences in degree (2)	Emic position (4) *Differences* in nature/ polycentric research

The issue of generalization is central in cross-cultural management research. There is a wide range of opinions about the matter of whether cross-national laws exist and whether there is any possibility of generalization across cultures. Farley and Lehmann (1994) speak of 'the myth that everything is different' (in the case of international marketing) and argue in favour of not confounding highly visible differences with the underlying patterns in market response which may be more generalizable than seems at first sight. Through an analysis of eighteen comparative studies in international marketing, they suggest two levels of generalization:

- inter-country comparisons in single studies;
- international generalization across different studies whose outcome variables, behavioural variables and technical characteristics can be calibrated in a meta-analytic way.

Others argue clearly in the opposite direction. Faucheux (1976), for instance, speaks of the 'generalization fallacy', giving examples of studies in experimental social psychology (a discipline widely used in several domains of management and marketing research) where the preoccupation for finding similarities has resulted in loss of meaning and spurious results. The first issue is in fact the status of generalization in the research undertaking. Amado et al. (1991) make a point that the search for universal variables and relationships, that is, valid cross-national laws can only be an aim and not a starting point. If the researcher, based on the assumption that universal knowledge exists (Cheng, 1994), is searching for universal laws as a starting point, she will have a tendency to crash down the complexity of phenomena and force her views upon realities that may not really fit with them. A second issue is to distinguish between three levels of generalization:

- in variables, how they are defined and operationalized;
- in the underlying models, that is, the theorized relationships among variables;
- the generalizability of the measurement process in order to test relationships (Rosenzweig, 1994).

These issues are treated in this chapter (for translation) and in Chapter 4 dealing with the search for cross-cultural equivalence. The search for generality is seen by almost all researchers as a legitimate endeavour. However, key words in this respect are complexity and emergent reality. Brannen (1996) insists on the complexity of describing micro-level cultural phenomena; any attempt at generalizing about culture seen as a monolithic whole (especially in the perspective of national culture) leads to reductionism and incomplete meaning. Complexity reduces the chance of getting any full generalization from a single study, however informed and well designed. The realities emergent of cross-cultural generalization can only appear at the multi-study level, involving researchers from different cultures and multiple research perspectives, and using an orientation towards knowledge as shared meaning rather than merely towards science as external truth. Emergent realities are generalized through a double increase in shared meaning: the comprehension of certain phenomena is enlarged while this understanding is shared by more and more people worldwide. Cross-culturally, general knowledge is better 'shared' than 'true'.

Role of the dominant culture in comparative studies
Adler (1983a, p. 35) quotes Hesseling (1973) stating that, 'to conduct comparative studies, researchers must assume that there is no dominant culture', and she continues, 'if the researcher either implicitly or explicitly assumes that one's culture's view of reality is superior to the other culture's, or that one culture's ways of solving organizational problems is superior, then he is conducting ethnocentric, not comparative research'. In fact, there is a dominant culture in management research, the USA, which many (including non-US researchers) consider spontaneously as superior because it has been legitimately prevailing in the field over the last seventy years with only minor challenges from Asia in recent years. Saying that it is dominant does not imply any negative value judgement. The American position lies much more in the latent and unavowed feeling of researchers from other countries of being inferior, rather than in the rarely expressed feeling by Americans of being really superior. The complex – and sometimes bitter – debate about who dominates is well phrased by Koza and Thoenig in the case of European researchers who are absent in US academic journals:

> Is it because they develop second-class research? In this case, this is fuelled by their US colleagues who either do not read other languages than English or may consider that the dominant and only relevant form of scientific achievement is to publish in their own domestic journals and according to routine established criteria. (Koza and Thoenig, 1995, p. 6)

The first basic link between culture and management, which is almost never mentioned, is in fact its dominant entrenchment in one particular national culture, that of the USA. Management concepts and practices, although partly originating from Europe, have been developed largely in the USA and later enthusiastically borrowed and adopted in many countries because these concepts appeared as powerful tools for developing and controlling businesses. In so doing, the importing cultures have often transformed management concepts and integrated them into their own culture. For instance, the success of the word 'marketing' gave a new image to trade and sales activities in many countries where it had often previously been socially and intellectually devalued, especially in Latin countries because of the relative lack of consideration of Catholicism for trade and business activities (Weber, 1958). Despite the success and the seemingly general acceptance of the term 'marketing', many examples indicate that there have been some basic misconceptions, especially in developing countries (Amine and Cavusgil, 1986). For instance, a survey of Egyptian business people indicated a clear lack of understanding as to what the word marketing really means (El Haddad, 1985). Either managers did not understand what marketing was all about or, if they did, they tended to believe that it had little relevance to their business. In fact, marketing is still seen in most parts of the world as mere selling, or as advertising and sales promotion. Although 'marketing' has been imported as a word, and even as a sort of slogan, its former cultural roots and precise meaning have been partly misunderstood.

In Japan, most of the books on marketing and management were borrowed from the USA and then translated directly without much adaptation (Lazer et al., 1985), at least in a first stage before the progressive integration of Japanese and American management concepts took place among both academics and managers (Beechler and Pucik, 1989). Survey techniques, the underlying concepts and the wording of questions, as well as questionnaire, interview and sampling techniques, were all widely imported. In fact more frequently the actual words have been imported rather than their whole sense and the social practices involved. The imported nature of management and marketing concepts and practices is clearly evidenced by the vocabulary, information and reference sources and the origin of literature on the subject, all of which demarcate it as an area of knowledge. Data, information sources and professional consultancy businesses (for auditing, advertising or market consultants, etc.) are mostly of American origin, even if they are far from being all American. Last but not least, the academic journals and associations are largely based in the USA. Academic journals also exist in the UK, Europe, Canada and Japan, but most of the research literature depicted in the reference section of the published papers is based on American materials. The percentage of US references in the bibliographies of a British, German or French reference list often reaches as much as 90 per cent . As Lazer et al. point out in the case of Japan (1985, p.71): 'What has occurred [in Japan] is the modification and adaptation of selected American constructs, ideas and practices to adjust them to the Japanese culture, that remains intact.'

They stress especially the importance of economic non-functionality which, in the case of marketing, 'emphasizes that marketing actions consider individual human factors rather than merely economic efficiency and business profits'. A similar situation is also to be found in France, where adaptation to the cultural context has now been broadly achieved by giving to management a logic and rational frame which fits with French society, where only Cartesian logic may give legitimacy and credibility to new knowledge.

That there is a dominant culture in business is merely a fact. However, it implies that the researcher has to address the issue of who compares what/whom for who using which theories, which kind of proofs? The research design is a compromise between the respective cultures of the researcher, the research field that informs him/her and the research publics who read the report, use the results, evaluate the findings and/or finance the research (Figure 2.1).

Figure 2.1   *Influences on the research perspective*

As Table 2.3 tries to show, basic orientations in comparative studies will result from more or less conscious choices of the researcher, from opportunities and constraints related to the researched field (for example, the cultural distance between researchers and their informants) and from the underlying theories which must fit with the intellectual style of the research clients, that is, anonymous reviewers in a peer review process or evaluators of a research project.

Researchers who undertake cross-national or cross-cultural comparisons have a personal involvement in the research and the researched. Previous knowledge of the cultural area being studied explains why the researcher often chooses a field which is culturally near to her. Researchers often want to explain their own cultural context and act as 'cultural mediators' in the area of academia. Such

Table 2.3   *Cultural influences on the research design*

	Theories (world views/ languages/frames of reference/codes/ instruments)	Data (facts/figures/ information/ evidence/statistics)	Proofs (hypothesis testing/ applicability)
Researcher	Home-country 'theories' versus dominant theories	Culturally accepted images of reality	Self-confirmation
Researched	Field–host country world views	Respondents' own views	Sympathy/ relationships
Research publics	Colleagues' own knowledge, paradigms, and research methods	Research reports, theses, articles, books, reports	Reviews/peer evaluations/ readers

is the case of comparative management researchers who study the Arabic/Muslim style of management and leadership (for instance, Baligh, 1991; Ali, 1993, 1995). Sympathy between researchers from different cultures helps them form a cross-border, joint-venture research project. Relationships such as those between ex-PhD students and their former advisor/supervisor who have developed a common understanding are key assets in comparative management research.

The researcher as comparison base

The issue of ethnocentrism in international management research is an important one. As emphasized by Adler (1983a, p. 35): 'Researchers must guard against imposing their own cultural perspective on the research design, data collection, interpretation, and analysis. This often means working with researchers from the target cultures and consciously masking one's own cultural conditioning.' Since a cultural conditioning is largely unconscious, it is important to be aware that the researcher's own background creates the real starting point for the research process, the real comparison base where she begins, implicitly or explicitly. Researchers in international management have therefore to address issues of ethnocentrism, stereotyping and prejudices and to question their own motivation in researching cross-nationally.

Researcher ethnocentrism
The concept of ethnocentrism was first introduced by Sumner (1906) more than eighty years ago, to distinguish between *ingroups*

(those groups with which an individual identifies) and *outgroups* (those regarded as antithetical to the *ingroup*). Ethnocentrism has been progressively extended at the individual level, describing the natural tendency of people to refer themselves spontaneously to the symbols, values and ways of thinking of their own ethnic or national group, their ingroup. The automatic and unconscious tendency to refer to one's own thought framework is mainly tied to national culture which, in general, people do not choose but which allows them to interpret situations, evaluate people, communicate, negotiate, or decide. Ethnocentrism may lead to disinterest and even contempt for the culture of other groups (Levine and Campbell, 1972).

One can transpose to management research the steps suggested by Lee (1966) in order to eliminate the ethnocentric bias related to self-reference criterion (SRC) when dealing with international business operations:

1   Define the problem according to the behavioural standards and ways of thinking of the researcher's culture(s).
2   Define the problems according to the behavioural standards and ways of thinking of the foreign country (the research field).
3   Isolate the influence of the self-reference criterion on the problem under investigation and identify the extent to which it complicates the research process or biases the results.
4   Redefine the problem, without the bias related to the SRC, and then find the solutions and make decisions which fit with the cultural context studied.

Although it may be a practical framework to operationalize the influence of cultural representations, the SRC is naive in assuming easy interpretation of a culture without being a native. Cultural expertise is complex and may be reached neither by experts from the source culture (in ignorance of the target culture), nor by locals being little aware of their own culture.

Ethnocentrism is largely inevitable. Others are easily perceived as ethnocentric, providing the self with a reassuring but misleading sense of objectivity. Obeying the norms of one's culture is almost unconscious and the cost of adopting the cultural demeanour of the environment in which one has been raised seems minimal because the costs incurred in the rearing, socialization and education are implicitly considered by accultured adults as *sunk costs*. On the other hand, the understanding and adoption of the traits of another culture are generally perceived as costly, evidenced by the difficulties encountered by immigrants. Ethnocentrism is not a cognitive limitation, it is also cognitive empowerment in the source culture. Jaeger (1983) shows, for instance, that multinational companies deliberately use cultural control by maintaining in the overseas location an emphasis on the 'home' language, English, by heavy use of expatriates and by offering local employees an extensive 'socialization' programme (p. 95). Underlying this is the tough issue of who adapts to whom, when economic and intellectual dominance as well as cultural violence (Galtung, 1990) play a key role. Galtung thoroughly defines what the process of cultural violence encompasses. In one section of his article (4.5) he argues about the role of Ricardo's doctrine (developed further by Hecksher and Ohlin, and others) as justifying the world division of labour: 'The principle of comparative advantage sentences countries to stay where the production-factor profile has landed them, for geographical and historical reasons' (p. 300). The law of comparative advantage has in fact almost completely eliminated the concept of culture from international trade theory. One may remark, as Galtung (1990), that: 'In short, this "law" [of comparative advantage] is a piece of cultural violence buried in the very core of economics.' Ignoring cultural differences, the law of comparative advantage imposes a paradigm of international trade which is excessively utilitarian: it assumes the complete pre-eminence of utility over identity. Yet real people do not live only with what is useful to them, they also live out of the maintenance and self-actualization of their cultural identity.

Stereotypes and self-shock
International comparative management research can induce culture shocks in the researcher. A good example is given by Clifford Geertz in *Local Knowledge* (1983), when he quotes a long passage from a nineteenth-century Danish trader, L. V. Helms, who accurately reports the ritual cremation of a dead man and his three (living) widows in India. He describes very carefully the background to the incident, which takes place around 1850. He is horrified by the ritual, amazed by the absence of reaction in the crowd attending the event and stunned by the lack of fear of the three women who throw themselves alive into the flames. Geertz emphasizes the relations of culture to moral imagination: what is seen as mere barbary by one culture is experienced as wholly normal by another. Implicitly researchers always compare and confront their own views to the foreign reality they are observing. This is why traditional international management research is unknowingly comparative.
    Stereotypes are important constructs in the relationship of the

researcher to her field. For instance, the French often perceive Americans as being tough in business and arrogant and the British as insincere (Gauthey and Xardel, 1990). The stereotype of American arrogance is related to a different hierarchy of values: American professional relations are centred on the task in hand to the relative exclusion of personal relations with the other party, which surfaces as the important issue in a French setting. Stereotypes represent a useful simplification, but their function of reducing and conserving our differences can make them dangerous. Stereotypes have both a cognitive function and an emotional function of self-defence against a difference that creates anxiety. It seems easier to stick to one's own values and to transfer onto foreigners the responsibility to change their views than to decentre oneself, that is, to leave one's system of reference and put oneself in the place of the other.

As shown by Zaharna (1989) in a review article on the culture shock experienced by people of different cultures, the problematic representation of the 'other' may evolve into a confrontation (equally problematic) with oneself. Zaharna calls this process 'self-shock'. Experiencing how others actually are may be somewhat destabilizing: identity confusion is a typical feature of culture shock (Oberg, 1972). Self-shock is probably one of the principal causes of stereotyping. Stereotypes often protect the self, much more than they really provide information on the other. In intercultural encounters one might think that the basic problem is 'getting to know the other', but there is in fact a 'progressive unfolding of the self' which can be attributed to 'a set of intensive and evocative situations in which the individual perceives and experiences other people in a distinctly new manner and, as a consequence, experiences new facets and dimensions of existence' (Adler, 1975, p. 18).

In cross-cultural research encounters, the necessary presence of otherness risks disturbing one's personal identity, which is put into question by a 'mirror effect'. Within the native cultural context people unconsciously build a self-image based on their observations and on the responses of others to their conduct. As emphasized by Erikson (1950, p. 13): 'Identity is the confidence gathered from the fact that our own ability to maintain interior resemblance and continuity equals the resemblance and continuity of the image and the sense that others have of us.' The cross-cultural researcher is therefore constantly confronted with issues in self-research, that is, inquiring into one's own prejudices, mindset and reference frame, which may be a disturbing task.

Variation in intellectual style across cultures

Many authors have noted distinct approaches to organizational research (for example, Faucheux and Rojot, 1978; Galtung, 1981; Cooper and Cox, 1989; Osigweh, 1989; Amado et al., 1991; Bendixen and Burger, 1995; Koza and Thoenig, 1995; Berry, 1996). Whether they speak about different 'intellectual traditions' or different 'research approaches', they highlight differences in the way of addressing issues, assigning a definite role to theory and defining what role data play in the whole process. Koza and Thoenig (1995), for instance, emphasize the difference between American and European researchers in the field of organization studies. They take the example of hermeneutics, deconstruction, postmodernism and anthropological interpretations which are popular among European researchers, more interested in qualitative and interpretive studies, and somewhat less familiar to the Americans. They argue further that European intellectual life is still dominated by the division of European languages and a deep loyalty to country-based academic milieux, which is reinforced by the stability of researchers' careers which are often spent in a single institution.

People, including researchers, tend to stick spontaneously to the values and representations of their national or disciplinary cultural grouping. Those who wish to enlarge their world view by freeing themselves, at least partially, from the mental programmes brought to them by culture, risk being misunderstood. By trying to escape their cultural programming, such people may be resented as exhibiting a lack of humility in setting themselves apart from the community. Furthermore, any relatively homogeneous human group, including academics belonging to scientific associations, organizing conferences and running journals, feels fairly threatened when members overstep the threshold of non-conformism.

A frequent misconception is to treat reality as external, and to assume that the ways in which we frame, interpret, act on and try to change our reality has no influence on it. This restricted view, naively linking perception and reality, is often called commonsense, that is, shared meaning which makes agreed upon sense in the cultural community simply because we share it, even though it may appear somewhat nonsensical or simply less valid and less important to people belonging to other cultural communities. Indeed our relation to the real world is heavily filtered by a series of convergent factors:

1   Our perceptual apparatus is partly culturally formed.
2   We implicitly privilege certain categories of facts *lato sensu*

(emotions, thoughts, actions and situations being regarded as facts) and interpret them based on our particular cultural background.
3   The truthfulness of these facts is based on a cultural consensus about their being a part of reality.
4   Even when facts have been established as true, there still remain different readings and interpretations, depending on culture-based values and social representations (Moscovici, 1976).

Johan Galtung (1981), a Norwegian by birth and a reputed scholar in peace research, uses the expression 'intellectual styles' and states that culture, among other factors, influences the investigation methods and criteria of good management research and good researchers. He contrasts the style of academics in major areas: theory versus data orientation, concepts of information, 'truthfulness' and 'proofs'. In intellectual processes, people may favour either *actual/empirical* reality, that is, the ways in which we experience reality here and now (or the way it is revealed by empirical science), or *potential reality*, that is, reality based on interpretation, speculation and imagination. Potential reality is in a sense the possible future of actual reality. Our sense of potential reality relies much more on imagination than on actual perceptions. Since potential reality is beyond the reach of our perceptions and cannot be experienced, we have to envisage it. Galtung (1981) uses this distinction between actual reality and potential reality in order to contrast what he calls the 'intellectual styles' of four important cultural groups: the 'Gallic' (prototype: the French), the 'Teutonic' (prototype: the Germans), the Saxonic (prototype: the English and Americans), and the 'Nipponic' (prototype: the Japanese and most generally Far East Asians).

Saxons prefer to look for facts and evidence which result in factual accuracy and abundance. Galtung deals with the intellectual style of academicians and describes them as 'ideal types' in a very European tradition since the seminal works of Max Weber. As Galtung states when he describes the intellectual style of Anglo-Americans:

> Data unite, theories divide. There are clear, relatively explicit canons for establishing what constitutes a valid fact and what does not; the corresponding canons in connection with theories are more vague. . . . One might now complete the picture of the Saxonic intellectual style by emphasizing its weak point: not very strong on theory formation, and not on paradigm awareness. (Galtung, 1981, pp. 827–8)

To the 'Teutonics' and the 'Gallics' the US research orientation often appears as excessively data driven. Berry (1996) gives good examples of how the US academic system works from a European perspective: the strongly competitive system and the rule 'publish or perish' lead to a high level of conformism based on 'mainstream' professional guidelines as to how research should be conducted. Galtung contrasts the Saxonic style with the Teutonic and Gallic styles, which place theoretical arguments at the centre of their intellectual process. Data and facts are there to illustrate what is said rather than to demonstrate it:

> Discrepancy between theory and data would be handled at the expense of data: they may either be seen as atypical or wholly erroneous, or more significantly as not really pertinent to the theory. And here the distinction between empirical and potential reality comes in: to the Teutonic and Gallic intellectual, potential reality may be not so much the reality to be even more avoided or even more pursued than the empirical one but rather a *more real reality*, free from the noise and impurities of empirical reality. (Galtung, 1981, p 828)

However, Teutonic and Gallic intellectual styles do differ in the role that is assigned to words and discourse. The Teutonic ideal is that of the ineluctability of true reasoning, *Gedankennotwendigkeit*, that is, perfection of concepts and the indisputability of their mental articulation. The concept of *Gedankennotwendigkeit* is typical of German thinking patterns, where abstraction is taken to its limits. It is not by chance that German philosophers have a worldwide reach. The German language is probably the richest in the world for abstract words. It favours pure conceptual thinking. The construction of *Gedankennotwendigkeit* is itself an illustration of this: *denken* means 'to think', Gedanken are 'thoughts'; *Not* means 'necessity'; *wenden* is 'to turn'; *-keit* is a suffix which abstracts the whole as 'the state of being'. As a result of this rebus, *Gedankennotwendigkeit* is something like *'the state of being turned into necessary (unavoidable, pure) thoughts'*. The Gallic style is less preoccupied with deduction and intellectual construction and directed more towards the use of the persuasive strength of words and speeches in an aesthetically perfect way (*élégance*). Words have an inherent power to convince. They may create *potential reality*.

Finally the Nipponic intellectual style, imbued with Hindu, Buddhist and Taoist philosophies, favours a more modest, global and provisional approach. Thinking and knowledge are conceived of as being in a temporary state, open to alteration. 'The Japanese rarely pronounce absolute, categorical statements in daily discourse; they prefer vagueness even about trivial matters . . . because clear statements have a ring of immodesty, of being judgements of reality' (Galtung, 1981, p. 833). It is especially important for western researchers when they research in Asian countries to have in mind where their theories originate from and where they are supposed to apply. That could be termed an evaluation of 'intellectual distance' which may call for the use of contingency theory (see, for instance, Shenkar and Von Glinow, 1994, who use the case of Chinese organizations to illustrate national contingency).

The issue of language in international business research

Different languages are used in the research process, those of researchers, informants, theories, questionnaires and instruments, clients or evaluators of the research. The resulting Tower of Babel is often simplified by the use of English as International Language (EIL), or by the mean of translation as a cross-language comparison process supposed to lead to similar meaning, leaving aside idiosyncrasies and irreductible differences. Faucheux (1976, p. 271) phrases the issue in a definitive way: 'The hope of doing language-free cross-cultural research is vain.' Comparing across cultures without awareness of language always results in biased and impoverished findings. At least three elements in language have an influence on the research process:

- words in as much as they signal specific meaning;
- words as they are assembled in sentences and text through grammar and syntax and work as codes that must in some way be 'translated' into other codes, when the researcher and the 'researched' do not share the same linguistic background;
- language, in general, provides the speaker with a particular world view.

Translation equivalence
Translation equivalence may be divided into the following subcategories: lexical equivalence, idiomatic equivalence, grammatical–syntactical equivalence and experiential equivalence (Sechrest et al., 1972). Lexical equivalence is that which is provided by dictionaries: for instance, one may discover that the English adjective 'warm' translates into the French *chaud*. The problem of idiomatic equivalence comes when you try to translate a sentence such as 'it's warm': French has two expressions, either *il fait chaud* (literally, 'it makes warm' meaning 'it's warm [today]') or *c'est chaud* (meaning 'it [this object] is warm'). An idiom is a linguistic usage that is natural to native speakers. Idioms are most often non-equivalent: for instance, the English present progressive (I am doing) has no

equivalent in French, except *je suis en train de,* which is highly colloquial.

Grammatical–syntactical equivalence deals with how words are
ordered in a language, sentences are constructed and meaning is
expressed. English generally proceeds in an active way, starting
with the subject, followed by the verb and then the complement,
avoiding abstractions as well as convoluted sentences. Many languages, including German and French, start by explaining the
circumstances in relative clauses before they proceed into the action.
This results in complex sentences (such as you may find in this
book) which start with relative clauses based on when, where, even
though, although, and so on. The Japanese language has a quite
different ordering of words compared to western languages since
verbs are at the end of the sentence.

Experiential equivalence is about what words and sentences
mean for people in their everyday experience. Coming back to
chaud, it translates into two English words 'warm' and 'hot': the
French do not experience 'warmth' with two concepts as do the
English, the Germans and many others. Similarly, the special experience of coldness expressed in the word 'chilly' cannot be
adequately rendered in French. Translated terms must refer to real
items and real experiences, which are familiar in the source as well
as the target cultures. Expressions such as 'dual career couple',
'decision-making', or even 'strategic plan' may face experiential
equivalence problems.

Another example of experiential non-equivalence is given by the
Japanese numbering system which reflects a special experience of
counting, where the numbers cannot be fully abstracted from the
object being counted (Chinese is similar to Japanese in this respect).
Most often the Japanese add a particle indicating which objects are
counted. *Nin*, for instance, is used to count human beings: *yo-nin* is
four (persons). *Hiki* is used for counting animals, except birds for
which *wa* is used (meaning 'feather'), *satsu* for books, *hon* for round
and long objects, *mai* for flat things such as a sheet of paper, textiles,
coins, etc., and *hai* for cups and bowls and liquid containers in
general.

A vivid illustration of translation problems is given by errors in
the case of a major scientific concept, 'reproductive health', widely
used for the UN world conference on population development held
in Cairo in 1994. The concept of 'reproductive health' was translated
into German as *Gesundheit der Fortpflanzung* (health of propagation).
The Arabic translators invented the formula 'spouses take a break
from each other after childbirth'. The Russian translators worded
this in despair as 'the whole family goes on holiday', and the

Chinese translators elevated themselves to the almost brilliant formula 'a holiday at the farm' (Bohnet, 1994).

Back-translation and related techniques
The back-translation technique (Campbell and Werner, 1970) is the most widely employed method for reaching translation equivalence (mainly lexical and idiomatic) in cross-cultural research. This procedure helps to identify probable translation errors. One translator translates from the source language (S) into a target language (T). Then another translator, ignorant of the source-language text, translates the first translator's target language text back into the source language (S'). Then the two source-language versions are compared (Table 2.4).

When back-translating, discrepancies may arise from translation mistakes in either direction or from actual translation equivalence problems which are then uncovered. Then a final target-language questionnaire (T_f) is discussed and prepared by the researcher (who speaks the source language) and the two translators. It is advisable that one translator is a native speaker of the target language and the other a native speaker of the source language; thus they are translating into their native language rather than from it, which is more difficult and less reliable.

However, back-translation can also instil a false sense of security in the investigator by demonstrating a spurious lexical equivalence (Deutscher, 1973). Simply knowing that words are equivalent is not enough. These literally equivalent words and phrases must convey equivalent meanings in the two languages or cultures. Another technique, blind parallel translation (Mayer, 1978), consists of having several translators translate independently from the source language into the target language. The different target versions are compared and a final version is written. Parallel and back-translation can be merged, as shown in Table 2.4. When two languages and cultures present wide variations, such as Korean and English, combining parallel and back-translation provides a higher level of equivalence. Translation techniques, even sophisticated ones, might prove incapable of achieving full comparability of data.

A more sophisticated solution to the problem of translation has been suggested by Campbell and Werner (1970). Research instruments should be developed by collaborators in the two cultures and items, questions or other survey materials should be generated jointly. After back-translation or an initial translation process has been performed, there is an opportunity to change the source-language wording. This technique, called *decentring*, not only changes the target language, as in the previous techniques, but also

Table 2.4 *Advantages and drawbacks of translation techniques*

	Direct translation	Back-translation	Technique Parallel translation	Mixed techniques
Process	$S \Rightarrow T$	$S \Rightarrow T; T \Rightarrow S'$ comparison S to S' $\Rightarrow$ final version T_f	$S \Rightarrow T; S \Rightarrow T'$ comparison T to T' $\Rightarrow$ final version T_f	$S \Rightarrow T; S \Rightarrow T'$ $T \Rightarrow S'; T' \Rightarrow S''$ comparison S' and S'', decentering of S $\Rightarrow$ final version T_f
Advantages	Easy to implement.	Ensures the discovery of most inadequacies.	Easier to implement in S country with T translators.	Ensures the best fit between source and target versions.
Drawbacks/ constraints	Leads to translation errors and discrepancies between S and T.	Requires the availability of two translators, one native in S and one native in T languages.	Leads to good wording in T, but does not ensure that specific meaning in S is fully rendered.	Costly to implement. Difficult to find the translators. Implies readiness to change source-language version.

Legend: S = source language; T = target language (translators or versions) allows the words and sentences in the source language to be changed if this provides enhanced accuracy. The ultimate words and phrases employed will depend on which common/similar meaning is sought in both languages simultaneously, without regard to whether words and phrases originate in the source or the target languages. A pre-test of the translated research instrument in the target culture is necessary until satisfactory levels of reliability on conceptual and measurement equivalence are attained (Sood, 1990).

The Whorfian hypothesis
In French, the sole term *pouvoir* means 'power', 'can' (physical ability) and 'may' (permission or possibility). Hofstede (1994a, p.8) contrasts four different models of organizations through four organization theorists, all born in the mid-nineteenth century: the Frenchman, Henri Fayol; the German, Max Weber; the American, Fredrick Winslow Taylor; and the Chinese, Sun Yat Sen. Fayol was a French engineer and wrote *Administration Industrielle et Générale* after retirement from his position of *Président-Directeur-Général* of a mining company. Hofstede quotes Fayol and Weber comparatively on the exercise of authority. Fayol's views reflect the strong emphasis on power in the high power-distance French society:

> We distinguish in a manager his statutory authority which is in the office, and his personal authority which consists of his intelligence, his knowledge, his experience, his moral value, his leadership, his service record, etc. For a good manager, personal authority is the indispensable complement to statutory authority. (Fayol, 1916, p. 21)

By contrast, Max Weber, a university professor with experience in the civil service, wrote: 'The authority to give the commands required for the discharge of (the assigned) duties should be exercised in a stable way. It is strictly delimited by rules concerning the coercive means . . . which may be placed at the disposal of officials' (Weber 1970, p. 650). The contrast found in the concept of authority (personal versus impersonal, bounded by statute rather than bounded by rules) is also reflected in the German language where, contrary to French, auxiliary verbs distinguish clearly between physical ability (*können*) and ability by rule permission (*dürfen*).

Language tends simultaneously to reflect and shape our world views. It contains preshaped images of the real world which partly condition our experiences and perceptions. The first proponent of the idea that language has a decisive influence on culture was the linguist Edward Sapir. Language creates categories in our minds, which in turn directly influence the things we judge to be similar and those which deserve to be differentiated. It is our *Weltanschauung* that will be determined: our way of observing, describing and interacting, and finally the way in which we construct our reality:

> The fact of the matter is that the real world is to a large extent unconsciously built up on the language habits of the group. No two languages are ever sufficiently similar as to be considered as representing the same social reality. The worlds in which different societies live are distinct worlds, not merely the same world with different labels attached. (Sapir, 1929, p. 214)

The linguist and anthropologist Benjamin Lee Whorf developed and extended Sapir's hypothesis. The Whorf–Sapir hypothesis contends that the structure of language has a significant influence on perception and categorization. The verifications of the Whorf–Sapir hypothesis seem to have been fairly conclusive, in particular those related to the comparative experiments based on Navajo children on the one hand and Anglo-Americans on the other. They both shared all principal sociocultural characteristics (education, family income, religion, etc.) except language (see the experiments reported by Ferraro, 1990, pp. 54–5). But although the empirical testing of this hypothesis seems to have been fairly thorough, it is not considered valid by many linguists. For example, the gender given to words is not necessarily indicative of a particular cultural meaning (for example, the gender of the earth, sun, moon, vices, virtues, etc.), for most often it seems to reflect an arbitrary choice. It may be the case, however, that this attribution of gender had a certain meaning at the genesis of the language, but that the meaning has since been lost.

An illustration of the Whorfian hypothesis is how languages reflect different patterns of time, a key variable in management. Time representations are conveyed through the medium of language, as a means of communication and therefore collective action. Whorf comments about the Hopi language in the following terms:

> After long and careful study and analysis, the Hopi language is seen to contain no words, grammatical forms, constructions or expressions, that refer directly to what we call 'time', or to past, present, and future, or to motion as kinematic rather than dynamic (i.e. as a continuous translation in space and time rather than as an exhibition of a dynamic effort in a certain process), or that even refer to space in such a way as to exclude that element of extension or existence that we call 'time', and so by implication leave a residue that could be referred to as 'time'. Hence, the Hopi language contains no reference to 'time', either implicit or explicit. (Carroll, 1956, pp. 57–8)

Time vocabulary tells a lot about the linkage between language and cultural representations. For those who have doubts about the existence of differences in cultural representations of time which are revealed, conveyed and reproduced by language, the example of the English/US word 'deadline' is very illustrative. A quick translation in French would give *échéance* [*temporelle*] or *délai de rigueur* (Langenscheidt, 1989), but would not render the intensity of this word. Taken literally, it seems to suggest something like 'beyond this [temporal] line, you will [there is a danger of] die [dying]'. It therefore gives a genuine notion of deadly urgency to what was originally a mere abstract notion (a point which has been agreed upon on a time line). The word deadline is used in French by many business people as such (*un deadline*), even though it is not in the official dictionary, because it conveys a typically Anglo-American sense of urgency that French people do not find in their own language.

Language also reflects (and preshapes) how people envision the future. In some African languages (Kamba and Kikuyu), there are three future tenses which express (1) action in two to six months; (2) action that will take place immediately; (3) action 'in the foreseeable future, after this or that event'. Commenting on the uses of these African tenses, M'biti (1968) demonstrates how coherence and sophistication in the accurate use of the near future, are important to African people.

> You have these tenses before you: just try to imagine the tense into which you would translate passages of the New Testament concerning the Parousia of Our Lord Jesus Christ, or how you would teach eschatology . . . If you use tense no. 1, you are speaking about something that will take place in the next two to six months, or in any case within two years at most. If you use no. 2, you are referring to something that will take place in the immediate future, and if it does not take place you are exposed as a liar in people's eyes. Should you use no. 3 you are telling people that the event concerned will definitely take place, but when something else has happened first. In all these tenses, the event must be very near to the present moment: if, however, it lies in the far distant future – beyond the two-year limit – you are neither understood nor taken seriously. (M'biti, 1968, pp. 8–20)

Levine, researching on Brazilian versus US time, highlights the ways in which concepts of punctuality are reflected in the language. He takes the example of the translation from English to Portuguese of a questionnaire containing the verb 'to wait':

> Several of our questions were concerned with how long the respondent would *wait* for someone to arrive versus when they *hoped* the person would arrive versus when they actually *expected* the person would come. Unfortunately for us, it turns out that the term *to wait, to hope* and *to expect* are all typically translated as the single verb *esperar* in Portuguese. In many ways our translation difficulties taught us more about Brazilian-

Anglo differences in time conception than did the subjects' answers to
the questions. (Levine, 1988, pp. 48–9; emphasis added)

There is a sort of continuum across languages in the accuracy of
description of the waiting phenomenon (a fundamental issue in
time experience). The French language, which lies somewhere
between English and Portuguese in terms of temporal accuracy,
uses two words: *attendre* (to wait) and *espérer* (to hope). To expect
has no direct equivalent in French and must be translated by a
lengthy circumlocution (*compter sur l'arrivée de*).

Languages in relation to actions, thoughts and emotions
Another example may be given of the language–culture link by the
Anglo-American way of dealing with action, especially in business.
There is a rich vocabulary to be used, which is often difficult to
translate into many other languages, if real equivalence of meaning
is sought. The words might include, for instance: *problem solving,
issue, matter of fact, down to earth, (empirical) evidence, to complete, to
achieve, feedback, to perform, achievement, individual, data, to check, to
plan, deadline, cognitive, emotional, successful.* Even such an elemen-
tary word as 'fact' is demanding: in English it must be an
established piece of reality; its French equivalent, *fait*, is less
demanding in terms of unanimously agreed-upon reality (*les faits
peuvent être discutés*, corresponding to a spirit of the facts being 'challenged' rather than just discussed); in German, a fact may be
translated by *Tatsache, Wirklichkeit, Wahrheit*, or *Tat* – it can mean
equally a piece of reality, a piece of truth, or a piece of action.

When translating, the difficulties extend far beyond the pure lexical and grammatical ones: they are cultural translation difficulties,
corresponding to what is often called the spirit of a language (in
French, *le génie de la langue*). Far from being merely a linking of a
chain of words, a language contains a series of stands taken on the
nature of our relationship to reality. Let us compare, for instance,
how the three most important western European languages express
ideas, facts and moods. One can tentatively suggest that German is
stronger than English in the expression of abstractions. In German,
word endings such as *-heit, -keit, -ung, -schaft, -tum, -nis*, allow the
'abstractification' of concrete notions. English is not only less able to
express pure concepts, but also less prone to. English is more action
and more outward oriented, with a view that data orientation and
facts based approaches allow a separation between feelings (inner)
and actions (directed toward the outside). French expresses inner
states more accurately, with an emphasis on emotions rather than
pure thoughts, describing the relationships between the self and

others with an underlying view that any action is related to emotions and affectivity. Stereotypically, we could say that English is
predominantly a language of action, French a language of emotions
and German a language of thoughts.

Language reflects status, hierarchy and a vision of what are
appropriate social relationships. The way to address other people
is another example of how language reflects social hierarchy.
There is only one word used in English for addressing other
people, 'you' most often with the first name; this is considered as
reflecting strong assumptions about equality and a preference for
informality. By contrast, the French often use the formal *vous* for
people they do not know well and people of higher status, while
the informal *tu* is reserved for family and friends. Thus the French
are reputed to be more formal. The Germans use *du* (second
person singular) in informal and personal settings and *Sie* (third
person plural) in formal address. The Germans, like the Spaniards,
have three forms of address: while the second person plural (*ihr*)
has been lost in practice in German, it remains in Spanish. In fact,
a closer look at these forms shows that the English 'you' was not
originally a second person singular, which was 'thou' in old
English (as in Shakespeare's plays), but the more polite second
person plural. This means that the only address kept in English is
based on an assumption of respect and formality and not on the
everyday and less formal form of 'thou'. In fact, the assumed
informality of Anglo interaction, advocated by many native
English speakers, is difficult to grasp for a Latin. In people being
called by their first name and together with 'you', the Latin sees a
different kind of formalism rather than true informality. Language
reflects quite complex assumptions about equality between
people. The French address *vous* reflects the strong emphasis on
hierarchical and status differences in French society, but it can be
nuanced, adding for instance *Monsieur* (formal *vous*) or simply the
first name (informal *vous*). It is naturally not simply because they
have long used the polite form that the French have a fairly hierarchical society. But the language context contributes to constantly
reframing culture-bound assumptions about hierarchy in the
society.

Consequences of the Whorfian hypothesis
The first consequence of the Whorf–Sapir hypothesis is that people
from different cultures not only communicate in different ways, but
also perceive, categorize and construct their realities differently. This
therefore supposes a 'state of alert' in communication, a readiness to
accept that words, even when translating well, offer only an illusion

of sharing in the same vision of reality. As many foreign words as possible should be kept in their original form, in order to recognize culturally unique concepts in the native language. Questioning translators, informants or foreign research associates about meaning in the local cultural context will allow identification of areas of shared meaning. For instance, an English term such as 'act of God' is not a strict equivalent of the French term *force majeure*. The Langenscheidt (1970) compact dictionary translates 'act of God' as *force majeure*, but it translates *force majeure* as 'overpowering circumstances'; Harrap's Concise does not include 'act of God' in the English section and translates *force majeure* as 'circumstances outside one's control'. *Force majeure* is used as such in English and US contracts.

An unfortunate consequence of the Whorf–Sapir hypothesis is that linguistic ethnocentrism is largely inevitable. It probably explains why natives of a language and culture mostly write about cultural topics for their fellow citizens. Famous anthropologists belonged to the cultures of their publishers and readers, not to the cultures they observed. The same holds true for area specialists, such as the American Theodore Zeldin and the Briton John Ardagh, both experts in French culture. An outsider to what is observed is better placed than a culture and language insider for reporting what has been noted. However paradoxical and provocative it may seem, it is more important to be understood than to understand. What is said by genuine cultural insiders is often difficult to understand unless their words have in some way been recalibrated in the linguistic/cultural background of the readers, which means a lot more than simply translated.

International management researchers are not required to have full command of several foreign languages for them not to be linguistically ethnocentric. What is important is the ability to catch what is unique in the structure of foreign languages and words; this does not require fluent reading and speaking. A look at a book of basic grammar and careful attention to specific words are a good start. Very often authors of books on Japanese business customs or management style keep Japanese words as they are originally pronounced when they want to signal a culturally specific meaning. Sometimes words are forged that partly bridge the cultural divide. Boye de Mente cites, for instance, the Japanese word *nominication* which is made up of the first part of the Japanese word *nomimasu* (to drink) and the last half of 'communication'. 'This Japlish word refers to business conversations and socializing that takes place in bars, cabarets, and other drinking establishments, and it is one of the institutionalized ways of "wisdom gathering" in Japan' (De Mente, 1990, p. 261).'

Culturally unique life concepts have a major impact on organization and decision-making issues. For example, original concepts in the area of labour management relationships are signalled by words such as 'management by objectives' for the Americans, *ringi* for the Japanese, *mitbestimmung* for the Germans, or *concertation* for the French. The same holds for the managing institutions of a company: a German *Aufsichtsrat*, often translated into English as 'supervisory board', should be considered a specific institution typical of German business culture, with particular consequences in the real life of real businesses (Schneider-Lenné, 1993). Although linguistic ethnocentrism is inevitable, we must strive for linguistic polycentrism by trying to keep original words as they are, understanding meaningful elements in the grammar (such as gender, tense, sentence construction etc.), and trying to behave as 'explorers' of the meanings and world views expressed by different languages.

EIL and international management research
In considering English as the lingua franca of management research (English as an International Language, EIL),[1] we have to differentiate between native and non-native English speakers. For non-native, English-speaking researchers, learning English and often one or two other languages is common. For instance, the Swedes, Finns, Danes and Norwegians often speak three or four foreign languages: English, another Nordic language, French, German or Spanish. The situation is very different for native English-speakers. Simon observes: 'The United States continues to be the only nation where you can graduate from college without having had one year of a foreign language' (1980, p. 2). Although regrettable, this may be explained and understood. The USA is a vast country with high linguistic homogeneity, despite the inroads of Spanish. There is no urgent need to learn foreign languages compared with Europe where most large cities are located less than 200 miles from a foreign-speaking area. Moreover, there is asymmetry in the efforts needed for learning foreign languages; a westerner learning Chinese or Japanese has to learn the characters, which implies a much greater effort than for the Japanese or Chinese to learn the Roman alphabet with its 26 phonetic characters. The *gaijin* (non-Japanese) has to learn two syllabaries of about one hundred characters each (*hiragana* and *katakana*, phonetic symbols) and about 1,850 *kanjis* (ideographic symbols). Finally, Americans easily find English-speakers during their travels, they can count on their foreign partners to speak English and they are tolerant towards the mistakes of their non-native counterparts.

Understandably, therefore, the impact of language differences has been systematically underestimated in international business research because of a single bias in Anglo-American culture. Most international business literature does not include a single fully foreign reference, that is, a foreign author in a foreign language. Foreign authors, when translated, will not be read in their original linguistic context and when not translated into English will not be considered. However, this regrettable situation also results from practical reasons for maintaining language homogeneity in sources, namely that the reader would not be able either to find or read references in foreign languages.

What is unfortunate, however, is that native English-speakers are at a disadvantage in the long term, although it may appear to be the exact contrary over the short term. The main disadvantage is that they cannot grasp the features of the foreign language in terms of world view and communication style. Many native English-speakers cannot imagine what it implies for their foreign respondents or research associates to express their thoughts in English with limited proficiency unless the native English researchers have themselves tried to learn and speak a foreign language. Thus native English-speakers have to develop an awareness of language barriers. The message to be conveyed cannot be simply and plainly to learn foreign languages. There is a difference between understanding and speaking a foreign language and grasping the consequences of language variations. Management researchers do not need to be multilingual, but rather to have an in-depth awareness of what language differences imply.

However, many foreign researchers or informants who are non-native English-speakers, although they seem to have a good command of English, still hold the kind of world view shaped by their native language. They may be somewhat misleading for their opposite numbers, looking quite the same, while being fairly different. In addition to their different mindset, they may be more proficient in oral than written communication, which may cause problems in discussing the written details of research or when writing for publication.

Assessing cross-cultural research: international marketing

The linguistic bias leads to a distorted view when assessing cross-cultural research; in the following section the example of international marketing is examined (Denis and Usunier, 1995).[2]

Under-representation of research on culture in international marketing

Two literature reviews have been performed which allow identification of the relevant articles that have been published on this topic during the 1980–90 period: Aulakh and Kotabe (1993) and Cavusgil and Li (1992). They provide valuable information in assessing the importance granted to culture in international marketing journals. The first was produced primarily with a view of assessing the recent theoretical and methodological development in the field of international business. The second includes an abstract for most of the entries recorded in the bibliography. Aulakh and Kotabe's survey covers 21 journals (published in English) and records 720 articles, 40 per cent being published in general journals and 60 per cent in international business journals between 1980 and 1990. They identify only 21 articles dealing with the cultural environment from a total of 607 pertaining to all aspects of international marketing. Out of these 21 articles only 8 dealt with empirical studies, which lead them to the following observation:

> The environmental research stream, one of the earliest research streams in international marketing, still continues to be descriptive and exploratory . . . A plausible explanation for this lack of theory-based articles is the inherent problem encountered in theorizing on cultural . . . factors that are extremely difficult to generalize cross-culturally and almost impossible to predict. (Aulakh and Kotabe, 1993, p. 16)

Cavusgil and Li consulted 30 journals published in English, most of them American. Their coverage is limited to the period of January 1982 to October 1991. Some 600 articles are included in this bibliography after a screening process so that only articles 'which offered the greatest relevance to scholars and practitioners' (p. viii) were selected. Only 17 articles were selected by Cavusgil and Li and entered under the heading 'Cultural and Social Environment'. Since some articles might very well deal with culture but could have been entered under another heading (there are no multiple entries in this bibliography), an examination of the other sections of the book resulted in identifying 25 additional articles dealing with culture. The conclusion to be reached on the basis of the work of Aulakh and Kotabe and Cavusgil and Li is that the cultural dimension does not draw the kind of attention among academics that one would expect, given the generally recognized central role of culture in international marketing. In the first source only 2 per cent, and in the second only 7 per cent of all the articles selected (roughly over a ten-year period) dealt with this topic.

International coverage: language, perspective and specification
The bibliographies of Aulakh and Kotabe and Cavusgil and Li both
suffer from some biases which result in an under-representation of
the cultural stream in the international marketing literature. These
surveys are admittedly American oriented. They cover almost exclusively American journals, European or Asian reviews being
considered only if published in English. Yet, especially since we are
dealing with cross-cultural marketing, worthwile contributions
should be expected to be found in non-English publications, such as
Marketing Zeitschrift für Forschung und Praxis published in Germany or
Recherche et Applications en Marketing and *Revue Française de Marketing*
published in France. A review of the national journals outside the
USA would yield a useful cross-cultural crop which would provide
greater diversity in the field. Some national publications edited in
English deserve consideration for inclusion in a review of the international marketing literature. For instance, *Japan Dentsu Marketing
Advertising* carries a wealth of information on the Japanese marketing
system, a topic which draws an interest worldwide. Such periodicals
are not selected in the two bibliographies for a number of reasons:
they are not known by American reviewers; they are not readily
available in North America; they would need to be translated to be
understood by solely English-speaking readers, and they are not written according to North American academic standards.

Another reason for the lack of inclusion of articles dealing with
culture is that they are often published in journals such as the
International Journal of Research in Marketing, *Journal of Business
Research*, *Journal of Retailing*, *Journal of Advertising*, *International
Journal of Advertising* and *Journal of Purchasing and Materials
Management*, which are not covered by Aulakh and Kotabe or
Cavusgil and Li. The bibliographers' viewpoint privileges a practical marketing management orientation and what is outside the
discipline or cannot be immediately translated into managerial
action is unlikely to be considered for inclusion. This is under-
standable since research in international marketing is performed
almost exclusively by academics teaching in business schools, and
who therefore would favour action-oriented inquiries over com-
placent intellectual speculation. The problem is however that
culture is both a wide and a marginal domain of inquiry (in each
discipline). As a result, it is likely that valuable contributions will be
widely scattered across a great variety of publications, most of them
outside of the realm of mainstream international business or even
marketing journals. For instance, a most interesting piece on advertising and cross-cultural convergence in Europe will fail to be
picked up because it was published in the *European Journal of*

Communication (Snyder et al., 1991). One of the few pieces on the impact of culture on pricing would be omitted for the same reason: it was published in the *Journal of Applied Psychology* (Peterson and Jolibert, 1976). This narrowness of viewpoint also leads to the exclusion of pieces relevant to culture even when published in journals canvassed by the bibliographers. For example, a number of articles published in the *Journal of the Market Research Society* in 1982 on cross-cultural marketing research issues are omitted by Cavusgil and Li, as well as an article comparing the Japanese and American ways of researching markets which was published in the *Harvard Business Review* (Johansson and Nonaka, 1987).

Researching the cultural dimension of international marketing requires to look into areas that are not mainstream or fashionable, in part because cultural differences may not have direct and obvious relevance to the study of business. Attempts at establishing direct and operational linkages in marketing management tend to discourage cultural explanations which are often indirect and difficult to translate into strategies. For example, the meaning of time is a topic which is considered as most important in international ventures by most practitioners. Differences in the perception of time have vast repercussions on negotiations, pricing and strategy implementation. Yet one of the very few articles on this topic (Usunier, 1991) was published in *Management International Review*, which is listed by Cavusgil and Li but not included in their bibliography. A comparative cross-cultural study of sales force motivations systems (Hill et al., 1991) is also not covered by them, even though it was published in *International Marketing Review*.

It is of course difficult to delineate what belongs to the cultural dimension of marketing and what does not. There is, for instance, a very substantial body of literature on the influence of 'made in' labels. Over a hundred articles have been published on this topic over the last fifteen years and they keep on coming. One might wonder why there is such an interest in this question since most often buyers are not even aware of the country of origin of the product they purchase, especially when these products are binational or multinational. The most likely explanation is that the topic has been and still remains fashionable in academic circles. Articles published in this area certainly do not appear under the heading of culture, yet some of them could: for instance, the articles by Shimp and Sharma (1987) or Han (1988), which deal with the issue of consumer ethnocentrism and patriotism. The point is that culture is omnipresent in international marketing and a strict classification separating the cultural environment from other sections such as marketing management, buyer behaviour or international market research like the one adopted by Cavusgil and Li results in an under-representation of the contributions of culture-related work. Although under-represented, a thorough tracking process would most likely indicate that compared to the overall research production in international marketing it still remains limited in spite of its relevance to the field. The production of such material is penalized by both the system in which it is produced, and by the researchers themselves.

Biases in production of cross-cultural research: systemic ethnocentrism

Much of the above criticism of the two bibliographies centres on the American system of research production. More precisely, we refer here to what we call a systemic bias in research production, resulting from the pressures applied by the academic system in which researchers perform that lead them to conduct and publish research in specific directions and according to specific methodologies. This bias affects both the quantity and type of research produced on culture. American researchers make a living, at least in part, with their research through the tenure track system which confers a rather substantial importance to publications. A 'proper' publication record results in promotions, postings at the more reputable institutions and, as a consequence, to greater prestige and in the end to higher pay. Paradoxically, the primary clients of researchers are not the management practitioners their research is supposed to enlighten but their peers who grant them tenure, respectability, honours perhaps, privileges often, and indirectly better salaries. There is no doubt that the American system will induce researchers to proceed according to the positivist and cumulative approach which is the established standard in the USA but much less adopted in Europe, Latin America or even Asia. This approach presents the following three salient characteristics:

1 *Professionalism.* It is a professional system where research production and diffusion are controlled by academic associations which organize conferences and manage journals, set publication, and in turn research standards.
2 *Emphasis on science rather than knowledge.* It is a system that emphasizes 'scientific' production confirming rather than rejecting previous research, and leads to a view of scientific knowledge where what becomes the accepted truth is essentially the result of cumulative confirmations.
3 *Praxis.* It must lead to applicable results. This is a legitimate concern since research is done by academics teaching in business schools, and thus preparing students for management careers. It

should be noted, however, that the practical relevance of academic research has often been questioned in business circles.

These three conditions do not favour academic inquiries into the incidence of culture in international marketing. The first, professionalism, imposes research frameworks which are difficult to apply to the cultural dimension. Clearly specified relationships between measurable dependent and independent variables are not easy to hypothesize when cultural dimensions are difficult not only to measure but also to define in the first place. Sometimes the urge to quantify backfires. For instance, some researchers have been unable to resist the temptation to use Hofstede's cultural dimensions as proxy measures for cross-cultural differences or cultural distance in international marketing (Kogut and Singh, 1988). Although these measures may have some relevance when applied to organization issues as intended by Hofstede, the clustering of countries based on their similarity in score pattern on the four cultural dimensions makes little sense for market segmentation. It is difficult to make any sense of the fact that Costa Rica is closer to Great Britain than it is to Chili or Guatemala, or that Pakistan is close to Denmark, and France to East Africa (see the clusters in Hofstede, 1983).

The second argument, emphasis on cumulative science, does not favour research on culture either since it promotes the inquiries into issues that are 'fashionable', and in addition in a conventional way as far as methodology is concerned. This explains why some topics have been over-researched such as the transaction cost approach in entry mode selection, the standardization/adaptation issue, and the country-of-origin effect. Culture is likely to appear non-mainstream and unattractive to researchers wishing to 'make it' professionally. Finally, the 'applicable now' syndrome does not help. Although culture is omnipresent, it is also difficult to provide prescriptions on how to proceed to take that dimension into account. Furthermore, cross-cultural studies need time (several years) to develop to full size, which is difficult for the young researcher given the pressures of the tenure track system.

Conclusion

The researcher in international management must be a cultural translator, that is, transfer meaning across cultures. This form of mediation is not easy, explaining why cultural mediators often come from the home country of their readers. The ability to cross the borders of cultures is a rare talent. An impressive example of a good cultural translator is Masahiko Aoki who has obtained great success in depicting and explaining the internal working of the Japanese firm in Anglo terms (Aoki, 1990). Another example is Ikujiro Nonaka from Hitotsubashi University, who has tried, often with western colleagues, to give a better understanding of how Japanese firms manage their relationships with markets, consumers and competitors (see, for instance, Johansson and Nonaka, 1996).

Is international research really international? I do not believe so. Language barriers and differences in intellectual styles and academic systems are major deterrents for cross-border management research. In this human rather than technological field of knowledge, meaning must be constantly fine tuned. The ability to take cultural diversity into account in international management research is heavily curtailed by the English-only bias. True international research, which is still quite rare, should always be the product of collaboration between native researchers coming from diverse cultural and linguistic contexts.

Notes

1 For more on language, culture and world views, see the special issue of the *International Journal of Intercultural Relations*, vol. 19, no. 2, 1995.

2 This section largely draws on Denis and Usunier (1995). Reproduced with permission.

3

Design and implementation of cross-cultural research in management

Designs in international and cross-cultural management research are understandably complex. The diversity of management, cultural and context variables to be taken into account makes them complex to conceive and researchers need to keep this complexity under control both at the conceptual and data collection levels. Overly complex designs result in failures during the implementation process since the researcher cannot collect the required data or control appropriately the relevance of the data collection process and generates either 'flat' data (almost no variance) or fuzzy data (variance is mostly measurement error). This is true of qualitative as well as quantitative approaches: if the design requires in-depth interviewees to elaborate way beyond their real experiences and their own mindset, they may smother their responses in a blanket of irrelevant statements.

The problems involved in monitoring the degree of complexity of an international cross-cultural research design cannot be solved by mere simplification. Simplification is tempting and to a large extent done by real world researchers in order to make the research project feasible. However to simplify the initial task of the researcher is to disentangle all the constructs, fields, variables and informants involved and try to make reasonable trade-offs as to what should be kept, given the key objectives of the study. Researchers generally have an initial thesis, that is, something they want to bring into light. The disentanglement process must have as an aim to reach the point where the chances successfully to confirm the thesis or disconfirm the contrary thesis will be high. There are basically two processual strategies for the disentanglement task that correspond roughly to criteria which are popular in operations research, maximin and minimax. The maximin approach starts from a very large number of variables, concepts, units, etc. (max) and reduces it to the minimal set which can achieve optimally the set research objectives. The other criteria, minimax, uses as reduced a base as is feasible (minimal) and progressively increases the degree of complexity for bringing relevance and feasibility up to a maximum point where marginal increases in complexity would be detrimental to the project.

There are various complementary content avenues for the disentanglement process. The first avenue starts with the formulation of research questions which must be stated clearly and concisely and obey to some basic rules, such as to have a potential audience. The choice of an appropriate avenue for explanation presupposes that alternative paradigms have been investigated and their implication in terms of field research methods assessed before the researcher chooses her favourite among them, that is, the one she believes will be the most meaningful. The researcher will also try to assess the degree of complexity in order to see where it can be reduced with minimal losses in relevance and meaning: the third part of this chapter proposes a framework for assessing the complexity of international cross-cultural management research designs. The fourth avenue is for the researcher to develop an awareness of how paradigmatic choices influence the researcher's relationship to her field: the overall coherence can be heightened by deciding clearly what the researchers will privilege: either the phenomenon under investigation, the key informants (people), the pure ideas that serve as conceptual reference points (ideas), or the research instruments that allow to generate data from people and situations ('research machines'). The last part of the chapter describes an avenue which is largely in use for addressing cross-cultural research issues by sharing complexity between researchers; it deals with the setting up of cross-national research networks. An appendix lists journals where researchers can find relevant cross-cultural management literature.

Formulation of research questions in cross-cultural management

Examples of research problems and consequent questions

Does it matter at all?   The initial question was to know whether culture, mostly viewed as national culture, had an influence or not on managerial attitudes (Haire et al., 1966; Harnett and Cummings, 1980; Kelley, et al., 1987). Nowadays, there are fewer such research questions since Hofstede's (1980a) study, *Culture's Consequences*, and many other studies (see, for instance, Bhagat et al., 1990) seem to have put an end to this question, at least as a broad interrogation. However, this question remains in actuality when it is applied to specific segments of management practices and managerial behaviour.

Replications   These are popular kinds of studies which offer the ease of having a preset design (the original study) and require only a new round of research implementation including new data collection. The research question is whether the replication provides the same findings; positive results promote confidence in the reliability of the original results (Hubbard and Armstrong, 1994). Replications, although not always considered to be major contributions, have the immense merit of verifying the accuracy of a given knowledge base. Hofstede's study has been the object of numerous replications (see Sondergaard, 1994) or it has been 'revisited' (see, for instance, Dorfman and Howell, 1988, on Hofstede's dimensions and their influence on leadership patterns). Cross-national or cross-cultural replications have the special status of a replication with extension because they try to assess whether the outcomes of the original study can be extended beyond the original context. The research question is then: Does it still hold true from here (source context) to there (target context)? Naive cross-cultural replications (I quote none) which ignored the extension aspect have been useful because they act as a major driver for the search for cross-cultural equivalence, developed in full length in the next chapter. Their findings have been typically inconclusive because of the relative lack of common comparison base; this has called for increased attention to the influence of context on replicability. Few researchers would now posit their research question too directly in terms of replication, because it has a distinct flavour of cultural insensitivity. However, most cross-cultural research designs still have an underlying replication component which needs to be recognized.

Transportability/transposability studies   Management seems more and more accepted as a human and social reality and not as a mere set of techniques; it is embedded in particular organizational and behavioural contexts. Illustrative of this is the case of the American system of management by objectives (MBO), which became in France the *direction participative par objectifs* (DPPO); it was transformed to fit with the high power distance and uncertainty avoidance of the French environment and was finally a failure (Hofstede, 1980a, 1991). The research question is then: Can a particular type of management practice, organization structure or employee motivation system be transported from its original context, where it proved efficient, to another context which imports it? This type of question has been studied in various directions, from west to west, that is, from the USA to Europe (see Hofstede, 1980b), from east to west, that is, from Japan and Far East Asian to western countries, and from north to south, especially when studying technology transfer to developing countries (Dadfar and Gustavsson, 1992).

This type of research question has two main variants. The first is very much an Emic type of research and has as an implicit, yet almost visible, assumption that management practices are not really transposable, the questions being: Why are the foreign management practices not transportable? Why and how are the studied practices context-bound? Examples of such studies are Amado and Vinagre Brasil (1991) on Brazilian organizational life, Ali and Wahabi (1995) on the value systems of Moroccan managers, or 'Management Made in Germany' (Ogilvie and Wilderom, 1993).

However, it is increasingly recognized that the question of transportability of management theories and practices must be set in an interactive setting where, for instance, Japanese quality circles are implemented in one of the European contexts. Japan is the first Asian country to have drawn the attention of the western world to the global growth of its enterprises. This is why extensive research has been undertaken to understand the Japanese culture and national character in the society at large as well as the Japanese style of management. These studies have been authored either by Japanese (for example, Nakane, 1973; Hayashi, 1988; Maruyama, 1990; Ichikawa, 1993), or by foreign observers of the Japanese reality (for example, Ouchi, 1981; Pascale and Athos, 1981; Whitehill, 1991). Whereas the degree of knowledge concerning the specificity of management in Japan is now fairly high, there is still relatively little knowledge of the degree of transposability of Japanese management practices such as quality circles or total quality management. The research question changes from yes or no, or why is it not transportable to how can it be transposed. Brannen (1994) has studied how the Japanese owners, after the takeover of an ailing paper plant in western Massachusetts, have negotiated with the local workers and managers a progressive introduction of Japanese management systems. In the same vein of 'how' management systems are transported across borders, Kantor et al. (1995) show the competing influences of the French and American accounting systems on financial reporting practices in Arab countries. While the American system is more influential because of its worldwide credibility and place in international standards harmonization, the French system is culturally more adequate for Arab countries and exerts influence through its initial import by Egypt, a central country in the Arab world.

Comparative attitudes: different solutions to common problems   This type of research question revolves around a common problem, such as decision-making, issues in labour–management relationships or business ethics. The researcher(s) then compare(s) how different countries or cultures solve a similar problem. Sullivan and Nonaka (1988) explore how strategic categorization issues vary between US and Japanese managers, especially whether they view strategies as opportunies or constraints and whether they prefer diverse or targeted information. Similarly, Tse et al. (1988) study how Chinese and North American managers adjust to risk in international marketing decision-making. Mattson et al. (1993) examine the influence of management in the purchase of key production equipment and materials (a common problem), in the USA, Sweden, France and five South East Asian countries. They assess the respective influence of top management and functional areas (technical staff, production, purchasing) in four successive steps that can be found consistently across nations/culture (information gathering, need recognition, search for suppliers, evaluation of suppliers).

'How to' research issues involving culture   Such research questions often start from a typically international problem such as how expatriates cope with culture shock (Oberg, 1972), especially in remote locations. Expatriates' adjustment has been largely documented by numerous articles in the domain of international human resources management (see, for instance, Mendenhall et al., 1987; Black et al., 1991). Some authors have argued that working abroad may involve few adjustment problems provided that there is cultural proximity or compatibility between the country of expatriation and the home country culture, and the expatriate worker has a certain level of communication skills, language abilities and intercultural relationship competence (Dunbar and Katcher, 1990). This is particularly true when the expatriation site is a very large city, where the foreign resident easily finds all the goods and services of the home country. However, many studies report a fairly high rate of early return among expatriates, that is a return before the normal term of their assignment. Concerning American expatriates who are the subjects of most of the literature the early return rate can be estimated between 25% and 40% (Tung, 1981, 1984a). When the host country is a developing one, the early return rate can reach 70% (Copeland and Griggs, 1985). The estimated company cost for the early return of an American expatriate manager has been estimated between $50,000 and $150,000 (Black, 1988). Since expatriates are susceptible to culture shock and their early return is costly for companies, it is worth studying a range of research questions dealing with how to

improve their adjustment (professional, personal, spouse and family adjustment, return to the home country).

Basic rules for formulating cross-cultural research questions
Five rules have to be followed when formulating international research questions:

1 They must be clear.
2 The addition of an international/cross-cultural dimension to a management research question must make sense; otherwise, it simply increases the complexity with little or no additional contribution.
3 The research question(s) must be meaningful not only to the researcher but also to the target audience.
4 The research questions should be 'researchable', that is, grounded in some kind of theory and related to data or facts which can be collected.
5 They must result in insightful results for both managers and academic audiences. It is important to phrase the research question(s) clearly because international research designs are complex and unclear research questions will lead to confusion at the stages of theorization or data collection.

Check 1: Is the research question clear enough?   A clear research question is often reflected in the title of a paper which includes a question mark. For example, when the title is: 'Do Cultural Differences Affect Management and Productivity?' (Morris and Pavett, 1993), the researchers affirm strongly what they will be doing. They explain that the research was conducted at five plants of a US multinational company which produces disposable medical products (Mexico, England, Spain, Italy, the USA) with identical products, standardized operations and a similar organization in the five plants; this design allows comparison across national contexts. To be clear, a question must be adequately formulated in the introduction of the research report or article(s) which is drawn from the research. It is easy to find examples in the introduction of research articles and look at how the author(s) proceed in a few lines to define their research question(s). For instance, Berggren and Rehder (1993) compare two new manufacturing projects, a 'loser', the Uddevalla plant (Volvo) in Sweden, and a 'winner', the Saturn plant (General Motors). Their research question is how to combine competitiveness and a humanistic orientation in manufacturing organizations. They argue that the closure of the Uddevalla plant by Volvo in 1993 was due to depressed markets and low capacity utilization rather than problems of competitiveness of the new plant. Furthermore, the Saturn plant has adopted some elements of the assembly plant of Uddevalla, showing that it was a misinterpretation to posit the trade-off between job enrichment/team working and traditional assembly plants as a mere opposition between humanistic concerns (as a supposedly typical Swedish preoccupation) and productivity (as a supposedly typical US concern).

Check 2: Does it make any sense to add the international dimension? The researcher must wonder whether it makes sense to add the international dimension to a research question or domain which does not necessarily need it. I have been involved in a cross-national research project which deals with services management, investigating the value put by service customers on personnel in contact versus automated service delivery. Despite high expectations of some members of the research team, the cross-cultural aspect did not appear as significant in a process where service technologies were fundamentally similar across countries at similar levels of development. Individual variables such as age, gender, key board literacy and level of education appeared as far more significant than any cross-cultural rationale (see also Marshall et al., 1995).

Cost accounting methods, for instance, are fairly universal. The concept of direct costing and the methods for computing complete costs cross the borders of nations and cultures, but the management control systems that derive from cost accounting can be more susceptible to cross-national variance (Hofstede, 1968). It seems more appealing to add the international and possibly cross-cultural dimension, if there is some conjecture of a possible cross-national variance. Recruitment techniques, for instance, would be a better exemplar of cross-national variance than cost accounting systems. The birthplace of applicants, their marital status, age, citizenship or language competencies are standard, non-discriminatory inquiries in most cultures where there is still some being orientation. Such questions to applicants, the request for photographs or handwritten letters (for graphologic analysis) are universally popular, but in the USA they would be considered as discriminatory when recruiting people according to a US affirmative action compliance programme (Chonko et al., 1992). The 'affirmative action, equal opportunity' motto lies on extremely strong doing and outgroup orientations, whereby it is seen as almost evil to describe persons as they are.

Check 3: Is there a public, an audience?   The worst result in this respect is met when the reader finishes the research report or article and says 'so what?' If we take the case of a cross-national investigation of recruitment techniques, for which public will it be insightful? What are the suggestions for action, managerial implications and/or the improved knowledge brought by the research? Good research questions have a certain public, not necessarily all potential publics. In the example of recruitment techniques, the researcher has to a certain extent to choose the employer's side or the employee's side.

Another problematic category is the 'self-destroying questions' which have to be avoided because they lose their audience at a definite point in time, for instance, research questions with a deadline such as how will the strategies of European banks be affected by the single banking market in the European Union (EU). Given the time required for the research to be completed, it may happen that the final answer is not given by the research itself but by the actual strategic moves of banks in the EU.

Check 4: Is it 'researchable'?   Some meaningful and interesting research questions cannot easily be investigated. Business ethics, for instance, seems to lend itself 'easily' to a cross-cultural perspective because it makes sense. However, business ethics is not easy to research because the difference in world views of the underlying morals can vary considerably across cultures and religions. Morals can be personal versus impersonal, group oriented versus individualistic, lenient vis-à-vis the sinner as in Catholicism versus relatively tough as in Protestantism, internal morals versus externally regulated. Another reason for such a topic to be difficult to research is that respondents do not easily deliver their true mind on moral issues and a large part of the data on infringements is publicly unavailable, or only partly accessible, such as for international bribery.

When the research design implies collaborations or co-operations that cannot be reached easily, the topic should be considered as less researchable. Designs which require hard-to-organize experimental designs are also difficult to research. For example, in international business negotiations it is recommended to have business people as subjects rather than students, because the reproach has been often made that experiments involving students as subjects (such as Kelley's, 1966, negotiation simulation) do not adequately represent the behaviour of business people and are therefore fraught with limited external validity. Feasibility becomes low if one adds that managers should come from different cultures and negotiate face to face in the experimental negotiation setting involving bicultural pairs, because the researcher targets intercultural interactions rather than cross-cultural comparisons (Adler and Graham, 1989). The rare case where such a situation can be found is an executive MBA where students are managers from different countries and cultures (Graham, 1985).

An additional impediment to researchability is the excessive search for general theories (see, for instance, Faucheux and Rojot, 1978, for a discussion of the difficulty in finding general theories in the field of industrial relations). Finally, an important aspect of researchability is the complexity of the research design, its 'height, depth and width', which are discussed further in this chapter.

Check 5: Is everything new? Is anything new?   If everything is new in the whole design, from research question, theories, data collection to countries covered, the researcher should worry about research feasibility. Conversely, if everything is old, outdated or over-researched, the project should be given up. For beginners, replication with extension at the international level of theories validated at the national level are a very down to earth way of generating valuable international/cross-cultural management research, if the questioning on the equivalence across contexts is properly managed (see Chapter 4).

The choice among substantive paradigms

It is important to choose among paradigms, not because one would be definitively superior to the other but because they have different implications in terms of data collection and research publics. They result in observing the same reality from quite different angles and are not necessarily compatible. Paradigmatic choices are also strong determinants of the 'labelling' of researchers. They largely define the abstract territory which the researcher shares with others who have a common world view. Last but not least, the personal appeal of a particular paradigm to the researcher makes sense in her choice. For the purpose of illustration, I will take below three examples from marketing, accounting and HRM.

The first example relates to consumer behaviour in a cross-cultural perspective. Paradigm one revolves around the *globalization of consumption* and sees it as an inevitable movement of worldwide homogenization of tastes and preferences (Levitt, 1983). Consequently, American consumer behaviour models are applied cross-nationally with some interest for issues of cross-cultural equivalence (Douglas and Craig, 1983), but basically with the view that quasi-universal theories apply worldwide. In a way typical of paradigm 1, Farley and Lehman speak of the 'myth of international differences' (1994, p. 111); research in paradigm 1 has been up to now the most frequent and uses mostly the psychometric approach which is dominant in marketing. Paradigm 1 serves as a contrast reference for other paradigmatic avenues in the field which offer alternative models based on:

1 The phenomenon of *ethnic consumption* (paradigm 2a) seen as an adequate avenue for describing the complex realities of world-wide consumption, marked by cultural borrowing, migrations and a unique mix of consumption habits (Gans, 1962; Hirschmann, 1985; Bouchet, 1995; Wilk, 1995).
2 The emergence of a *postmodern consumer* (paradigm 2b) who invents new identities through multifaceted consumption experiences (Firat, 1995) and buys meanings rather than simply commodities (McCracken, 1991).

A third more radical paradigm centres on *consumer culture* (paradigm 3), and investigates the consequences for traditional societies of the incoming mass-market commodities; it critically questions the basic theories underlying consumer behaviour such as the hierarchy of needs (Maslow, 1954). Belk (1988), for instance, describes a Third World consumer culture and emphasizes the hedonistic attraction for conspicuous consumption, even when basic utilitarian needs have not been met. A growing body of literature relating to marketing and economic development, in the vein of paradigm 3, emphasizes a marketing system which 'must design deliver, and legitimate products and services that increase the material welfare of the population by promoting equity, justice and self reliance without causing injury to tradition' (Dholakia et al., 1988, pp. 141–2). Paradigms 2 and 3, contrary to paradigm 1, tend to make great use of ethnographic approaches, rely on direct observation and concentrate on meaning rather than numbers. However, actual choices are not as clear-cut as they may appear in this short discussion of alternative paradigms in cross-cultural consumer behaviour. Paradigm 1, for instance, is increasingly open to assumptions about the influence of deep-seated cultural values on consumer behaviour with special emphasis on Asian values (Yau, 1988; Wong and Yahuvia, 1995).

The second illustration comes from the area of accounting where the movement towards international standardization fuels cross-national or cross-cultural comparisons. Hofstede speaks of the 'culture of accounting systems' and presents a series of hypotheses for the linkage between culture and accounting systems (1991, pp. 155–8). He explains that 'from a cultural point of view, accounting systems are best understood as uncertainty-reducing *rituals*, fulfilling a cultural need for certainty, simplicity, and truth in a confusing world, regardless of whether this truth has any objective base' (p. 155). In fact, if one looks at the comparative accounting literature there seems to be three paradigms. The first is a *technical* paradigm of accounting which deals with the cross-comparison of accounting and auditing procedures (for example Brunovs and Kirsch, 1991 on goodwill accounting; Jones and Karbhari, 1996, on auditors' reports; Abdulla, 1996, about Bharaini annual reports) looking at the treatment and the disclosure of specific information. This factual comparison tries to stay far away from any interpretive stance. Comparing the various possible categories of addressees of the auditors' reports across nations (shareholder, board of directors), Jones and Karbhari (1996, p. 139) note that 'twenty-three percent of French auditors' reports were addressed to "ladies and gentlemen"'. They finally conclude that there is 'considerable national harmony' and 'tremendous international disharmony', which leads them to call for increased international harmonization.

At the other extreme is a *cultural* paradigm of comparative accounting, much in the line of Hofstede's quotation above, which has been developed by Gray (1988). This paradigm has been applied to accounting systems in developing countries by Baydoun (1995) in the case of the French accounting and reporting systems, or by Baydoun and Willett (1995) in the case of Lebanon where the French unified accounting system (*Plan comptable général*) has been applied because of historical rather than cultural reasons. The cultural paradigm of comparative accounting is taken at its extreme by Shaari et al. (1993) who discuss in detail the influence of religion, in their case Islam and its economic concepts and institutions, on accounting systems.

In between the two polar positions expounded above is a paradigm which tries to explain how combined legal, economic and cultural variables contribute to the development of national accounting systems. Such a model of accounting development is exposed by Doupnik and Salter (1995, pp. 192–3); it allows in particular for the influence of intrusive events such as colonization or a change in economic system. This avenue for comparative accounting tries to balance various influences in the process of accounting development (see, for instance, Kantor et al., 1995).

The third example deals with the modalities of personal adjustment in expatriation experiences using two main categories of situations, those related to personal life (*personal adjustment*) and those relating to work and to the adjustment in the expatriate job assignment (*work role adjustment*) on which the literature has mostly focused (Black et al., 1991). Constance Befus (1988) distinguishes four theoretical models for explaining expatriate adjustment that are in fact alternative paradigms. The first is a *psychoanalytical* model which suggests that culture shock results from nostalgia, melancholia and even a mourning of the lost native culture. This is further reinforced by threats on personal identity which are induced by the problematic encounter with the host country culture (Loss, 1983). Those who have described these adaptation difficulties from a psychoanalytic perspective go so far as to mention a sort of 'disintegration of the personality' (Adler, 1975) following deep-seated anguish caused by the necessary and problematic reorganization of personal behaviour, the feeling of loss of stable landmarks built around the native culture and a sharp reduction in self-esteem caused by the self-concept being directly challenged by the values and behaviours of the host country's culture (Loss, 1983).

The second paradigmatic avenue is a *behaviourist* model, where the basic mechanism of culture shock is seen as a consequence of 'punishments' experienced in the host country culture (David, 1976). Expatriates have no knowledge of what is considered locally as appropriate behaviour and are therefore at a risk to experience negative stimuli (*aversive stimuli*) through reactions of local counterparts who resent the expatriate's behaviour without suggesting the ways and means to solve the problem. In a third avenue, the culture shock experienced by expatriates has also been envisioned as a *manifestation of adaptation to stress* (Barna, 1983). The intellect of the expatriate is under severe stress during the expatriation experience because he has an enormous amount of information to process and to organize. She would be exposed to a sort of 'cognitive overload' situation. Language barriers and communication problems play an important role in the difficulties of personal adjustment. Thus, in the case of Japanese expatriates Okazali-Luff (1991) cites a series of studies which show that the Japanese, whose language structure is quite different from western languages, tend to experience strong communication difficulties with the local population. This results in a psychological distress which embodies psychosomatic symptoms such as loss of appetite, fatigue, a state of irritability or nervousness.

The fourth paradigm is a *phenomenological* model which proposes that culture shock is to be seen as a 'transitional experience' (Adler, 1975). Adler explains that culture shock, although often depicted as a negative experience may be considered in fact as a positive experience, which accompanies the learning process and resulting personal development. Culture shock is then presented as a process of change and transition in personality. It starts with the rejection of the host country culture, but as the expatriated person improves his/her autonomy, knowledge of and familiarity with the new culture, it is then possible for him/her to accept the self as an individual within the new culture, and thereby compromise and integrate the values of the two cultures. The stage of 'personality disintegration' quoted above will be followed by a phase of 'reintegration', except in the case of early return and failure of the experience.

The last model directly offers a representation of the adjustment to the host country culture as a function of time, the *U-Curve* which plots the degree of adjustment against the duration of stay. The expatriate typically starts with a somewhat misleading stage called *'honeymoon'*, which corresponds to the pleasant discovery of new places, new people and an exotic culture. It is new, therefore enjoyable. Interest in the new culture supersedes all other impressions. Moreover, the expatriate is often taken care of during the first days or weeks after arrival, which eases all the interaction difficulties. Then comes a phase where the discovery of the new culture leads to culture shock; the perceived degree of adjustment will diminish. Finally, in a third phase, the expatriate will gradually adjust. The 'U-Curve' adjustment model is globally supported by empirical studies, but without all the results being in clear favour of it (Black and Mendenhall, 1991). Most of the expatriation literature relies in fact on paradigm 2 (behaviourist) and paradigm 4 (phenomenological approach of a transitional experience), with a quite distinct distaste for the first paradigmatic avenue, the psychoanalytical approach.

Choices concerning complexity of research design

What is compared across which units?
The researcher should be aware that she has to define as clearly as possible the precise unit(s) of comparison across which the final contrasts will be made. The following units are basic alternatives in international comparative management: nations, cultures, individuals, organizations, or studies themselves. Nationality is one delimitation of individuals belonging to a large group, operational and obviously convenient. However, the direction of causality between the concepts of nationality and culture is not self-evident. Historically, shared culture has been a fundamental building block in the progressive construction of modern nation-states. As soon as these states began to emerge, they struggled against local customs, cultures and patois and tried to homogenize institutions. As argued

earlier, an attempt to equate culture directly with the nation-state or country would be misguided for a number of convergent reasons:

1 Some countries are deeply multicultural, for example, India which is made up of highly diversified ethnic, religious and linguistic groups.
2 Some nation-states are explicitly multicultural – Switzerland, for instance, with a strong emphasis on the defence of local particularisms in the political system.
3 Colonization and decolonization have resulted in borders which are sometimes straight lines on a map, with little respect for cultural realities; for African countries, 'ethnic culture' matters whereas 'national culture' is in many cases meaningless.

The researcher has the choice to compare across groups/cultures or to compare across individuals. The issue of national character and modal personality (Clark, 1990) is important in this respect. If the researcher believes, after due examination of the literature, that personalities can be averaged in a particular cultural grouping, then it makes sense to consider that the mean score of a group of culturally homogeneous individuals represents a score for the culture. However, Hofstede (1991) has added an appendix entitled 'Reading Mental Programs' in *Culture and Organization: Software of the Mind*, where he clearly explains that samples of cultures should not be confused with samples of individuals. He draws attention to the risk of abusive stereotyping, whereby country characteristics are considered as individual characteristics: 'Mean values are calculated from the scores on each question for the respondents from each country. We do not compare individuals, but we compare what is called central tendencies in the answers from each country' (Hofstede, 1991, p. 253).

When using a 'multiple culture perspective' (Boyacigiller et al., 1996) the researcher may also try to compare across organizations. In his PhD dissertation, Trompenaars (1981) combined different types of organizations as regards size and industry. This can be useful to control or take into account corporate culture. However, in such designs, especially if data are collected at the individual level, it becomes difficult to attribute the observed variance to a definite level (individual, organization, industry, culture, nation). Finally, comparing across studies is rarely done but could be extremely interesting. This type of comparison deals with cross-nationally common and cross-culturally robust issues such as motivation and pay systems. This kind of meta-analytic venture would look mainly at the existing literature in various large cultural contexts (USA, the UK, France, Germany, Italy, Japan) and would try to assess how people tackle a certain research issue in different cultures, what concepts and theories are preferred, what type of data collection is used locally. Such a project is still rare because the barrier of languages and the issues involved in terms of translation and conceptual equivalence are probably too complex for researchers to overcome.

Dimensions of design in cross-cultural management research
We start here from the perspective of a researcher or a group of researchers looking for universal knowledge (Cheng, 1994). This search would imply to envisage the generalization of findings across several layers of the management process, from strategy to implementation (height), across successive units from individuals to countries through organizations and industries (width), and based on which more or less in-depth rationales ranging from explanations at the level of business practices to the deepest cultural assumptions (depth). Figure 3.1 represents the three co-ordinates of the cross-cultural research design as in a geometrical space. This figure has no other purpose than to clarify the options in research designs and outline the potential complexity involved in choosing too many levels of analysis at the same time.

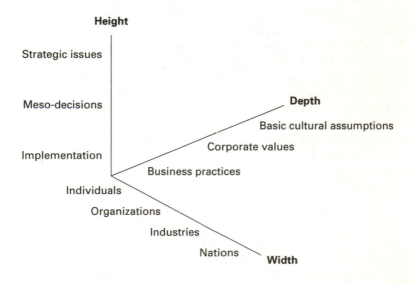

Figure 3.1   *Dimensions of the research design*

Depth choices: cultural explanations from sea level to deep abysses

Depth relates the level of independent variables to the level of explanatory variables. Explanations may be more or less deep-seated and therefore relatively far away from the behaviour or practices they are supposed to explain. One may wonder how basic cultural assumptions or values (possibly from their roots such as adaptation to climate and geographical conditions) can be related to management procedures, company rules and business practices. Assuming that the variable to be explained is efficiency/performance or others such as satisfaction or motivation, a typical depth choice is whether the researcher goes very deep into the explanations, uses several successive layers of explanations and tries to relate culture to values and then to managerial practices (see, for instance, Derr and Laurent, 1989). There is a sort of continuum from very deep-seated explanations to the final aspects of management concerned, with profound explanations at one extreme and daily managerial reality at the other.

The depth dimension deals with the underlying patterns of explanation, which can be made explicit or remain largely implicit such as assumptions about cultural convergence or the latent opposition between modern and traditional societies, the latter being supposed to disappear in the long run. Here, the researcher's choices convey her view of the role of culture on management. The depth choices also depend on the degree of managerial implications looked for by the researcher: deep explanations rarely produce findings applicable now. If the researcher inquires profoundly into values or more fundamental basic assumptions in the Kluckhohn and Strodtbeck style, she incurs the risk of being far from any implementable recommendation, at least as perceived by an audience of business people or even of management colleagues. The final aim of cross-cultural management can be to provide managers who sell abroad or work in multinational companies with operative knowledge about concrete behavioural and organizational differences and the way to deal with them in interactive settings. In this respect, a choice to be 'nearer to the surface' (I do not mean superficial) can make sense.

When defining the depth of the cross-cultural investigation the researcher needs to decide whether she looks only at *what* differs, or whether she addresses also the issue of *how* it differs and, possibly, *why* it differs? What–how–why choices result in increased complexity. It is important to keep in mind that the question 'does it differ?' is already a significant research issue and should not necessarily be followed in the same research piece by 'why?' and 'how?'.

Consequently, researchers often use a preframed explanatory framework (for example, the national scores for Hofstede's four dimensions) in order to account for deep cultural explanation in an operational and implementable way. If looking at the 'why and how', the researcher must in any way find a specific explanatory framework, possibly with an ad hoc conceptualization (for instance, entrepreneurship as embedded in societal and cultural context, Berger, 1991; or the difference between the legal systems of common law and code law as explaining Franco-American organizational contrasts, Amado et al., 1991). Ad hoc conceptualizations may help to avoid the traps of going so deep that it becomes difficult to find convincing rationales for linking the profound explanation to the behavioural level. For instance, the difference between shame and guilt which is especially meaningful for Asian and western cultures (Ha, 1995) can be used for contrasting ethical attitudes in business (Chapman, 1992) or relational patterns between business partners.

An additional interrogation concerning depth is to what extent the scope of potential explanatory variables is enlarged, say to historical, sociological, political or legal explanations. Problems related to the operationalization of a large set of explanatory variables explain why researchers tend to be somewhat parsimonious about the scope of deep explanations. Historical explanations have little success among cross-cultural management researchers: for instance, the hypothetical view that human resource practices in Japan would be linked to the feudal system in ancient Japan. However, they may surface at times in the interpretive part of the research. The relative lack of appeal of historical explanations (except in specialized journals such as *Journal of Business History*) is probably explained by the fact that they are not replicable and are likely to disappear with convergence. Religion is sometimes used as providing a deep rationale for observed differences. Lessem and Neubauer (1994) use it to explain a significant part of management differences across European countries. Religion has been claimed to be a confounding cultural element in the international harmonization of accounting (Shaari et al., 1993) with the example of Islam's influence on accounting practices in Islamic countries. Rodriguez (1995) studies the influence of religiosity on consumer behaviour in the case of Peru. The final interrogation of in-depth issues is how to treat other explanations, especially economic or institutional, which often have a most profound impact aside from culture. A solution is to contrast economic versus cultural factors as rival explanations in the research design. In the case of Turkey, Kozan (1993) contrasts the respective influences of culture and industrialization on leadership attitudes of Turkish managers.

Width: choices concerning empirical settings

Width is the 'across' dimension. Width choices concern the possible units of analysis, ranging from individuals, organizations and industries to megagroups such as nations or regions. Hofstede (1995) has argued in favour of such 'multilevel' research where the combination of different levels allows a better 'discovery orientation' than the mere study at one level, for instance, that of individuals as carriers of culture. If sampling procedures are used, samples will pile up as Russian dolls: samples of individuals within organization, of organizations within industries, of industries within countries. To the best of my knowledge, nobody has ever attempted this kind of research undertaking. As an 'across' dimension of the research design, width is important because it has a lot to do with the complexity of conceptualization and data collection, that is, with the implementability of the research project. Typical contrasts in width will be between large-scale surveys such as Hofstede's, with large samples both of countries and individual respondents within each country, and small-scale, two-country designs (Amado et al.,1991), or the study of a single organization in several countries (Morris and Pavett, 1993).

There is some discussion on the issue of whether two-nation studies constitute a cross-cultural design. Nath (1968) in an early review of cross-cultural management research reported that 54 per cent of the 57 studies that he reviewed involved only two nations. Researchers favouring the Etic approach consider that only studies of several cultures give us a better and deeper understanding of the effects of culture on behaviour. This is what Hofstede (1980a) called 'ecological correlations', correlations related to observed mean scores of different national or cultural groups.

The researcher must be aware that both deep and wide research designs are most likely to be unfeasible if the structure uses traditional quantification approaches. Choices of parsimony must be made. For industry or organization, one can control by taking the subsidiaries of the same multinational company on a worldwide basis (Hofstede, 1980a). If samples of individuals are considered, rival explanations by socio-demographic variables must be controlled, especially for sex, education or age, and their remaining influence must be assessed by techniques described in the next chapter. The relevance of the units examined must be carefully assessed. For instance, Al-Aiban and Pearce (1995) show that public organizations offer a better reflection of cultural differences in their management practices than private ones; the impact of local values on management practices in the public sector is shown to be stronger than in private organizations in both Saudi

Arabia and the USA. Finally, if the researcher chooses a multiple culture perspective (Boyacigiller et al., 1996) with different type of cultures, especially organizational culture, intervening at different levels of analysis, she will be obliged to stay far away from survey research, representative samples and close-end questionnaires because they are not adequate instruments for capturing multiple influences and assessing how they combine. When confronted with quite new and complex phenomena, Parkhe (1993, 1996) argues in favour of what he calls 'messy research', taking the example of research on international joint ventures and theory development in the field.

Height choices
Height refers to the level of aggregation or disagreggation in the whole management process of the research issues involved. Leadership, strategic decision-making and organizational design are typical 'high key' issues, while reporting, accounting, motivating salespeople, or adapting products to foreign markets are 'lower key' issues. However, top management/strategic issues and implementation/ancillary management tasks should be related to each other. Height is important because of the possibility of discrepancies at different levels of the management process: imitation and cultural borrowing at the top management level may be contradicted at implementation levels by actual behaviour inspired by local cultural patterns.

When combined, height, width and depth of the research design express the necessary trade-off between what would be desirable and what is feasible. The quest for the Holy Grail is a phantasm common to many cross-cultural researchers who would like to find both profound and universal dimensions that would explain behaviour across a wide array of countries. If starting from a rather positivistic perspective, a reasonable strategy is to posit the design at only one level on each of the three dimensions and attempt to control variables intervening at other levels. Hofstede, for instance, chose nations as units and controlled at the individual level by similar composition of national samples. Trompenaars has followed a different line in his PhD thesis, also trying to account for some variance across organizations and industries, which proved in fact difficult to manage. Another way of dealing with complex research designs is to use an in-depth, grounded approach which privileges internal validity, studying in full length only one case involving two cultures and one organization (Brannen, 1994) at the expense of possible claims for external validity (Eisenhardt, 1989, 1991).

Role played by ideal types in simplifying cross-cultural
research designs

Since cross-cultural designs can lead to a high level of complexity, the researcher is spontaneously in search of some axes of simplification. Ideal types provide such a basis. Ideal types were introduced by Max Weber who was in a sense the first true cross-cultural researcher. Weber (1958), originally a sociologist and historian of religions, defines ideal types as systematically composed forms which cannot be found in the real world but allow one to draw clear conceptual borders between aspects of reality. There is some artificiality involved in the process of 'ideal typing'. For instance, Hofstede's dimensions or his depiction of organizational forms as village markets, pyramids of people, well-oiled machines and families are cultural ideal types (1991, p. 141). Part of the game of cross-cultural research is to find the most appropriate ideal types which allow optimal contrast across cultures (see for a challenger of Hofstede, Trompenaars, 1993). Individualism and collectivism are probably the strongest polar ideal types which are in wide use in cross-cultural research. A standard ideal-typical statement is given by Kanungo and Wright:

> The behavioural patterns and customs of the Japanese people have been deeply influenced by Confucianism, which stresses a rigid, hierarchically arranged collective society. Members of each collectivity are expected to maintain absolute loyalty and obedience to authority and to the group in the fulfillment of their obligations. (Kanungo and Wright, 1983, p. 121)

Ideal types are both useful and dangerous. They are useful because they allow simplification of the conceptualization process and hence the research design. They provide polar reference points to analyse complex realities. However, ideal types can easily border on stereotypes, especially when they undergo a process of over-simplification: either the original works of those who have authored these miniatures of complex reality are not read with enough care, or some salient traits of the ideal type become over-emphasized in a successive citation process which gradually ends in caricaturing the original concept. For instance, the contrast between the typical traditional American organizational form (type A), the typical Japanese (type J) and the modified American type Z (Ouchi, 1981; Jaeger, 1983), reduces the height of the research design. These ideal types presuppose total coherence from daily working practices to strategic management. Additionally, since all Japanese organizations, irrespective of their industry, are supposed to be typical of the J model, the width of the design is also reduced. A, J and Z types lend themselves easily to becoming organizational stereotypes of both countries' companies – and this despite the best intentions and care of the original authors.

Ideal types are dangerous because they may imply a return to stereotypes and ethnocentrism under scientific coverage. The 'far-away' syndrome is one of the reasons for slipping from ideal to stereotypes ('all these Confucianist countries in Asia'). Sometimes, because ideal types rely on broad statements, they can lead to significant divergences in interpretation rather than agreement on their implied meaning. Kanungo and Wright (1983, p. 120) state: 'British managers perceive authority as vested in the person, presumably because of their liberal training; whereas French managers perceive authority as vested in the organizational role.' This is in fact largely a contradiction of what Hofstede would say about French managers in contrast to British managers (see quotation of Fayol by Hofstede, 1994b, p. 8, in the next chapter).

Ideal types also tend to border on the stereotype when they fulfil pure purposes of operationalization because of the ambiguous relationship between conceptual simplicity and measurability. That is why de-stereotyping ideal types is an important task of cross-cultural management research. De-stereotyping helps to avoid broad generalizations about the management style of a large group of countries, seemingly similar, at least as seen from Europe or the USA. For example, a study of Korean management (Chang, 1989) allows fine tuning of the influence of Confucian philosophy on Far-East Asian management styles by comparing China, Japan and Korea. Similarly, Tung (1996) compares Chinese, Japanese and Korean business negotiation styles and highlights both significant commonalities and some clear differences. Another avenue for de-stereotyping ideal types is to search for an increased in-depth understanding of their underlying dimensions. Singelis et al. (1995) distinguish between the horizontal and vertical dimensions of individualism and collectivism, based on the acceptance of inequality in a society (vertical) versus an emphasis on equality (horizontal). They have operationalized and measured these new constructs.

Constraints related to applying theories and collecting data internationally

The choice of cross-cultural research designs is to a large extent guided by the constraints of data collection. There are naturally methodological debates about the question of the best way to generate new theoretical insights (see, for instance, Dyer and

Wilkins, 1991, arguing in favour of single case studies, who take a critical view of Eisenhardt's (1991) suggestions for generating better constructs through case studies). These debates are largely common to management research in general. I shall concentrate on issues which are more specific to international/cross-cultural research.

Theories: the case for national contingency
Very often theories are typically taken from a toolkit based on existing literature, mostly generated from western contexts. The main issue is whether they are applicable in context, especially when a multitude of variables differ. Shenkar and Von Glinow (1994) use the case of organizational research in China to illustrate national contingency. They note distinct conceptual differences as concerns the Chinese work unit, which works a total institution 'situated within a walled, gated and guarded compound. Its employees depend on the unit for everything from social insurance and medical care to provision of ration cards for basic food staples' (p. 61). They also show that the basic motivation theories used in the west (Maslow's need theory, expectancy theory or equity theory), cannot be used blindly. Their use is contingent upon evolution in the Chinese context that may make them applicable, but cannot be assumed without prior verification. The (too) broad question of whether a theory makes sense when transposed into another context cannot receive in fact a clear-cut answer.

Research instruments/data collection techniques
The same research instruments are available as compared with the domestic research but they face a problem of cross-cultural equivalence which has been discussed in great detail in the literature (see the next chapter); and they become more difficult to implement because of a series of practical problems deriving mostly from the absence of familiarity of local informants with survey research. Figure 3.2 posits various data collection techniques as they pertain to key aspects of the research design. The vertical axis opposes the phenomenon to the ideas: if the researcher is deeply engaged in describing and respecting the realities of the phenomenon under investigation, she will tend to choose research instruments that favour a thick description of the phenomenon. Conversely, a strong emphasis on pre-set theories (ideas), including not only the concepts and their articulation but also their operationalization, will induce the researcher to choose an instrument which reflects an intellectual picture of the phenomenon, suitable for measuring key pre-set dimensions rather than for coming directly to grips with reality.

The right side of the horizontal axis highlights the preoccupation of the researcher with her informants, when and if she considers them as the key element of the research process. In this view, the data collection process must allow informants, as much as possible, to reveal their world views, deliver their true mind and give their own interpretations, probably at the expense of codifiability since the collected information cannot be easily transformed into quantified variables. At the opposite side on the horizontal axis, the research design is instrument centred to collect the informants' views in a codified form. Operationalized variables are a direct output of the data collection process, however, at the expense of relevance (the categories proposed in the questionnaire may be far from the informants' own views), and exhaustivity (significant pieces of information may be lost because of an imposed research instrument).

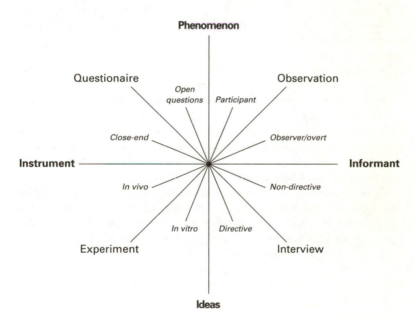

Figure 3.2   *Research instruments as they pertain to key aspects of the research design*

The north-east quadrant of Figure 3.2 corresponds to context-embedded research designs where the emphasis is on the phenomenon and the informants. Their application to cross-cultural business research implies a great deal of observation, including participant observation, diaries and journals which are then analysed for generating new insights. This is rarely used in international/cross-cultural research because it is highly demanding in terms of familiarity with and knowledge of the research context. Examples can be found in management in Brannen (1994) who studied the take-over of an American plant by a Japanese company. An American by birth, Brannen was raised in Japan and is therefore bilingual, which was a key skill for her research undertaking (Brannen, 1996). In consumer behaviour, examples of such research approaches are given by Wilk (1995) and Arnould (1989). Like Brannen, both have a background in anthropology and a good command of the language of their field of research (Spanish for Wilk, French for Arnould).

The south-west quadrant of Figure 3.2 features decontextualized studies: the choice of context-free research instruments does not imply that the researcher is unaware of cultural issues, nor that apparently context-embedded approaches are automatically taking their context into full account. Participant observation can be undertaken with little understanding of the field's culture, while experiments can be organized so that they take into account some influences related to culture, by explaining the instrument, organizing the experiment differently, or observing the subject's behaviour during the experimental process. Among the quasi-experimental research instruments, the *in vivo* category tries to reproduce real life situations while the *in vitro* category is nearer to a 'scientific' experiment. Typical *in vivo* instruments are vignette research or basket instruments.

Vignettes are systematically elaborated descriptions of concrete situations which precede questions and allow the respondent to produce more reliable answers than the conventional abstract questions (Alexander and Becker, 1978). Vignette research has been used by Becker and Fritzsche (1987) for studying comparative business ethics issues linked to illegal payment on three sample groups of businessmen, from the USA, Germany and France. The scenario was as follows:

> The Rollfast Bicycle company has been barred from entering the market in a large Asian country by collusive efforts of the local bicycle manufacturers. Rollfast could expect to net 5 million dollars per year from sales if it could penetrate the market. Last week a business man from the country contacted the management of Rollfast and stated that he could smooth the way for the company to sell in his country for a price of $500,000. If you were responsible, what are the chances that you would pay the price? (Becker and Fritzsche, 1987, page 89)

While the replies from the French and German managers differed little, those of the Americans indicated that they were, by and large, less prepared to pay the secret payment. Similarly, Tse et al. (1988) have used an in-basket instrument simulating a decision to be taken to assess cross-cultural risk taking and decisiveness of executives from Asia and North America.

The north-west quadrant of Figure 3.2 is very popular in cross-cultural management research. Those adopting the 'toolkit' approach described in Chapter 1 tend to generate survey data through questionnaire administration, Hofstede (1980b, 1991), Trompenaars (1981, 1993), Smith and Peterson (1988), Smith et al. (1993) Peterson et al. (1995) and many researchers in organizational psychology (see Bhagat et al., 1990) also use this approach. Finally, the south-east quadrant is popular among cross-cultural researchers who undertake in-depth interviews which are often within the framework of complete case studies (Parkhe, 1993). Observation data, documents, meeting reports and contracts, can be typically tri-angulated with in-depth interviews in order to generate reliable insights into the phenomenon under investigation.

The real world of cross-cultural data collection and research instruments is fortunately more complex than the previous presentation would have us believe. First, the same research issue can be approached typically in all of the above ways, but generally by different researchers. International business negotiation is a good case in point. Let us compare three well-known researchers in the field: John Graham, Steve Weiss and Rosalie Tung. John Graham has widely used Kelley's negotiation simulation game (1966), typical of the instrument/ideas approach (Graham, 1985); samples of business people from various cultures have played the dyadic negotiation game to generate negotiation data. Over several years, repeated experiments generated cross-national data which was re-analysed by Graham et al. (1994) in order to describe how the negotiator behaved comparatively in ten cultures, taking into account explicitly the American origin of Kelley's research instrument. Weiss has used mostly in-depth interviews and has observed complete international negotiations, often as single case studies (Weiss, 1987, 1993, 1996a, 1996b), while Rosalie Tung has often used survey data based on mail questionnaires to companies negotiating internationally (for instance, Tung, 1984b). Researchers quite often use research instruments taken from two adjacent half-quadrants over an axis line. They combine, for instance, overt observation and non-directive, in-depth interviews (as in the case of Steve Weiss) or an *in vivo* laboratory experiment, Kelley's negotiation game with close-end questionnaires distributed to participants at the end of the survey (as in the case of John Graham).

However, it is much more difficult to combine data collection techniques which are in opposed half-quadrants because they may imply quite different underlying research philosophies. Graham (1985) has combined observation by a video camera with Kelley's game, but he did not observe a real-world phenomenon and the content analysis of the video records using Angelmar and Stern (1978) categories proved costly and complex. Brannen (1996) reports that she has been using a questionnaire survey with close-end questions in conjunction with observation data generated from overt participant observation. On similar issues the two research instruments resulted in seemingly contradictory outcomes which induced some re-analysis before a final interpretation was possible.

As a very general, and highly provisional conclusion of this section, I would suggest the following advantages and drawbacks for each of the four broad categories (underlined in Figure 3.2). Observation is most susceptible to allow cross-cultural discovery, but also the most dangerous because it needs both familiarity with the research context and an ability to distance oneself from the observed phenomenon. Experiments (or quasi-experimental instruments) are most likely to be adopted when universality is assumed. Respondents are considered as subjects of the experiment and the test is (supposed) to be culture free, which may result in largely crashing down the cross-national differences (see differences in negotiation behaviour reported by Graham, 1996). Questionnaires are typical for the search of cross-cultural equivalence. They are widely used for the search of common conceptual dimensions valid across culture differences, with differences only in degree; 'country scores' are the result of such research undertakings, with a lot of operational and practical value. Their main disadvantage is that partly they tend to hide conceptual differences across cultures. Finally, interviews are probably not as popular in cross-cultural research as they are in domestic research settings because the language barrier renders them quite difficult. If undertaken through interpreters, it produces noise, artificiality and an absence of tempo in the conversation which can be quite detrimental to the quality of the materials collected. However, cross-border research co-operation, implying a multinational research team, can allow them to overcome these limitations. I discuss at greater length in Chapter 5 the issues of cross-culturally friendly versus cross-culturally unfriendly research instruments; research approaches that favour similarities versus those which favour the emergence of differences.

Implementation of cross-cultural research in management by international networking

Forms of cross-border research collaboration and problems involved

It is a frequent practice to promote cross-border research co-operation in order to increase research feasibility, especially at the data collection level. This results sometimes in huge research teams (more than twenty for Peterson, Smith et al., 1995) which are not easy to manage, especially when one or several key researchers bring with them the research questions, underlying theories and research instrument and the collaborators bring mostly their capacity as local insiders and data collectors. Cheng (1996) proposes a prescriptive approach of cross-national research teams, where he distinguishes three basic situations according to the basic research motive, whether it is to develop culture-free theories (by replications), culture-specific theories (single culture studies with a certain degree of cross-national collaboration) or to develop contextual theories which integrate input from a variety of different cultural settings. In the first case, the primary research task is simply to replicate an earlier study in a new cultural setting, in fact the most frequent case in cross-national collaborations. The replicating researchers (call them 'targets') will in fact have limited initiative, except that of adapting existing instruments and data collection procedures if needed, while the initial researcher (call him/her 'source') will retain the greater responsibility and generally provide the publication outlet. Mutual learning according to Cheng (1996) is limited in this case. However, there may be a learning process for the replicators who are often given access to state-of-the-art research procedures which can accelerate quite strongly their own maturation as management researchers.

The second case of cross-national collaborations for single culture studies is more rare, but still exists in practice, for instance, the Swedish/Japanese venture between Johny Johansson and Ikujiro Nonaka, who try to understand the unique aspects of how Japanese companies deal with markets and consumers (Johansson and Nonaka, 1987, 1996). This may quite largely improve the understanding of the phenomenon under study, since the two researchers can confront their interpretations. The third case (developing integrated contextual theories) assumes that there is equality between the research partners, source(s) and targets, which was obviously not the case in the replication case. Responsibility is shared and the research process itself is a true cross-cultural challenge because the researchers, coming from diverse cultures, must in some way

discuss and calibrate their views and interpretations of the phenomenon under study in order to generate new insights, valid
across the various national/cultural contexts. As we will see in
Chapter 5, this is a promising avenue for future cross-cultural collaboration. However, this type of research co-operation does not
really exist up to now.

I have 'e-mail interviewed' Peter Smith, who has been involved in
several large-scale research projects in cross-cultural management,
and asked his opinions on the matter:

> I have now found some time to reflect on the questions that you posed to
> me concerning the management of large-scale, cross-national projects in
> our field. First, I would put what I might call the nature of colleagueship.
> The projects in which I have been involved have relied upon the creation
> of a network of peer relationships between investigators in a wide vari-
> ety of cultures. However, the colleagues within that network have
> differing conceptions of what is an appropriate way to participate in
> such a network. Colleagues from low Power Distance nations expect to
> be fully involved in key decisions as to hypotheses and design. Those
> from high Power Distance nations are more likely to be deferent toward
> Western researchers and not to question designs or hypotheses, even
> though there may well be objectively stronger reasons why it would be
> good for them to do so. Where a project has a large scope, collective
> planning of the project becomes both very expensive and very difficult,
> and the most typical consequence is that one or two researchers from
> Western nations take on a major role in decision-making. This may well
> undermine the validity of the results to a certain extent, but it could also
> be a necessary price if the project is to come to fruition. I shall welcome
> the time when researchers from other parts of the world find themselves
> in these leading roles.
>
> Second, comes the problem of sampling equivalence. The more pre-
> cisely one specifies the desired sampling frame within a given nation, the
> more certain one becomes that it will be impossible to satisfy that crite-
> rion within at least some of the nations which it is desirable to include.
> Furthermore, matching respondents on something readily measurable
> like age may ensure that they are less well matched on other less tangi-
> ble attributes like seniority, since age and seniority structures vary by
> culture. I have pursued a policy of not trying to match samples precisely,
> and I note that the GLOBE project has also specified a range of popula-
> tions to sample rather than just one. It is however crucial to have
> a demographic profile of respondents. Thirdly, I know of no way of
> evaluating the relative adequacy of different translations and back-
> translations. In each case one tries to ensure that the process is carried
> through thoroughly and professionally. But at the end of the day, some
> translations are probably a lot more difficult to do than others, and they
> introduce an unknown and uncontrollable amount of error variance.
>
> Fourthly, timing. All large projects take a long time to complete. Data
> are thus collected at different sites at quite different times, and may thus
> lose another dimension of comparability. When an international project

becomes known, by being presented at conferences and elsewhere, additional researchers offer to join the project. Waiting for them to complete their part then delays final publication of results, which frustrates those who have contributed much earlier. My overall feeling is that the conduct of these types of project is fraught with all types of difficulty, many of them without any possible resolution. The best that we can hope for is that a series of studies each of which has its own weaknesses will nonetheless converge upon some relatively consensual findings. I see some progress towards that goal in recent years.

Practical aspects of cross-national research collaborations in management

Starting from the beginning, the first question is how to find collaborations. I propose here a modest view based on human motivations, some of which are beyond the ideal world of research. In the first place, I assume co-operation between people who have some sense of their 'inequality', of the asymmetrical relationship as concerns the management of the research process and the responsibility for finding a publication outlet. Good potential 'targets' are often young researchers who have done their PhD in the USA, England, Sweden or the Netherlands because they have a good command of English as the language of research and publication; and they were educated in the dominant research cultures and have made a first exercise. Targets are often recruited as cultural insiders from their country of origin. Either they have been recruited as assistant professor in the country where they presented their dissertation (and want to return home sometimes) or they have been hired in their home country or elsewhere and want to keep a link with the place where they did their doctoral work.

Across countries there are huge gaps in resources for universities and research which create differentials in academic levels that are in practice difficult to overcome. That is mostly visible in three areas:

1 The emphasis on research versus teaching, reflected in annual teaching load and administrative charges related to teaching.
2 Access to literature, library stacks, journals received, library opening hours, information search systems, etc.
3 Access to databases, software and computation (manuscript managers, for example, are unavailable in most countries in the world).

The gap is surely decreasing worldwide but still exists. A few years ago I was invited to a conference on the seventh anniversary of its foundation by the University of Nouakchott, the capital of

Mauritania, one of the poorest countries in the world. It was clear that teaching higher education contents had an absolute priority over the creation of new knowledge.

The sophistication of research facilities increases almost continuously from an absolute low in very poor countries such as Mauritania to industrializing countries such as Brazil, Thailand or Tunisia, to some Latin European countries and Japan, and at the top North America. Some countries have concentrated resources on two or three key places, often supported by both public and private funds, while the average university has limited funding for research and cannot easily participate in cross-national collaborations. Such is the case of Spain with well-funded places like IESE and ESADE in Barcelona, or Turkey with private universities like Bilkent University in Ankara or Boyazigci University in Istanbul which benefit from a favourable research environment.

GNP per capita is surely not the only reason for resources dedicated to research. Another reason is the place of management in the local academic scene. Despite the growing legitimacy of management research due to globalization of the academic model in business studies, it is still not recognized as a fully legitimate field of knowledge in some countries:

1 There is little local tradition for management education and research.
2 Management is mixed with money seen as too earthly.
3 Management is seen as practical in focus and an art rather than a science.

Moreover the degree of involvement of the business community in the process of promoting management research, through financing or by offering a research field, varies considerably across national contexts. The Dutch, for instance, are very good at cross-cultural research exercises and their companies are supportive of such research undertakings (for example, Shell in the case of Trompenaars). The Dutch have a long tradition of cross-cultural research, probably because they are also superbly located, right in the middle of different cultures. Their businesses are spontaneously sensitive to cross-cultural and intercultural issues because they make sense for them.

Cross-national differences in intellectual style must also be acknowledged when co-operating with colleagues. The issue of who adapts to whom is not a major issue for the time being because co-operation patterns are mostly asymmetrical. It could become a more critical issue in the future. However, similarity between researchers as pure individuals is a key asset which can compensate for the cultural gap and allow better cross-cultural dialogue. The lack of familiarity of some target collaborators with management research methods (not from intellectual knowledge but as a practical experience) must be considered in advance. The richer must not confuse poverty with inability: intellectual talents as such do need little support. But the source researchers must be aware that levels of professionalism do differ in the sense of ability to mobilize resources along definite standards of quality and performance set by the profession. If a gap in professionalism exists, it must be filled in some way.

I now take the point of view of the potential target who seeks to be targeted. The task may appear difficult if the target is in a place with less lustre: she is in an unknown university in a small country which is not well located, especially for after-hours activities. These potential targets still have a major competitive advantage because they are in remote locations which may offer fine settings for cross-cultural research in terms of implied variance: Thomas (1996), for instance, advocates in favour of 'research in forgotten locations'. The target will use existing questionnaires and concentrate on the quality of the data collection. Modesty is a key asset for targets whose imitation behaviour is necessary at the beginning. For targets who want to make contacts with potential sources, the solutions are multiple. The participation to international academic conferences is a good starter for de-provincializing oneself. Subscription to journals, even to only one international academic journal, is a must since it generally allows simultaneously to become a member of an academic association and to be listed in its directory. However, target researchers will go through a series of practical obstacles: email, for instance, is heavily controlled by public authorities in a broad array of countries such as China or Tunisia; problems of foreign exchange control may render uneasy the subscription to journals or purchase of books by international mail order. If possible, the resources of the Internet must be used as early as possible, including email, participation to discussion groups and access to home pages and working papers. Participation in specific networks (such as 'marketing and development' or 'organizational symbolism and corporate culture') is also an interesting avenue, but carries the risk of belonging to too-narrow groupings which do not reach the critical mass of larger academic associations. For potential targets, the solution to invite academic 'stars' is not worthwhile for a one-day conference, because it is costly and offers little return. It is a better solution if the star can come to the foreign location for some weeks, because she (star is feminine in French) may be interested in extending existing theories to a new challenging cultural context.

In cross-national research co-operation the problem of equality between researchers is in fact constantly posed, even if implicitly. Ranking and competition are standard practices in the management area. It is popular in the UK and USA to rank business schools or faculties according to their research publication records or teaching excellence. This is somewhat less the case in France where, however, universities are rather underscored compared to the top *Grandes Ecoles*. This is not at all the case in Germany where the university system is very homogeneous in quality. Let us, however, assume now the case of equality between researchers. I would suggest that the research contract, even if not written, must be fairly clear from the start in order to avoid misunderstandings later in the process (objective, methods, research philosophy, distribution of tasks, authorship). David Buisson from the University of Otago in New Zealand, who is a leader in the Interprod research project involving more than twenty countries, states that clear protocols should define who owns the data, where the central data point is to be, what is required from each of the partners and how the data is to be collected and analysed (email, 14 March 1997).

Writing the research can be problematic when researchers have quite different levels of language proficiency. The language gap can be somewhat problematic for Asians except when they come from English-speaking areas such as India or Hong Kong. Writing and dissemination can also be a problem when there are different requirements from the local audiences. Easterby-Smith and Malina (1997, p. 9), in the case of a ten-year UK–China research project, note that 'the UK team was under pressure to publish theoretical work within refereed journals' while 'the Chinese were expected to demonstrate how theoretical observations could be implemented within Chinese enterprises'. Publication in the form of co-authorship or acknowledgement in a footnote must be decided at the beginning under the condition that the respective assigned tasks have been properly performed. Financial aspects of the cross-national collaboration can be tricky, especially when the source researcher is not allowed to spend public research funds by transferring part of these resources to research associates abroad, which is the case in many countries. Some researchers are able to collaborate on the basis of peer exchange and joint publication. Elsewhere, resource shortages are acute and data can only be collected if some payments are made, either to researchers or their subjects. Since the cost of living is usually much lower within those nations which are most lacking in resources, the transfer of quite small sums of money can have a disproportionally positive effect.

Conclusion

The great danger in cross-cultural management research is the quest for the Holy Grail, that is, the search for simplified frameworks that would nonetheless allow a deep understanding of a wide range of cultures. This quest is, in my opinion, largely doomed to failure, because it results in very complex designs which are hard to implement. Hofstede's research appears in this respect as the exception rather than the rule. In addition, the researcher's own culture remains a central determinant of the instruments and ideas which most often force behavioural diversity (phenomena and informants as people involved in them) to fit into a preset comparative framework. In order to generate cross-culturally valid knowledge, it is advisable to start from a more limited research question and find robust ways to address the issue, find collaborators in other cultures and have with them a truly equal co-operation. This process can go so far as to redesign original research questions in a way quite analogous to that of decentring (Campbell and Werner, 1970).

Appendix: Where to find literature for cross-cultural business research

An additional complexity of cross-cultural research in management is the diversity of sources where it is possible to find relevant literature. Key words such as 'cross-cultural', 'culture', or 'comparative management' give relatively poor results in information searches with large databases on CD-ROM (ABI-inform, Business Periodicals On-Disk). This search is useful but clearly not sufficient. Many academic journals regularly publish comparative, cross-national or cross-cultural contributions, although not as a mainstream focus. The only exception to this is *International Studies of Management and Organization (ISMO)*, which is edited by Jean Boddewyn who has been involved in comparative business studies for quite a long period of time (Boddewyn, 1966). *ISMO* publishes a majority of comparative cross-national or cross-cultural studies. I have noted in Table 3.1 which journals most commonly carry cross-cultural literature in international business, marketing, HRM, management, or accounting and finance topics. The list is not exhaustive and I may have overlooked some publications outlets. Apart from journals, dissertation abstracts in journals such as the *Journal of International Business Studies* can prove quite useful. Annual volumes, especially those edited by JAI Press, Greenwich, CO, are good sources. They offer relevant research which is less filtered by the scientific criteria of major journals; contributions often appear more sound conceptually, much more personal in tone and therefore richer in meaning. The 'Advances' volumes published by JAI Press comprise, inter alia, *Advances in International Comparative Management*, *Research in Organizational Behavior*, *Advances in International Marketing*, *Advances in International Accounting*. Finally, some specialized proceedings volumes are quite valuable sources, for example, those of the Symposium on Cross-Cultural Consumer and Business Studies or the proceedings of the International Conference on Organizational Symbolism and Corporate Culture. Also worth consulting are the annual proceedings of the Academy of Management Annual Meeting or the conferences of the Association for Consumer Research.

Table 3.1   *Academic journals publishing cross-cultural business studies*

Cross-cultural and general	General management and miscellaneous
American Sociological Review	Business Horizons
Cross-cultural Research	California Management Review
International Journal of Psychology	Harvard Business Review
International Journal of Intercultural Relations	Human Systems Management
Journal of Applied Psychology	Journal of Business Venturing
Journal of Cross-Cultural Psychology	Journal of Operations and Production
Mind and Language	Management
	Journal of Purchasing and Materials Management

Marketing	Organization, HRM and management
Dentsu Japan Marketing Advertising	Academy of Management Review
European Journal of Marketing	Academy of Management Journal
International Journal of Advertising	Academy of Management Executive
International Journal of Research in Marketing	Administrative Science Quarterly
International Marketing Review	Human Relations
Journal of Advertising	Human Resource Management
Journal of Advertising Research	Human Systems Management
Journal of Consumer Policy	International Journal of Human Resource
Journal of Consumer Research	Management
Journal of International Consumer Marketing	International Review of Industrial and
Journal of the Academy of Marketing Science	Organizational Psychology
Journal of the Market Research Society	International Review of Strategic Management
Journal of Marketing	International Small Business Journal
Journal of Marketing Research	International Studies of Management and
Marketing and Research Today (formerly	Organization
European Research)	Journal of Business Ethics
Marketing Science	Journal of Business Research
Marketing – Zeitschrift für Forschung und Praxis	Journal of Management Studies
Psychology and Marketing	Journal of Organisational Behavior
Recherche et Applications en Marketing	Long Range Planning
	Management Science
	Organization Science
	Organization Studies
	Strategic Management Journal

International Business	Accounting
Columbia Journal of World Business	Abacus
International Business Review	Accounting, Organizations and Society
Journal of International Business Studies	Financial Accountability and Management
Management International Review	International Journal of Accounting

4
Methodological issues in cross-cultural management research

The search for equivalence and comparability across nations and cultures appears as a natural undertaking in cross-cultural research, whether in psychology, sociology or management studies. If researchers want to compare across cultural contexts, they need to use concepts and research instruments that are understood in similar ways in all the cultures studied. Moreover, they need to check that the same data collection procedures do not result in biased findings in one of the contexts under investigation. The search for equivalence is therefore the most important methodological aspect of cross-cultural management research. Studies which strongly favour purely Emic techniques easily forget that there is always a need for a minimal level of commensurability, at least with the readers' views of the research findings. A general problem in the search for cross-cultural equivalence is the relevance of western models which generally offer the implicit starting base for the comparison process. The issue here is not to criticize them but rather to face a paradoxical situation, namely that the dominant culture in terms of theories, language used and cultural origin of the researchers tends to frame the relevance of the topics, methodologies and concepts used, while at the same time sincerely trying to generate new insights in culturally different contexts. The search for cross-cultural equivalence is in this respect a somewhat self-contradicting process.

I do not argue in this chapter in favour of *tabula rasa*, based on the assumption that everything being specific no single piece of managerial or consumer behaviour could be compared. As a general statement, that would be false and lead to inertia. I argue in favour of being aware of problems of equivalence across national and cultural contexts and making fairly conscious choices in the research design. The issue of cross-national/cross-cultural equivalence is especially important in survey research because questionnaires tend to impose strong frames on informants in comparison, for instance, to depth interviews or observation.

The first part of this chapter explains when it is necessary to undertake a search for equivalence across the contexts under investigation; when the issue addressed is largely culture free it is not necessary. However, the mere use of the term 'cross-national' in a culture-bound comparative study is not enough for researchers to excuse themselves from the search for equivalence across contexts. Then the categories of cross-cultural equivalence are defined. The second part presents two key areas, conceptual and functional equivalence, which allow assessment of whether the theories used will be transportable over borders without major changes. The equivalence of measures used for secondary data or for surveys (units, scales, etc.) is examined in the third part. The following part deals with the issue of finding comparable samples and is followed by a discussion of problems in collecting data: respondents' motivation, response styles, familiarity with research techniques, etc. The last part discusses more generally the equivalence in the whole measurement process, especially when sophisticated statistical techniques are used to assess whether the dimensions of a construct are similar across the cultures studied.

The search for universality and nature of differences

Examples of research involving cross-national/cross-cultural equivalence issues
Seringhaus and Botschen (1991) made a comparative study of the views of Canadian and Austrian companies about their public export promotion services. They state very clearly that it is a 'cross-national' study. It is in fact an issue between organizations (the exporting companies) and public authorities; no individuals are involved as such. The export promotion techniques are fairly similar across countries and cultures (Raimbault et al., 1988). Since the two countries compared are both western countries it can be considered as a culture-free comparative issue. On the other hand, some studies claim to be cross-national (for the purpose of avoiding the pains involved in the search for equivalence) whereas they are partly culture bound. For instance, Peterson et al. (1988) investigated the situation where husband and wife report disagreement in consumption-related surveys that deal with the entire family. They do it across three national contexts: the USA, France and Libya. It is obvious that the disagreement between husband and wife is a culture-bound issue, at least different in the two western countries in comparison to the Muslim country considered, Libya. There is no consideration of cultural differences except to state that Libya

differs substantially on several macro-level factors, including cultural traditions, and that 'the difficulty of collecting valid and reliable data in a nation such as Libya limited the number and scope of variables that could be investigated' (p. 128). It is obviously convenient to call a study 'cross-national', because it seems to save the pains of critical self-examination, but the research findings may then be difficult to interpret.

The determinant of the decision to search for cross-cultural equivalence in a comparative design is whether the research is culture free versus culture bound (or culture embedded). It cannot be decided arbitrarily and has to be based on observation, honest self-questioning and discussion with insiders of the target cultures. The search for cross-cultural equivalence is not a convenient position and involves:

- a world view (that language and culture matter, not always but often);
- a philosophical position (that differences are the main riches in the fabric of reality);
- a decision about what to research.

The final meaning of the search lies in the fact that the researcher wants to discover not only differences in degree, but is also ready to discover differences in nature. Differences in degree are largely spurious when differences in nature have not been previously assessed.

There are topics where culture progressively imposes itself as relevant for explanation. For instance, the issue of quality management and the quality–cost trade-off philosophy have been studied comparatively in Japan and the USA (Reitsperger and Daniel, 1990). The quality recipes of Juran and Deming have been borrowed and developed by the Japanese and then re-imported by US companies. However, some conceptual differences progressively appear in quality management (Yavas and Marcoulides, 1996). Prasad and Sprague (1996) address the issue of whether total quality management is a global paradigm and explain that empirical studies in the 1970s and 1980s have shown that US managers believed that cost increased with quality while the Japanese held an opposite view. Americans view quality management as an economic process, a trade-off whereby companies try to balance costs incurred in quality improvement against costs related to a definite percentage of defective products. The optimal level is reached when marginal costs on both sides are equal. The Japanese view quality as an absolute strategy which targets zero-defect regardless of the costs. Since quality will reduce failures and product returns and increase customer satisfaction and finally sales volume, it will result in decreased costs. A joke on this subject tells of an American company that asks a Japanese supplier to provide one million parts with maximum 1% out from the exact specification. When the American company receives the order it discovers that 10,000 parts are out by the exact dimensional bracket. When asked about this, the Japanese respond that they supplied what they were asked for! However, these differences are not unlimited because the problem is common, and partly culture free. Both costs and technical defects are culture free, but the approach to them may be culture bound. Brannen (1994), for instance, has discussed the intercultural issue of a Japanese company transferring its quality management system to its US subsidiary; her investigation was mostly based on participant observation. Differences in nature can be interpreted in fact as absolute differences (the whole construct is different) or dimensional differences, that is, a construct such as quality management can be understood as having the same basic dimensions across cultures (say, technical perfection and economic quality) but these dimensions receive different weights depending on the culture considered.

Categories of cross-cultural equivalence

The researchers must in some way choose theories and constructs and decide how data will be collected about the phenomenon under investigation. Consequently, a sound process for the collection of data is vital, especially at the international level. The first step in the research process is a clear and concise statement of the research problem. The relevant literature comprises many studies which explore the issue of cross-cultural equivalence (Sekaran, 1983; Douglas and Craig 1984; Leung, 1989; Poortinga, 1989; Peng et al., 1991; Van Herk and Verhallen, 1995; Mullen, 1995; Polonky et al., 1995; Singh, 1995; Cavusgil and Das, 1997). Non-equivalence may be a cause for the non-comparability of data across contexts. Table 4.1 presents the various levels of cross-cultural equivalence. They are further explained in this chapter, except for translation equivalence issues which have been presented in Chapter 2.

An important difference between the various kinds of cross-cultural equivalence categories is whether they should be addressed before or after the data collection takes place. The issue of *ex-ante* versus *ex-post* examination of equivalence across contexts is in practice overlooked. For the correspondence at the meaning level, it is always more advisable to proceed *ex ante*. However, since it is difficult to uncover all areas of possible inequivalence from the start, it is advisable also to check *ex post*. The last part of the chapter discusses this issue in more detail.

Table 4.1   *Categories of cross-cultural equivalence*

A Conceptual equivalence	B Functional equivalence
C Translation equivalence • Lexical equivalence • Idiomatic equivalence • Grammatical–syntactical equivalence • Experiential equivalence	D Measure equivalence • Perceptual equivalence • Metric equivalence • Calibration equivalence • Temporal equivalence
E Sampling equivalence • Sampling unit equivalence • Frame equivalence • Sample selection equivalence	F Data collection equivalence • Respondents' co-operation equivalence • Data collection context equivalence • Response style equivalence
G Measurement process equivalence	

Conceptual and functional equivalence

The underlying meaning of apparently identical concepts
A basic issue in cross-cultural research is the determination of whether the concepts used have similar meaning across the social units studied. Problems of *conceptual equivalence* are frequent when testing the influence of certain constructs on behaviour. For instance, the hypothesis of the cognitive theory that consumers do not willingly behave contradictorily may hold true in the USA while not being applicable to some other countries. Consumer behaviour centres on persons as individuals, as a member of a group (ethnic groups, social classes, families), or as members of the society at large. Emphasis can be on the individual, group or mega-tribe and this may be viewed as a difference in kind or simply in degree. The following statement from Geertz (1983) gives a slight feeling of how difficult it may be to reach true conceptual equivalence between cultures and insists on difference in nature:

> The Western conception of a person as a bounded, unique, more or less integrated, motivational and cognitive universe, a dynamic center of awareness, emotions, judgement and action, organized in a distinctive whole . . . is, however incorrigible it may seem, a rather peculiar idea, within the context of world's cultures. (Geertz 1983, p. 59)

Basic concepts such as autonomy, beauty, leadership, friendliness, motivation, honesty, satisfaction, wealth and well-being are often used in management and marketing research questionnaires where perceptions and motivation for action are related to self-image and interaction with other people in a particular social and cultural setting. Words are seemingly universal when one looks at a dictionary. However, it is always advisable to question the conceptual equivalence of all these basic words, especially when designing a cross-cultural questionnaire survey. In accounting, for instance, the conceptual equivalence of 'goodwill accounting' has been discussed by Brunovs and Kirsch (1991) in the framework of the harmonization of international accounting standards. They conclude that the most significant conceptual difference is between the UK and Ireland on the one hand and the various countries examined on the other.

> The UK standard advocates that goodwill be eliminated immediately on acquisition by write-off directly against reserves, whereas the other countries require goodwill to be carried forward in the balance sheet and systematically amortized against income over the estimated useful life of the goodwill. This difference is not just an inconsistency, but rather represents the chasm of conceptual division as to the underlying question of what goodwill represents. (Brunovs and Kirsch 1991, p. 155)

Let us add that in the case of France, which is not studied by Brunovs and Kirsch, the term 'goodwill' finds no equivalent and is most often used directly in English, despite the traditional reluctance of the French to do so. The French have no equivalent for so intangible an asset as goodwill.

Another example is the concept of trust which is now increasingly widely applied, especially in the areas where intercultural interaction are frequent (for example, joint ventures, international business negotiations). Sullivan and Peterson (1981) have studied the relationship between conflict resolution approaches and trust in a cross-cultural setting and further discussed the factors associated with trust in Japanese–American joint ventures (Sullivan and Peterson, 1988). Choi (1994) has discussed the role of trust in contract enforcement across cultures. However, trust is considered as conceptually equivalent across cultures in most of the literature and the linguistic equivalence of the concept of trust across cultures is never questioned. Only the tip of the iceberg is considered, which may be dangerous.

By looking at how trust is expressed in four languages (English, French, German, Japanese), we can derive some insight into which aspects of the concept are put to the forefront by the corresponding cultures. The English concept of trust is reliance on and confidence in the truth, worth and reliability of a person or thing. Reliance is central to the Anglo-Saxon concept of trust, which is why the legal institution of trust has been highly developed in the common law tradition, whereas it was non-existent in the Roman–Germanic tradition until very recently. The German concept is based on two verbs, *trauen* and *vertrauen*, both of them meaning literally to trust.

But in fact the Germans use the first form, *trauen*, mostly in the negative sense, *'Ich traue Dir nicht'* (I do not trust you), and the second in the positive sense, *Ich vertraue Dir* (I trust you). The prefix *ver* indicates a transformation and this informs us on the picture which is behind the German concept of trust: the initial position is distrust; only after a favourable change has occurred can trust be established. The French notion of *confiance*, as in other Romance languages, is based on the Latin *confidentia*, a compound of *cum* (with, shared) and *fides* (faith, belief): the notion of sharing common beliefs, religion or group membership is central to the Latin concept of trust. The Japanese word for trust is *shin-yô* meaning literally sincere business: it is based on a compound of *shin*, a character for 'sincerity' and *yô* which means literally 'something to do, a business' (Sakade, 1982).

We can still assume that the central concept of trust is the same cross-culturally, but that languages favour a facet of it. Concepts of trust largely overlap across culture but the dominant emphasis may be revealed by linguistic investigation, at least as a potential track to be verified. A first possibility is to gather insights from the four languages/cultures reviewed, to derive the facets of the concept of trust:

1 Trust is reliance on and confidence in people, words and things.
2 Trust is inseparable from distrust. Since obvious showing of distrust is detrimental to the establishment of trust, every culture has to deal with the paradox of their inseparability.
3 Trust is about sharing common faith, beliefs, possibly education or group membership.
4 Trust is directed to common and future achievements, even though this does not deny the value of the lessons of the past.

Another avenue is to build on the etymology of the word trust in various cultures and discuss its variations. With the English 'trust', that is remitting one's interests into another's hands, one may wonder to what extent trust is seen as reciprocal and under which conditions and circumstances. The doing orientation will result in seeing the appropriate solution as the writing of a detailed contract.

The French *confiance*, as shared beliefs, insists much more on being and membership, implying that if they are to trust each other people must share a common religion, the same educational or social background, possibly a common national or ethnic affiliation. This poses the question of extent to which similarity between partners is a condition for a trustful relationship.

The German *Vertrauen* evokes the process of changing an initial trustless situation into one where the parties have built confidence into the relationship. It is very much akin to the human nature orientation of Kluckhohn and Strodtbeck (1961), with an implicit view that the starting base of human nature is bad.

The Japanese *shin-yô* insists on the orientation of trust towards the future, a common enterprise and the sincere expectations of the parties. Time orientations play a role in shaping cultural views of trust building. Both past performance and long-term orientation and continuity over time are essential in the Japanese concept (see the Makimono time pattern as presented by Hayashi, 1988).

It is a useful game to question words and expressions and try to find the real concepts (shared meaning in the cultural and language group) which is conveyed by them. Shenkar and Von Glinow (1994) note, for instance, that when interviewing Chinese employees, a word such as 'autonomy' which is a key concept in organizational research 'cannot be adequately translated into Chinese, or that alternate Chinese terms, such as "right of self-determination" (*zi zhu quan*) convey a quite different meaning' (p. 67). Examples in previous chapters illustrate the practical difficulties in dealing with the conceptual equivalence of constructs, especially when they are used in survey research. When looking at the underlying dimensions of a construct across countries, one often realizes that they are not equivalently weighted or articulated in the total construct. For instance, in the construct 'waiting in line' (to be served), relevant to services management, the dimension of 'losing one's time' may be emphasized in a time-conscious culture, whereas it may be almost non-existent in a culture which has little concern for the economic dimension of time. When 'waiting in line', the dimension of 'guilt for pushing in' is more developed in guilt-oriented societies. Often the conceptual equivalence of several basic interrelated constructs has to be questioned, inasmuch as they relate to idiosyncratic behaviour.

Concepts which have a moral connotation such as bribery do not offer conceptual equivalence. Patronage can be viewed differently in the Anglo world in contrast to the Mediterranean world where a system structured around kin-based loyalties, involving patterns of reciprocal obligations, provides the natural bases for a patron–client relationship (Chapman, 1992), elsewhere considered somewhat immoral. Shame and guilt, key concepts in intercultural interactions (Tangney, 1995), are understood differently according to the cultural context. They need to be examined for conceptual equivalence across cultures, such as the role played by shame in Asian versus western cultures (Ha, 1995). A particular concept may also largely lose its initial meaning because it is transferred into another context. For example, the concept of 'consumer ethnocentrism' (Shimp and Sharma, 1987) and their psychometric scale (CETSCALE) refer to situations where consumers associate the purchase of foreign products with the potential loss of jobs in domestic industry and consequently refrain from buying foreign. It applies fairly well in developed countries to regions in industrial decline where some people, especially the working classes, may resent foreign-made products because they feel that their jobs are threatened by competitive imports. The same logic prevails in European countries, which is probably why Netemeyer et al. (1991) have successfully replicated the CETSCALE in other developed countries. But the basic rationale underlying the concept of consumer ethnocentrism is somewhat different in less developed countries.

Similar concepts performing different functions: functional equivalence

Concepts or constructs used in management research can be activity outcomes, products, practices, rites, rules, activities or relationships. They may be conceptually similar but do not perform the same function. For example, targets may serve as realistic objectives or be motivators for surpassing oneself by setting unreachable performance levels. The primary purpose of meetings can be to solve precise tasks in the agenda or to be social gatherings aimed at building and maintaining group consensus. Other basic concepts in management such as reports, deadlines, relationships and friendship, while conceptually similar, can serve different functions according to the cultural context. Diplomas, for instance, can serve to assign status or to ascertain task-related abilities. The difference in functional use of common concepts is not necessarily dichotomous, but rather the dominance of a particular functional aspect in a definite culture. The function of friendship is essential to the Chinese for doing business, while it is considered somewhat unfair to exploit friendships for business purposes by many westerners (Pye, 1986).

If similar activities perform different functions in different societies, their measures cannot be used directly for the purpose of comparison (Frijda and Jahoda, 1966). A concept such as authority (the right to give orders and the power to ensure obedience) can be conceptually equivalent, but the functional use of authority can be different according to the context – whether authority is used directly by giving detailed instructions, or indirectly by setting target achievements and leaving room and autonomy to the employee for implementation. Activity concepts frequently used in market surveys, such as preparing a meal, are not necessarily functionally equivalent across countries. When asked what dishes do you cook or prepare with tomato juice, Italians and Danes will not think of the same experience.

Products, because their use is context embedded, are good examples of problems of functional equivalence across cultures: a watch, for instance, may be used as wrist jewellery or an instrument for handling time and daily schedules. The same holds true for a fountain pen. In some countries its function may be as a simple general-purpose writing instrument; in others it may be regarded as an instrument for signing documents. Elsewhere it may be considered purely non-functional since it needs time and care to refill and often leaks over one's fingers. A similar product may perform different functions: a bicycle in one country may be considered a transportation vehicle (in the Netherlands, for instance) while in other countries it may be only a leisure or sports item. Stanton et al. (1982) illustrate this functional equivalence problem by taking the example of hot milk-based chocolate drinks. Whereas in the USA and UK they are considered best before going to sleep, in much of Latin America a 'chocolate caliente' is a morning drink. Functional equivalence is reached neither in the consumption time period nor in the purpose for use (waking/energizer versus sleep/relaxer).

Many other examples could be given such as wine (everyday beverage accompanying meals versus beverage for special occasions), beer (summer refresher versus all-year standard 'non-water' beverage), perfumes (covering bodily odours versus adding a nice smell after a shower). The word 'coffee' covers a range of beverages that is enjoyed in very different social settings (at home, at the workplace, during leisure time, in the morning or at particular times during the day), in quite different forms (in terms of quantity, concentration. with or without milk, cold or hot), prepared from different forms of coffee base (beans, ground beans, instant). The function of the Brazilian *cafezinho*, very small cups of rather strong coffee drunk every hour in informal exchanges with colleagues, cannot be compared with the US coffee which is very light and drunk mostly at home and in restaurants. One of the best ways to investigate functional equivalence is to examine the social settings in which an activity takes place and what it means for the people involved.

Measure equivalence

Perceptual equivalence
Perception varies across cultures. There is a wide range of practical research issues where perception has an influence. If the

research deals with a comparative study of working conditions, the ways in which people perceive space, shapes, materials and smells and interpret them within the native cultural community will have a deep influence on their evaluation and assessment of their own working conditions as respondents. Colours are also differently perceived according to cultures, that is, people do not have equivalent sensitivity to the various parts of the colour spectrum and the corresponding languages do not qualify colours in exactly the same way. The next step (after colour identification) is its symbolic interpretation, which varies widely. The same is true for smells. The first issue in equivalence is whether people perceive them physically and mentally, related to the training of their olfactory apparatus; the second issue deals with the kind of interpretation they vest in these smells. When researching packaging and perfumes for washing liquids or other products where perceptive clues are important for product evaluation, a key research issue is to formulate the questions so that interviewees can express their native views on the smell or colours. Rather than ask them whether they like the scent of lavender, it is better to ask them first to recognize the smell, then to comment on what it evokes for them.

Metric equivalence
The validity of a rating scale in a cross-cultural study is affected by the metric equivalence of the scales and by the homogeneity of meanings (Albaum et al., 1987). Pras and Angelmar (1978) did a comparison of verbal rating scales (semantic differentials) in French and English. They showed that difficulties can occur in determining lexical equivalents in different languages of verbal descriptions for the scale. It is also difficult to ensure that the distances between scale points (adjectives, for instance) are equivalent in the two languages (metric equivalence). In this case the standard deviation for the French respondents was significantly smaller than for US respondents due to a greater cultural homogeneity in France. It is naive to use a differential semantic scale originally written in English, French or any other language and translate it lexically (simply with dictionary-equivalent words) into other languages. Pras and Angelmar favour decentred measurement (Campbell and Werner, 1970), which means constructing reliable and valid scales for all the countries under survey. In this case the original wording of the scale may be changed if it provides better measurement equivalence across countries/cultures.

Sood (1990), studied the metric equivalence of nine scale terms (from 'excellent' to 'very bad') across eight languages (English,

Arabic, Chinese, Farsi, French, German, Korean, Spanish). He evidences two facts:

1 Some languages have fewer terms to express gradation in evaluation (for example, Korean), whereas others have a multitude (French).
2 There are large discrepancies in the 'value' of these adjectives, measured on a 0–100 scale. For instance, the Spanish *muy malo* was 58% higher than its supposed English equivalent of 'very bad'. Therefore the best solution is not to try and translate scale terms but rather to start from local wordings based on scales used by local researchers.

Calibration equivalence
To calibrate is to mark the scale of a measuring instrument so that readings can be made in appropriate units. When secondary data – especially published statistical data – are sought there may be some difficulties in comparing these across countries. Differences in categories, for instance, age brackets, income brackets or professions, or differences in base years, when some countries have no recent data, can cause calibration equivalence. A typical calibration equivalence problem relates to monetary units, especially in high-inflation contexts where daily prices change constantly and cannot be directly compared over a year with those of a low-inflation country. Exchange rates and units of weight, distance and volume cause calibration equivalence problems.

A good example of calibration equivalence is given by Marchand (1993) when he discusses the issue of defining and measuring working time cross-nationally, and particularly the problem of assessing the length of working time in a way which makes it comparable across nations. Reasons for inequivalence can be related to different bases for computation: legal or conventional working time, length of working time for which one is paid, hours during which a firm is open for business, full length of the working day including break times and travel time from home to work, time devoted to training. The same holds true for pay systems as to whether they are based on hours, day, week or month and whether they include benefits or bonuses (for instance, the treatment of semester bonuses in Japan). The search for equivalence of hourly wages for workers is especially difficult since the calibration of qualification levels and categories across countries will add complexity to the already observed sources of inequivalence in both pay and working time.

Calibration equivalence mixes with perceptual equivalence, for instance, how many colour classes are recognized by people from a particular country? This might prove useful for a packaging test or a product test. Western subjects, for example, have more colour classes than African subjects and some people have only a two-term colour language. The Bantu of South Africa, for example, do not distinguish between blue and green. Consequently, they do not discriminate between objects or symbols in these colours (Douglas and Craig, 1984). Calibration equivalence problems also arise when different basic units are being used as well as from compound units based on different computation systems. Most Europeans, for instance, use the metric system, counting distances in kilometres and liquid volumes in litres (one cubic decimetre). Fuel consumption is measured in litres/100 km at an average speed. In the USA, 'gas mileage' is based on the inverse calculation: how many miles can one drive with a definite fuel volume, namely a gallon? Calibration needs to assess which gallon it is: the British or imperial gallon (4.55 litres) or the US gallon (3.79 litres), and which mile, a statute mile (1.609 km) or a nautical mile (1.852 km), make an inverse calculation and try to finish with 100 km as the denominator.

Temporal equivalence
Temporal equivalence is near to calibration equivalence because it deals with the calibration of dates and time periods. Information ages differently across countries. In a country where the annual inflation rate is 1 per cent, income and price data are comparable across years, whereas in a country with 200 per cent annual inflation rate it is necessary to indicate on which exact day or week the data were collected and what the price indexes and exchange rates were at that exact date. Temporal equivalence also deals with differences in development levels and technological advancement. Certain countries are 'equivalent' to what others were twenty years ago. Assessing time lags may be useful for making analogies: such a market may now develop in South Africa as it did in the USA fifteen or twenty years ago and the product life cycle may be similar, even though the two countries are at different points on the curve.

Sampling issues

The main problem in the cross-cultural sampling process is the selection of samples that can be considered comparable across countries. Reaching perfect comparability is very difficult – in fact almost impossible. These limitations should be considered when interpreting research findings. An initial issue to be addressed is the two-level type of sampling:

- first level: sample of countries or cultures;
- second level: samples of individuals within these countries or cultures, i.e. national samples.

Hofstede clearly explains that samples of cultures should not be confused with samples of individuals. He draws attention to the risk of abusive stereotyping, whereby country characteristics are considered as individual characteristics: 'Mean values are calculated from the scores on each question for the respondents from each country. We do not compare individuals, but we compare what is called central tendencies in the answers from each country' (Hofstede, 1991, p. 253).

In much the same vein, that is trying to delineate what is at the individual and what is at the group level, Leung and Bond (1989) distinguish four different ways of combining samples of individuals coming from different cultures:

1 a *pancultural* sample consists of pooling the data for all the individuals regardless of which cultural sample they belong to;
2 a separate *within-culture* analysis of individuals in each sample;
3 an *ecological* analysis based on the mean scores of each cultural group, in the same way as Hofstede's indication above;
4 a purely *individual* analysis, by deducting, for each variable, the mean score of the cultural sample from individual scores or by standardizing the data.

In cross-cultural settings a number of issues have to be addressed if the researcher has different national samples which are to be used for comparison purposes:

1 What is the sampling unit? Who should the respondent be?
2 What are the sampling bases?
3 How are the samples drawn from the sampling base?
4 What do the samples represent and are they comparable across cultures?

An important criterion is the choice of respondents. Selecting a unit of analysis is a key issue in the conceptualization of comparative research designs. For instance, the role of respondents in the buying decision process (organizational buying, family buying, information and influence patterns) may vary across countries. In the USA it is not uncommon that children have a strong influence when buying cereals, desserts, toys or other items, whereas in countries that are less child oriented, their influence on the buying decision will be much smaller (Douglas and Craig, 1984). The same holds true for the extended family pattern in South East Asia which heavily influences individual buying decisions. It is therefore of primary interest first to assess the basic equivalent sampling units: for instance, when researching about industrial markets, by comparing the position, role and responsibility of industrial buyers throughout different countries. Similarly, in the area of management, the role of direct supervisors may vary considerably across cultures as concerns their responsibility for evaluating their immediate subordinates.

Sampling is a basic step in many surveys. A complete census, where the whole population of interest is researched, generally proves too costly. Therefore it is advisable to infer the characteristics of the whole population from a limited sample. During this process the following tasks must be carried out:

1 Find a sampling frame, the basic characteristics of which are known (a telephone directory, an electoral list, a business directory).
2 Draw a sample from this frame by a method which may be either probabilistic or non-probabilistic.
3 Check that the selected sample is representative of the population under study.

A second issue is the representativeness of each sample in each country or culture. In cross-cultural research it seems a priori relevant to follow a systematic procedure, the same in every country, to achieve reliability and comparability of data. Unfortunately, demographic definitions do not correspond exactly from one country to another; age does, of course, so long as people know their birth dates, but occupation, education and socio-economic status usually do not. If data are presented in categories, say for income or age bracket, these will most likely not correspond exactly across countries (category equivalence). Religion and tribal membership will also have to be added to traditional demographics as they are of the utmost importance in some less developed countries (even if this appears politically incorrect to some researchers).

The researcher then constructs a sample which represents the population of interest. However, a sample split into 50 per cent men and 50 per cent women conveys a different meaning in a country where women's rights are recognized compared to that in more traditional countries where women's status is lower. As such, the expression 'representative sample' makes little sense if one does not clarify which traits and characteristics this sample actually represents. For instance, shopping behaviour is very different worldwide: in some countries men do most of the shopping, in others women shop for the family; this depends also on other factors such as income level, type of product, employment patterns, etc. The samples must represent actual shoppers rather than men and women as they are in the general population of potential shoppers.

In order to define a sampling procedure for cross-cultural research, one must select a method which is based on several national/cultural samples, each being fully representative of the population(s) of the country/culture which it attempts to represent, and furthermore provides comparable data across countries/ cultures. Douglas and Craig (1983) stress the limited availability of an exhaustive sampling framework which corresponds exactly to the characteristics of the population at a global (multi-country) level. The data collection procedure by local census bureaus can be biased for reasons such as non-exhaustive census or inadequate sampling procedure, causing sampling frames which are often biased. A sample drawn from the electoral list in Bolivia may over-represent men since women are not as likely to vote (Stanton et al., 1982). Tuncalp (1988) states that most sampling frames in Saudi Arabia are inadequate: there is no official census of the population, no elections and therefore no voter registration records, and telephone directories tend to be incomplete. Tuncalp suggests further that non-probability sampling is a necessary evil. Douglas and Craig (1983) also suggest that an empirical method (non-probability sampling procedures) may prove as efficient as probability sampling when researching cross-culturally. Data can be collected at reasonable cost, compatible with the objectives of the survey. Therefore the final criterion for selecting the sampling procedure(s) will remain the comparability of results across countries.

Estimating sample size also appears as a critical step. The use of traditional statistical procedures such as constructing confidence intervals around sample means or hypothesis testing is difficult to implement in cross-cultural settings inasmuch as they require precise estimates of the variance of the various populations compared. This variance estimate is often unavailable in countries which have poor census data. The most frequently used procedure is therefore the selection of sample size, country by country, taking into account their respective peculiarities. If research starts from a domestic survey, where the home country representativeness has been emphasized, and is then extended to other countries it may be difficult to achieve comparability. Although true random sampling is necessary for the successful completion of research projects, studies using non-random samples (quota sampling, for instance) can also be valuable if they include all the characteristics of the subjects and environment that could potentially influence the results or their interpretation (Calder et al., 1981).

Finally, one may conclude that representativeness and comparability of cross-cultural samples can be better achieved by using different samples and sampling techniques which produce equivalent levels of reliability rather than by using the same procedure with all samples. The main problem (before any statistical procedure is implemented) is to secure equivalence in meaning: does it make sense to represent the same populations across various countries? Do the samples actually represent these populations in the same way?

Equivalence in data collection

Why do respondents respond? Why do people participate as respondents in a survey? What motivates informants to deliver their true mind on subjects defined – and worded – by the researcher, with whom they may have little familiarity or sympathy? Albaum, et al. (1995) test the role of response behaviour theory in survey research strategy of research practitioners across three countries: Australia, Hong Kong and the Philippines. In the literature, the three most cited theories for participation or non-participation of respondents to surveys are exchange theory (individuals are motivated to respond by returns or rewards they expect from others), cognitive dissonance (failure to respond creates a state of anxiety which will be reduced by answering), and self-perception (people respond to be consistent with their view of themselves as helpful and responsible persons). It appears from their data that the most popular combinations of techniques among research practitioners include, in addition to one of the three theories cited above, another theory – that of involvement/commitment (Albaum, 1987). Informants will be more likely to respond 'if the topic, sponsor, or researcher is relevant to them. Their level of involvement will determine their level of commitment to survey response' (Albaum et al., 1995, p. 49).

When primary data are concerned, survey or interview data in particular, discrepancies in response patterns across countries may cause data unreliability and limit direct comparison. We assume at this stage that, through any of the translation procedures described in Chapter 2, the researcher has been able to develop equivalent language versions of a common questionnaire/interview guide for a cross-cultural business study, and that the samples are consistent and equivalent. However, response equivalence problems may appear such as secrecy/unwillingness to answer (respondents' co-operation equivalence); response biases (data collection context equivalence), or differences in response style (response style equivalence). Error measurement sources related to response styles are multiple and may directly create discrepancies between observed and true measurement. Some basic precautions may help to avoid generating data with a great deal of measurement error.

Respondent's co-operation equivalence

Reluctance to answer Respondents sometimes feel that the interviewer is intruding upon their privacy. They prefer not to answer, or they consciously bias their answers, fearing that their opinion could later be used against them (Stanton et al., 1982). Many cultures have strong privacy/intimacy patterns, where the family group is protected from external, impersonal interference, especially when interviewers are considered as outgroup people. Tuncalp (1988) explains that the very private and reserved nature of Saudis is not conducive to personal interviews. Being independent, Saudis do not relish the possibility of being exposed to justifying or explaining their actions when answering a barrage of questions.

Biases resulting from the relationship with the interviewer Sexual biases between interviewer and respondent are also an important source of reluctance to grant interviews (Kracmar, 1971). In many countries, housewives are reluctant to grant interviews to male interviewers. Ethnic bias may also exist between the interviewer and the respondent: a Chinese person may feel uncomfortable when interviewed by a Malay (Kushner, 1982). Much response bias may result from the interviewees not understanding that the process of interviewing them is in order to generate objective data. Informants may perceive the purpose of research as a very long-winded form of selling, especially in developing countries (Goodyear, 1982).

The objective and process of the interview must often be explained at the beginning. When briefing native interviewers (management students) in Mauritania, I was asked the following question: 'What do you want us to tell the interviewee to answer?' It was necessary to explain to the interviewers that interviewing was a distanced and objective process, where interviewees had complete freedom of response. The idea of objective truth, external to personal relations, was unfamiliar to Mauritanians. Furthermore, among the Mauritanian interviewers, the Maures of Arabic descent clearly explained that they would not interview Black Africans. Fortunately, there were some Black Africans who were potential interviewers for their own ethnic group. Strong ingroup orientation implies that group membership has to be shared between interviewer and interviewee for the process to take place. Maruyama (1990) explains in the same vein, that Japanese managers in Indonesia tend to recruit Bataks because their characteristics resemble those of the Japanese, although they are not necessarily liked by other Indonesians and may perform poorly as data collectors.

Data collection context equivalence

There is inevitably a social and cultural context to questions – they are never completely culture free. Contextual equivalence relates to elements in the context of the data collection process that have an influence on responses. As Douglas and Craig explain (1984, p. 109): 'In the Scandinavian countries, for example, respondents are considerably more willing to admit overdrinking than in Latin America. In India, sex tends to be a taboo topic.' Any question that deals directly or indirectly with social prescription needs to be worded so that people can elaborate a response without feeling embarrassed, and responses have to be screened in order to know whether they reflect actual realities or simply a view of what is socially desirable. Some well-disposed and open-minded interviewees may be questioned further to deliver their true mind on the question. Lack of familiarity with the research instrument is another cause for problems of data collection: Shenkar and Von Glinow (1994) note that the Chinese are not accustomed to complete a detailed questionnaire in multiple choice format. They have a problem with hypothetical questions and tend to reserve the most important points to the end of the interview. Similarly Easterby-Smith and Malina (1997), in the case of a UK–China research project, note that the Chinese were surprised at the informality and short duration of the interviews in British companies. The Chinese view was that interviewees had to prepare the answers in advance in order to be able to answer the questions. According to the British, interviews in China were more like lectures where managers read prepared reports and questions usually came only after each speech was finished. Interviewed about this, the Chinese managers answered that a spontaneous exchange of ideas would lead to ill-prepared answers.

In the researcher's quest to embed the data collection process in the local context, she may be tempted to employ local researchers rather than from the home country. The strength of local researchers is that they know the country and its people and can usually establish rapport easily. Knowledge of the local language allows the researcher to interact much better and to understand what is said. Language can be an enormous barrier, as anyone who has tried to interview through interpreters must recognize. If local researchers are familiar with the country and language where the survey originated, they can also interpret the significance of what is said and explain differences across cultures (Goodyear, 1982). Local researchers also have weaknesses, often having less research experience than their equivalent in more developed countries. They may find it difficult to adopt the kind of neutral, objective stance with reference to informants or clients because they do not see the value of objective truth resulting from a distanced position in the interaction. They may want to be didactic in groups and may well prefer to distort findings to reflect a more educated picture of fellow countrymen than exists in reality. Alternatively, they may seek to distance themselves from the 'average consumer' by exaggerating their foibles and lack of sophistication, especially if the researcher is from an educated family and out of touch with his countrymen. Finally, the local researcher may be unwilling or unable, even for business reasons, to cross traditional barriers of class, religion or tribe (Goodyear, 1982).

Response style equivalence
This is an important step in the search for equivalence, in direct relation with the informants' world. The four main concerns for response style equivalence are:

- yea-saying pattern (and, symmetrically, nay-saying pattern);
- item non-response pattern;
- median response style;
- extreme response style.

In the 'yea-saying' pattern (Douglas and Craig, 1983), response scores tend to be inflated and the mean scores of the respondents are biased towards the positive end of the scale (in questionnaires) or they make exaggerated/hyperbolic statements in interviews. Some respondents, especially in Latin American countries (Stanton et al., 1982) tend to present a 'courtesy bias' by answering in order to please the interviewer. Respondents tend to tell the interviewer what they think the interviewer would like to hear. This response pattern may be more frequent in countries where people are not familiar with surveys and questionnaires. When they accept, it can be through some kind of personal favourable sentiment towards the interviewer. If the courtesy bias is high on average a 'yea-saying pattern' bias may be found. Van Herk and Verhallen (1995) evidence such a bias when interviewing Greek and Italian housewives on their cooking behaviour. There is a systematic tendency in the Greek sample to give more positive answers in psychographics, as well as in product-related questions, than the Italian sample. The yea-saying bias translates into a higher mean score on almost all questions. Standardizing scores across cultures allows elimination of the 'yea-saying' pattern, although it is fairly difficult to differentiate whether people were striving on average to the positive end of the scale or are agreeing strongly with a particular item. Thus the 'yea-saying' pattern can only be diagnosed when it is consistent across almost all the questions.

Face saving issues, especially in Asia, can bias the response in the sense of what seems locally as socially desirable. Adler et al. (1989) note the tendency of the Chinese to respond a desired rather than an actual state. Social desirability is a strong bias, even in domestic settings, but is in fact increased by the cross-cultural setting. The Chinese, and most Asians, tend to respond by using their group as a reference rather than speaking their own mind. The acceptable discrepancy between ideal and actual behaviour varies across societies and therefore the tendency to respond after the ideal rather than actual behaviour is especially strong when informants have to self-report their behaviour. Grunert and Muller (1996), when measuring values in international settings, address the issue of whether respondents are thinking about 'real' life or 'ideal' life. They contrast the scores of Danish and Canadian respondents who are asked to report on their ideal values ('imagine an ideal life for yourself') and actual values ('that which persons may strive for in their day-to-day life'). They evidence a discrepancy between ideal and actual values in both countries.

Item non-response is another important source of bias in cross-national surveys. Respondents may be unwilling to respond to some questions, such as those relating to income or age. Douglas and Shoemaker (1981), studying non-response of different items in a public opinion survey in eight European countries, found evidence of higher non-response on income in the UK and Ireland, whereas the willingness to respond to political questions was highest in Germany and Italy. Some questions such as income or age, which appear as relatively easy to respond to in certain cultural contexts, are sensitive issues in others and cannot be asked directly.

Item non-response is also a source of information for the researcher because it evidences possible inadequacies of the research instrument which can be due to culture or language.

Where a culture values moderate behaviour in general and self-effacement in particular, respondents will tend to use the median value on questionnaire scales (see Shenkar and Von Glinow, 1994, in the case of the Chinese) or to soften their position and avoid being affirmative as interviewees. An opposite bias results from significant extreme response style (ERS), the overall response pattern in a particular sample being marked by higher standard deviation. People in the USA, for instance, tend to respond with more enthusiasm and therefore present a more extreme response style in answering than the Japanese (Zax and Takashi, 1967) or Koreans (Chun et al., 1974). This produces a bias in the standard deviation of data, increasing it artificially in cultures where people tend to over-react to questions, compared to other cultures where people may tend to suppress their opinions, whether positive or negative. Marshall, et al. (1995) test extreme response style across seven countries (Australia, China, India, Indonesia, New Zealand, Singapore, USA) contrasting across cultural groups and across genders within the country samples. They find substantially high ERS in India and Indonesia in comparison to the other five countries in the sample, and little difference in ERS between men and women.

Cross-cultural coding issues
Coding issues are important for a series of data collection procedures where a content analysis is done. In the study of international business negotiations, dyadic interactions between negotiators are observed by video-camera (Graham, 1985) and the records are content analysed using a classic classificatory scheme of attitudes in business negotiations (Angelmar and Stern, 1978). The categories of the content analysis are not neutral and no leeway is given to coders. The necessity to assess intercoder reliability (a measure often asked for in positivistic cross-cultural research) will result in the coders being strictly instructed by the researcher as to the segments being observed and the possible categories in which they can be coded. This will automatically reduce the capacity of the coders, as cultural insiders, to give new insights and will consequently favour the emergence of cross-cultural similarities. What is important in the coding process is that the final data are not raw, but have been derived from the content analysis process.

For instance, Alden et al. (1993) compare the use of humour in advertisements across four different cultures (Korea, Germany, Thailand, USA) and use a common model of forms of humour for the four cultures studied. For the identification of what is humorous in the advertisements under investigation, they use three bilingual coders in Germany and four in the other countries who have received the coding instructions in their own language. They state quite clearly that they have not asked the coders to assess on a personal basis whether they judge the advertisement to be humorous or not, but to code the humorous intention in order to reduce their 'subjectivity'. Such a coding procedure will naturally let the global dimensions of humour emerge rather than the culture-specific segments. It is obvious that coding instructions will have a very strong influence on the final results of a cross-cultural study.

Measurement across cultures: assessing comparability in cross-national and cross-cultural research

An example of a typical cross-national study is given by the Meaning of Working study which was conducted by a collaborative research team across eight nations, Belgium, Israel, Japan, the Netherlands, UK, USA, the then West Germany, and Yugoslavia (Bhagat et al., 1990). A number of conditional variables have been retrieved such as sociodemographics (age, sex, occupational level), career history and socio-economic variables at the society level. The underlying model was that the meaning of working, as perceived by individuals, was determined by the interaction of their personal background with their work experiences and the social, economic and cultural environment. The study enabled the researchers to highlight six dimensions which appeared cross-culturally: work centrality (importance of work relative to other areas of life), entitlement norm, obligation norm, economic functions of work, expressive working outcomes and social relations in a work setting. The main issues to be addressed in assessing the cross-cultural validity of the whole measurement process are:

1   Where do we start from in terms of theories and previous research?
2   How to control for intervening variables other than culture?
3   How to assess the level of cross-cultural comparability?

Transposition/replication versus new instruments
Most often comparative studies are based on the transposition of an existing instrument (questionnaire, items, psychometric scale) which pre-defines, at least partially, the concepts used, the measurement system and the data collection procedures which have to

be implemented in the foreign context studied. In this case, there is some transposition in the sense that the team of researchers discusses the basic concepts and research procedures in a way which offers side avenues for improving the level of cross-cultural comparability. The ideal solution would be to design a new instrument on a cross-national basis from the very start. The worst is probably mere replication, that is, administering a research instrument to a quite different economic and cultural context compared to where it was developed, without any adaptation. Direct replications assume wrongly that there are no differences in nature and only differences in degree, while reality lies somewhere in the middle because there must always be a starting point in terms of items for a possible common questionnaire or theme list for interviews. Most of the literature dealing with measure equivalence is based on psychometric research instruments. Key words are then: items, scores, factor analysis, factor loadings, measurement error and reliability of psychometric scales (Bhalla and Lin, 1987).

Accounting for other intervening variables and differences in
response styles across data sets
The general problem is how to control that variance in the data can really be attributed to cultural differences. The risk is to compare individuals rather than nations/cultures. Variance can be due to age or gender, which are quite significant explanatory variables in most social science research; it can also be related to the type of organizations surveyed (size, industry). What Hofstede calls 'ecological correlations' (correlations across mean national scores), like most cross-cultural research, requires matched samples across national or cultural groups. The first step therefore is to control for sociodemographics, generally by quota sampling, that is, non-probabilistic sampling with similar distribution in age brackets, gender, occupation, level of education, or hierarchical position within the organization if superior–subordinate relationships are studied. If several organizations are surveyed they must share common characterics across countries; researching in only one organization sets to zero the variance related to corporate culture (Hofstede, 1980a).

The second step is to try and avoid biases due to the divergence in response styles described above (for example, if the Greeks respond systematically more positively than the Italians). The traditional recommendation is to standardize the data in national data sets: standardized scores are adjusted so that they are normally distributed with zero mean and unit standard deviation. The underlying assumption is that, in the absence of response biases, the mean scores for the various groups would be equal. Therefore the standardization of individual responses in each national data set serves the purpose of avoiding yea-saying biases or extreme response style in some countries; it brings the various data sets to a common metric. However, it is clear that this procedure has quite strong effects: it throws the baby out with the bathwater by eliminating possibly significant differences in mean across national samples. Alpert et al. (1987) remark that this *ex-post* adjustment may raise problems while solving others; standardization within individuals tends to invalidate comparisons between individuals. Singh (1995) argues that standardized coefficients reflect an Emic comparison standard because standardization ensures a within-sample common metric, but not across national samples (which is what many researchers believe, because the standardization of coefficients is often undertaken with an Etic, comparative perspective). Singh argues that unstandardized coefficients reflect the true Etic perspective, because they really assume cross-cultural equivalence at the various levels described above. He recommends that researchers use standardization in each national data set only if there is suspicion of inequivalence, especially in response style, but to keep unstandardized coefficients for interpretation and substantive inference.

Assessing cross-national/cross-cultural comparability

Variations in the reliability of research instruments due to measurement error　Measurement reliability is a threat to cross-national comparability and has been investigated by Davis et al. (1981) for three types of consumer behaviour measures (demographics, household decision involvement and psychographics) across five country markets, utilizing three different reliability assessment methods. Their findings show that it is easier to obtain measurement equivalence between demographic variables than between psychographic variables such as life styles. Assessment method and the nature of the construct may be two causes of measurement unreliability across countries.

Variations in knowledge and familiarity with concepts or attitudes, have a deep impact on the equivalence of measures. Parameswaran and Yaprak (1987) have compared the attitudes of respondents in two countries (USA and Turkey) towards the people and products from three countries of origin (Germany, Japan, Italy) using three products (cars, cameras, electronic calculators). They demonstrate that the same scale may have differing reliabilities when used by the same individual in evaluating products from differing cultures. The cars reviewed are the Volkswagen Golf (Germany), the Honda Civic

(Japan) and the Fiat 128 (Italy). Cameras considered are Leica (Germany), Canon (Japan) and Ferrania (Italy). The brands of electronic calculators are Royal (Germany), Canon (Japan) and Olivetti (Italy). Parameswaran and Yaprak explain that:

> Differing levels of awareness, knowledge, familiarity and affect with the peoples, product in general, and specific brands from a chosen country-of-origin may result in differential in the reliability of similar scales when used in multiple national markets. . . . Two alternative courses of action may alleviate this problem. Measures to be used in cross-national market comparisons may be pre-tested in each of the markets of interest until they elicit similar (and high) levels of reliability. . . . Alternatively, one might devise a method to develop confidence interval (akin to statistical spreads based on sample sizes) around the value of the measure based on its reliability. (Parameswaran and Yaprak, 1987, pp. 45–6)

In order to account for differences in meaurement error at the level of individual variables, say X and Y, Singh (1995) suggests computing corrected correlation based on their mutiplication by an adjustment factor using their reliability estimates (Cronbach's alpha):

$$1/\sqrt{\alpha_x}\,\sqrt{\alpha_y}$$

Indicators of similarity across countries There are a number of techniques for diagnosing measurement equivalence, most of which should be applied *ex ante*, especially techniques that ensure translation equivalence (discussed in Chapter 2). A basic step for measuring metric equivalence is to compare reliabilities across national data sets, as has been affirmed above. A more sophisticated procedure is to test for equality of measurement error variances (δ) using multiple group LISREL (Bollen, 1989; Jöreskog and Sörbom, 1993). Mullen (1995) uses this technique to reassess the results of Lincoln and Kalleberg (1985) who have studied the concepts of organizational commitment (loyalty) from a job or work perspective in the USA and Japan. Satisfaction was measured on three items, while job loyalty was measured with five items. The original samples were based on a large survey of both Japanese (3,735) and US workers (4,567). Multiple group LISREL basically consists of estimating a model for the two separate data sets and testing the assumption that the loadings of the items on the factorial dimensions (that is, how measurement variables contribute to a particular theoretical, latent construct) are invariant across the two data sets. Mullen uses the differential in χ^2 between the two models which must be statistically insignificant if it is to provide support for the invariance hypothesis. In fact, verification, whether done through multiple group LISREL or through optimal scaling, indicates that measurement equivalence exists for job satisfaction but not for job loyalty, leading to a reassessment of the Lincoln and Kalleberg study and possibly to a search for the conceptual equivalence of the construct of job loyalty between the USA and Japan. A similar approach, but in a different domain and with new data, has been followed by Durvasula et al. (1993) to assess a cross-national model of attitudes towards advertising.

Invariance of factor structure: levels of cross-cultural comparability   It is quite obvious that among positivistic researchers the most advanced approaches for cross-cultural/cross-national measurement revolve around the issue of factorial dimensions of constructs and loading of items on the factors (Nunnally, 1978; Churchill, 1979). Grunert et al. (1993) distinguish different levels of cultural comparability. If we assume a LISREL model, where X is a vector of q observed measures, μ a vector of q mean values in the population, Λ a matrix of q x n factor loadings relating items (measurement variables) to the construct, or the dimension of the theoretical, latent construct ξ, a vector of n factors, and δ a vector of q error terms, we have:

$$X = \mu + \Lambda\,\xi + \delta$$

Assuming that ξ and δ are independent, the matrix of variance-covariance of X, Σ is defined as:

$$\Sigma = \Lambda\Phi\Lambda' + \Theta\delta$$

If we have two national/cultural data sets, with variance-covariance matrices Σ_1 and Σ_2 and mean values μ_1 and μ_2, then the underlying structure of the two groups of respondents can be compared. If both the Σs and the μs are equal, one can speak in Grunert et al. (1993) terms of 'strong cultural identity', a condition difficult to find in the real world. If simply the Σs are identical but the mean values μs differ, then there is a case of 'weak cultural identity'. If the Σs differ, then, if the Λs are equal (similar items load in the same way on the same factorial dimensions) as well as the Θs (identical distribution of error terms), then there is 'strong cultural comparability'. Further, if the Θs, that is, the distribution of error terms, differ across national data sets but the loadings Λ are still equal, there is a case of 'weak cultural comparability'. Finally, if all measures differ (Σ, Λ, Θ), there is no cultural comparability. However, Grunert et al. (1993) consider the case where Λs are very roughly similar – a frequent case in practice – as a situation of 'minimal cultural comparability'. They test these hypotheses of cultural identity/comparability on five national data sets (USA, divided into four regional US subsamples, Japan, France, Denmark, Germany) where respondents have been exposed to the List of Values (Kahle et al., 1986). In most cases the items do not load exactly on the same factorial dimensions across the various data sets. Even in the case of the US subsamples there is no cultural comparability, even in the weakest condition. Across the five national data sets there appears to be no cultural comparability, even minimal. Only the dyad of Danes and Germans achieves strong cultural comparability.

Singh (1995) has reassessed the study by Dubinsky et al. (1992) of the influence of role stress on industrial salespeople's work outcomes in the USA, Japan and Korea, and the influence of two independent constructs (role conflict and role ambiguity) on three dependent constructs (job performance, job satisfaction and organizational commitment). Singh re-analyses the data of Dubinsky et al. which was mostly analysed by multiple pairwise comparisons and regression analysis. He takes into account the measurement error, using an approach similar to other authors (Grunert et al., 1993; Durvasula et al., 1995; Mullen, 1995), except that he computes estimates of the various national models through the EQS software (Bentler, 1989) rather than LISREL. Not taking into account measurement error, Dubinsky et al. have underestimated the explained variances in all cases and have both over-estimated and underestimated the magnitude and significance of several path coefficients. Singh shows further that the authors in the original study have committed one type-I error, that is, inferring a spurious cross-national difference, when they stated that job performance had an influence on job satisfaction, and two type-II errors, that is, overlooking a significant cross-national difference.

In much the same way as Grunert et al. (1993), Singh (1995) distinguishes three successive steps in construct equivalence assessment: establishing 'factorial similarity', which is reached when the scale items load on the same factor across nations (that is, 'minimum cultural comparability' in Grunert et al. terms); 'factorial equivalence', which corresponds to identical factor loadings for each scale item across nations (that is, 'weak cultural comparability'); and 'measurement equivalence', when the factor loadings and error variances are identical for each scale item across nations (that is, 'strong cultural comparability' in Grunert et al. terms). Additionally, Singh (1995, p. 604) states very clearly: 'Issues of functional, conceptual and instrument equivalence need to be addressed *before* cross-national data collection, while equivalence assessment is only possible *after* the data collection stage . . .the aim of *after* procedures is to probe the degree of success of *before* procedures.' That is why we explain in the next section some avenues for investigating *ex-ante* construct equivalence, by using the example of the consumer dissatisfaction construct.

Cross-cultural transportability of a construct at meaning level: of consumer dissatisfaction

The word 'construct' relates, in general, to a concept which has several underlying dimensions and may be measured quantitatively by identifying these various dimensions. The construct 'consumer dissatisfaction and complaint behaviour' (Richins, 1983, reported in Richins and Verhage, 1985, p. 198) identifies five domains of attitudes toward complaining:

1 Beliefs about the affect experienced when one complains.
2 Perceptions of the objective cost or trouble involved in making a complaint.
3 Perception of retailer responsiveness to consumer complaints.
4 The extent to which consumer complaints are expected to benefit society at large.
5 The perceived social appropriateness of making consumer complaints.

Constructs such as consumer dissatisfaction have been used for assessing cross-cultural differences in consumer attitudes. Richins and Verhage (1985) have studied differences between American and Dutch consumers relating to their dissatisfaction and complaining behaviour. They look for conceptual equivalence of what it means, socially and individually, for Americans and the Dutch to be dissatisfied with a product or a service. Their questionnaire was reviewed by a panel of Dutch experts and some minor changes to the wording of the questions were made. Richins and Verhage found 29 per cent of the variance to be attributable to national differences, the most salient being:

> Dutch consumers perceive more inconvenience and unpleasantness in making complaint than do American consumers . . . Dutch consumers were less likely than Americans to feel a social responsibility to make complaints . . . Seemingly contradicting this finding, however, Dutch consumers are more likely than Americans to feel bothered if they don't make a complaint when they believe they should, a sort of guilt. Perhaps this seeming contradiction indicates that Dutch respondents tend to feel a personal rather than social obligation to make complaints. (Richins and Verhage, 1985, p. 203)

A scale of consumer complaint behaviour (CCB) has been also developed by Singh (1988). US respondents were asked to express their degree of agreement or disagreement on a six-point Likert scale to the items listed below (possible behavioural responses to dissatisfaction with a consumption experience). Factor analysis allowed to distinguish three dimensions for CCB:

- 'Voice CCB': forget about the incident and do nothing; definitely complain to the store manager on your next trip; go back or call the repair shop immediately and ask them to take care of your problem.
- 'Private CCB': decide not to use that repair shop again; speak to your friends and relatives about your bad experience; convince your friends and relatives not to use that repair shop.
- 'Third party CCB': complain to a consumer agency and ask them to make the repair shop take care of your problem; write a letter to the local newspaper about your bad experience; report to the consumer agency so that they can warn other consumers; take some legal action against the repair shop/manufacturer.

Questioning the cross-cultural transposability of such a scale implies investigating mostly the meaning, situations, institutions and behaviours depicted by the items. At first sight, the relevance of the three dimensions seems fairly robust because they are based on major alternatives that exist consistently across nations and cultures: to keep silent or to complain; to decide to go back to the shop, complain and ask for redress; to speak to friends and diffuse negative word-of-mouth communication (a way to take revenge as well as to please one's friends by giving them good advice); to make an official, written complaint to a newspaper or a consumer agency. However, the third dimension, 'third party CCB' is, on average, not very robust. Consumer agencies do not exist in all countries and newspapers may be concerned with myriad topics other than individual consumers complaining about the hairdryer or the washing machine. Writing such pieces may appear socially ridiculous because the world of things is despised and materialism is taboo.

Macro and micro dissatisfaction are also two aspects to be considered. People often do not complain at the micro level because they quickly make an attribution that something goes wrong at the macro level (inflation, political instability, inappropriate regulation, bribery, educational system), causing dysfunctions at the micro level that cannot be attributed to manufacturers, shopkeepers or maintenance people. Cavusgil and Kaynak (1984) have proposed an interesting enlargement of the consumer dissatisfaction concept in the case of developing countries. They distinguish between micro-level sources (excessive prices, misleading advertising, lack of performance, etc.) and macro-level sources of consumer dissatisfaction (low income, inflation) with the possibility of interaction between the two levels. They state: 'In general micro-level sources appear to lead, over time, to a diffuse, latent discontent with the state of the marketplace; that is to a macro-level dissatisfaction. Unsatisfactory experiences with specific products and services seem to be reflected in a disillusionment with all institutions in the society' (Cavusgil and Kaynak, 1984, p. 118). Moreover, the complaining behaviour does not have the same meaning at all in the case where buyer and seller know each other personally, either as acquaintances or relatives: 'Personal relationships with vendors often prove advantageous. Usually food shoppers get to know how far they can trust a food retailer, and can negotiate prices and other terms' (Cavusgil and Kaynak, 1984, p. 122).

Potential problems in transposing psychometric scales cross-culturally can be encountered in the following areas:

1 Adaptation of existing items (wording, experiential equivalence).
2 Basic cultural assumptions that distort responses to the items or the subsequent interpretation by a non-native researcher; high individualism, low power distance, a strong belief in free market forces and a materialistic culture are key value orientations which underlie most of the CCB literature.
3 A problem of missing items: macro satisfaction and its impact on micro satisfaction should probably be considered.

Table 4.2 illustrates some possible contextual and cultural influences on the items of the scale.

Conclusion

This chapter has presented the technicalities of cross-cultural research. The researcher must keep a critical eye on the pursuit of absolute cross-cultural or cross-national equivalence which may simply end in crashing down relevant information. There is something vaguely ethnocentric in the absolute pursuit of 'zero-bias' in cross-cultural research, inasmuch as differences are not meant as useful information, but rather as a disturbing phenomenon for the research process that must in some way be eliminated, so that concepts, instruments, respondents and their responses are made comparable across nations and culture and systematically viewed as

Table 4.2 *Possible problems of cross-cultural equivalence for Singh's (1988) CCB scale*

Items	Contextual and cultural influence
Forget about the incident and do nothing.	Fatalism may induce people to accept and keep silent.
Definitely complain to the store manager on your next trip.	Corresponds to low-context/explicit communication cultures (Hall, 1959, 1960, 1976).
Go back or call the repair shop immediately and ask them to take care of your problem.	Difficult in sellers' markets – the shopkeeper will argue that the product has been misused or is correct.
Decide not to use that repair shop again.	Availability of alternatives/personal linkages (if the repair shop is that of a friend or a relative).
Speak to your friends and relatives about your bad experience.	Social desirability (the speaker may appear ridiculous or uselessly negative).
Convince your friends and relatives not to use that repair shop.	Social influence: negative WOM may backfire, the complainer being accused of defaming respectable people.
Complain to a consumer agency and ask them to make the repair shop take care of your problem.	Existence of consumer agencies (CA)/ literacy/ influence of CA/free versus paying complaint procedures.
Write a letter to the local newspaper about your bad experience.	Functions of the press vis-à-vis businesses/power distance/degree of freedom of the press.
Report to the consumer agency so that they can warn other consumers.	Independence of the consumer agency; CA's means to spread information and battle against manufacturers.
Take some legal action against the repair shop/manufacturer.	Existing legal texts/power distance.

different in degree rather than different in nature. Wright (1996, p. 63) arguing for and about qualitative research in international management, quotes Friedrich Hayek (1978): 'Unlike the position that exists in the physical sciences, in economics and other disciplines that deal with essentially complex phenomena, the aspects of the events to be accounted for about which we can get quantitative data are necessarily limited and may not include the important ones.' However, qualitative researchers must also be concerned with conceptual and measurement equivalence because in such approaches the researcher herself is the instrument. The rivalry between positivistic/survey/quantitative research and ethno-graphic/observation/qualitative researchers is traditional in most individual domains of the social sciences. As I will argue in the next chapter, the two broad research traditions are complementary rather than competing in the area of cross-cultural research where both avenues can be merged in order to look simultaneously for meaning as differences in nature and differences in degree.

5
Strategies for improving the relevance of cross-cultural research in management

Eighteenth-century writers were active in exploring fantasy foreign territories, like Swift with *Gulliver's Travels* or Voltaire with *Candide*. In so doing they began the first explorations of cultural differences. In the *Persian Letters*, Montesquieu (1721) wondered, humorously, how it is possible to be a Persian, while letting Rica write the following lines: 'They [Europeans] are very keen on the pursuit of knowledge here, but I cannot say that they know a great deal . . . The majority of Frenchmen have a mania for being clever, and the majority of those who want to be clever have a mania for writing books' (1973, p. 134). A culminating point of such fantasied travels was reached by Xavier De Maistre with *Voyage autour de ma Chambre* (journey around my room), published in 1795. De Maistre died in St Petersburg in 1852, which tends to show that, in the meantime, he had travelled. In fact, our fascination for overseas locations, foreign peoples and their strange ways is also located within the observer, within ourselves. When travelling internationally and collecting data constantly, we compare, confront and finally enrich our inner gestalts. Culture is in fact suffusing the whole scene, it is located everywhere, that is, not only in the object under investigation, but also in the observer and the context of the observation.

True international research must therefore be based on some awareness of one's own biases and a readiness to accept new ways of seeing the world. That is why deconstruction, in the sense of a radical questioning about the ideological foundations of one's own thoughts, is an absolute necessity (first part of the chapter). If a researcher does not question herself about her preconceptions, she is quite likely to impose preframed views upon the foreign reality; the example of cross-cultural research on risk and decision-making is offered as an illustration of such a deconstructionist enterprise. Language, as I have argued throughout the book, is a key asset for discovering hidden meaning and searching for equivalence across contexts. In the second part of this chapter I give examples of how language can be used to deconstruct preframed meanings and generate insights on differences in concepts.

Combining qualitative and quantitative approaches seems a significant avenue in cross-cultural business research, because both the assessment of differences in nature and the assessment of differences in degree make sense. This type of multi-method approach is difficult because the two 'religions', the positivistic/quantitative and the humanistic/phenomenological research paradigms, are in somewhat constant conflict. Although the two traditions tend largely to remain separate, it may be adequate to use the two approaches in parallel. In the fourth part, I explain what should be avoided in cross-cultural business research if one is to generate valid cross-cultural findings. That is, between which rocks or icebergs (a large part being invisible) the ship of the cross-cultural researcher should be guided. Finally, I suggest some ways and means to enlarge perspectives in cross-cultural business research.

The necessary deconstruction of multiple cultural realities

Culture, being socially constructed, is a highly complex kind of reality. Culture is often opposed to nature with the Rousseauist view that people living near to the primitive simplicity of nature would be fundamentally 'better' than those who live in sophisticated modern cultures. This naive opposition hides the complex nature of arrangements between nature and culture within real-world human systems. Subjects and objects of culture are in the same global ocean and culture is highly 'natural' while nature is now highly 'cultured'. An example of this can be found in our relationship to the environment and the ecosystem, as it is constructed by the environmentalists, especially the highly environment conscious Germans with their concept of *Umweltfreundlichkeit* (the fact of being environmentally friendly). An initial preoccupation with nature ends in a typically German list of prohibitions when people trek in even a tiny piece of forest, while thousands of cars can be stopped in a major traffic jam one mile away, polluting the whole area. That is why the first step is to be sceptical about what is natural and about nature itself. What is our true nature anyway?

Introspective self-inquiry and fears of deconstruction
Taking the perspective of 'doing what comes naturally' (Lincoln and Guba, 1986) seems to be a friendly piece of advice but is in fact somewhat dangerous for cross-cultural business research. What is

more natural is to use our own culture as an interpretive framework, because it is a system of preconceptions and prejudices which allows a short cut to conclusive findings. In this respect, qualitative research is as susceptible to bias as quantitative, and in some respects even more so, because the researcher is directly in charge of interpretation and bears even greater responsibility for possible biases. One may wonder whether 'doing what comes naturally' is not simply built in the researcher's own background and/or in favourable circumstances. Some personal backgrounds can be useful for cross-cultural research because they are multicultural and multilinguistic in nature, such as those of Fons Trompenaars, with a French mother and a Dutch father, or Mary Yoko Brannen, who was raised in Japan until she was 7 years old.

Most of the cultural fabric is invisible, like the immersed part of an iceberg, while cross-cultural research situations involve encounters between instruments from one culture and informants from another, employees and managers from different cultures, etc. For this reason it is necessary to start with a phase of pre-research inquiry which has a lot to do with self-inquiry. In this enterprise, the key word is 'foreign': what or whom is foreign to what or whom? Cultural deconstruction is not a philosophical enterprise (although the word 'deconstruction' seems to be proprietary to some French philosophers like Derrida), but involves a systematic investigation of the basis on which the research design will rest, including a self-assessment of the researcher's own part in terms of underlying concepts and theories, as well as attitude towards the research practices. The employment system, as argued in Chapter 2, is an element of the iceberg and needs to be recognized in the deconstruction process. People are bound to produce a certain kind of research in line with the local scientific consumer culture, for instance, the dominant, national and professional culture of the supervisor and members of the dissertation committee. Such deconstructionist investigations are little developed in the cross-cultural domain where they would be useful because researchers are systemically afraid of challenging the dominant assumptions. They believe that the whole research system rests on these assumptions and that their own survival depends on the employment system which they perceive as tightly bound to a certain style of research. Stated otherwise, they fear that deconstruction may be destructive. This results in enormous mental blocks whereby differences are prudently searched in degree rather than in nature. I believe that this view is largely mistaken. The quality and the durability of the academic system rests only on the relevance of the intellectual debates, on the soundness of the theses advanced and the quality of the arguments, data or theory brought in favour of them. Open debate will make the academic system stronger rather than weaker in the long run.

Another fear has to do with the lack of directly applicable results coming from the deconstruction process. If it results in highlighting key explanatory variables that cannot be easily manipulated in further managerial action (language competence, for instance), it is considered as good for nothing and to be rejected. The lack of content orientation is also an apparent drawback of deconstructionist approaches. They seem to destruct knowledge, especially if knowledge is assumed as universal, content based and static, and to exist per se, not in the interaction between people in a context-dependent relationship. One comes to the contrary conclusion, namely that deconstruction is constructive, when one considers knowledge as basically process oriented, local in nature within a particularist approach to the progressive construction of knowledge. Then deconstruction becomes a constructive undertaking, even a necessary initial step for designing cross-cultural research, for instance, through open discussion with colleagues from other cultures.

Deconstruction is a critical investigation into one's own research approach. For instance, my own lack of data orientation, which may have some drawbacks, is typical of the French intellectual style (see Chapter 2). I have largely corrected this bias by continuous exposure to other intellectual and research traditions. In the deconstruction process, it is also important to envision what could be alternative assumptions and explanations, including multiple cultures, professional and corporate, as well as basic sociodemographic variables that can often explain more than national culture itself. In a sense, fundamental sociodemographic variables such as age or sex represent cultures in themselves. The contrast between masculine and feminine cultures is surely the most fundamental cultural divide, crossing largely the border of national cultures. In 1948, Margaret Mead published *Male and Female*, which drew on her in-depth knowledge of several South Pacific and Balinese cultures. The book depicts the organization of relationships between men and women, the division of labour and roles in the community, and explains how these patterns may be compared to those of contemporary American society. *Male and Female* is a detailed introduction to gender cultures. Although rarely mentioned in this book, the difference between masculine and feminine cultures is in fact the most basic cultural distinction, fundamentally under-researched despite its in-depth influences on organizational life, leadership patterns, or conflict handling modes. Similarly, in today's societies age cultures become more and more significant. People are strictly grouped by age classes who live together as distinctive tribes and the interaction with individuals from other generations is often considered as irrelevant, useless or even ill-mannered.

Cross-cultural research in risk and decision-making (CCRDM)
The perception of risk is a significant area of research which makes sense for finance, insurance and consumer behaviour. The concept of risk is pervasive in the whole field of business. How risk is perceived and how it influences decision-making has been studied in a cross-cultural perspective, starting from an American model of perceived risk (Slovic et al., 1984, 1985; Slovic, 1987). The Slovic model consists originally of a psychometric technique based on 81 risks and hazards grouped in nine dimensions of risk evaluation. These risks and factorial dimensions, with some variation in the number of hazards and dimensions across studies, have been further used for cross-cultural comparisons between the USA and Japan (Kleinhesselink and Rosa, 1991), Hungary (Englander et al., 1986), Norway (Teigen et al., 1988), Poland (Goszczynska et al., 1991), and France (Karpowicz-Lazreg and Mullet, 1993). Hovden and Larsson (1987) have started investigating, at a conceptual level, the cultural aspects of risk issues and their influence on decision-making with a basic divide between risk exposure and risk handling, quite typical of the western linear model of 'think first, act then', often a nice reconstruction of the real world. Later, The acronym for cross-cultural research in risk and decision-making (CCRDM) has been progressively introduced to propose a framework for research in the area (McDaniels and Gregory, 1991). However, the psychometric approach of CCRDM has been challenged by other methods, for instance, respondents being asked to list in their own words as many risks of personal concern as they could (Fischer et al., 1991) which could seem a better technique for generating cross-cultural contrasts in this field. Similarly, Holtgrave and Weber (1993) have compared a model of conjoint expected risk (CER) model with the Slovic psychometric model in order to see which one highlights more efficiently the dimensions of risk perception for financial and health risks. They conclude in favour of the CER model.

However, the dominant paradigm in the area is the Slovic et al. psychometric model based on American items and a factor-analysis approach, centred therefore on the search for differences in degree rather than nature. When one looks at such research undertakings with a critical deconstructionist perspective, the cultural relativity of the starting assumptions is obvious. First, individualism is assumed in its strongest form. Risks are best understood as individual risks, experienced at an individual rather than family or group level; risks are at best shared with other individuals in a mutual form, that is, based on impersonal rather than personal solidarity. The individual is supposed to be future oriented and time projections are more or less assumed to be similar around the world. The 'doing' orientation (Kluckhohn and Strodtbeck's, 1961), permeates the whole Slovic model. The seven variables are related to *activities* (Slovic, 1987):

- voluntarisness (degree to which the *activity* is voluntary);
- dread (degree to which negative consequences of the *activity* are dreaded);
- control (degree to which the person engaging in the *activity* has control over the consequences);
- knowledge (degree of knowledge which the person engaging in the *activity* has about the associated risks);
- catastrophic potential (worst case disaster severity of the *activity*);
- novelty (degree to which the *activity* is new and novel or old and familiar);
- equity (degree to which the consequences of the *activity* are fairly distributed).

These items have nothing to do with being, identity, belonging, membership or status. Moreover, perception of risks has been shown by this literature to be situation specific, with an underlying model of individuals identifying and assessing particular risks related to their activities (especially through some kind of subjective probability assessment) and then handling these risks by some kind of hedging strategy. This whole model is typical of a purely rational human being engaged in mastering his own destiny.

CCRDM is mostly cross-national rather than cross-cultural research. The 3A framework (Anglo-American Assumptions) which suffuses this research stream is not wrong as such. It is probably the best applicant for generality. However, there is no real discussion on the underlying assumptions and the 3A framework is imposed on other people: thanks to the psychometric approach, differences in nature are largely hidden, as well as the differences in degree. In a deconstructionist approach, the search for conceptual equivalence would have to be undertaken for the concepts of risk, hazard, peril, risk assessment and risk handling, and their articulation in either linear, circular or holistic models. In risk perception, the issue of the controllability of real-world situations cannot be addressed without referring to fatalism and to locus of control issues which may be key variables in such research. The over-rational approach is apparent in many ways:

1 *Risks can be dimensionalized*: the basic assumption is that of divisibility and relative independence of the parts into the whole, evidenced in psychometry by the search for relatively uncorrelated factorial dimensions (which is actually not the case).
2 *Measurement orientation*: to a large extent risk is viewed as measurable, with a high emphasis on probability assessment and predictability of events.
3 *Risk handling*: the ways to cope with risk are limited to linear and sequential solutions and do not envisage flexible adaptation to reality based on context-embedded solutions, such as those which can be observed for motor insurance in developing countries.
4 *Cost-benefit analysis and economic rationality*: the expected value of risks can be balanced against the discounted value of insurance premiums over a period of time.

Language as a tool for discovery of potential meaning

The dominant position of the English language in business and international trade must be the starting point of a discussion about language as a tool for the discovery of cultural meaning. It is also a fantastic avenue for deconstruction. The special qualities of English (fairly simple from a grammatical point of view, precise, action and facts oriented) make it an ideal language for business, in fact the ideal language because there is no other competitor for the worldwide leadership. It is not by chance that English has become the true universal language of business. It is built mostly on the merger of a Latin language, French, and a Germanic language, spoken by the English before the Norman conquest. However, the constant recourse to English as lingua franca tends to blur differences across cultural contexts. A contrast must be constantly made between the world views expressed by English as a native language and as an international language, and the world views expressed by local languages. The importance of this linguistic perspective for revealing world views has been well expressed by Levi-Strauss in the introduction to *Anthropologie Structurale* (1974), where he explains: 'When building this volume, I came up against a difficulty on which I must draw the attention of the reader. Several of my articles have been written directly in English, it was necessary therefore to translate them. Yet, while doing this work, I have been impressed by the difference in tone and structure between the texts conceived in either language. From this results heterogeneity which, I fear, jeopardizes the balance and the unity of the work' (1974, pp. 7–8). Language reveals world views in the form of underlying assumptions, inferred key situations, typical interactions, views of adequate inputs, of desirable outcomes and of the appropriate (positive and normative) transformation processes which link inputs to outcomes.

Language: a window on world views
How languages other than English try to express responses to common problems can be contrasted by the mean of *untranslation*, that is, avoiding to translate when the meaning would be fundamentally altered by the translation process (and keep the original word or expression in the source language) or translate when the meaning is only slightly altered (and keep note of the meaning lost or distorted). The Italian proverb *traduttore traditore* (translator traitor) contains a moral and a pragmatic message: it is better to adopt a form of sophisticated honesty and try to uncover the meaning lost in the translation process. The objective of *untranslation* is neither to be down to earth, nor to be applicable now. The benefits to be gained from *untranslation* are indirect and take time to be reaped. They consist basically in an increased understanding, a profound rather than superficial knowledge of why other peoples behave and interact differently in situations which are largely similar. If we start from a metaphor of *mise-en-scène*, language may be seen as staging the scenario or scripts of our lives: individuals and groups, as carriers of culture, are players and they have to learn their text by heart before the dress rehearsal (see Figure 1.1). Culture indicates the stage setting as well as, through language, a shared text, composed of scenes and acts, and it explains to the players the ways in which scenes begin as well as end. Culture stages people, because they have learned their roles, and people are staged by cultures because individual roles fit together in the whole theatre piece. That is why intercultural communication is not an easy task. If language was strictly about differences in words, there would be no or little differences, and in some rare cases this may be true. We simply do not play the same plays.

Language is especially useful to investigate conceptual and functional equivalence and hence instrument equivalence. It allows to generate insights into possible differences which can be progressively verified. Meaning differential can be investigated across languages for apparently similar words and utterances in the following areas:

1 Multiple meanings of a word.
2 Central, most important meaning (modal meaning).
3 Frequency of use of certain words.
4 Latent value judgements put on words, positive and/or negative, and in which context; pejorative meanings indicate a normative orientation.
5 Meaning subtleties: context of use of words and experiential aspect (for this, insert individual words in sentences which are culturally typical).
6 Idiomatic expressions.
7 Sometimes even phonology can be useful because it may be suggestive.
8 The study of grammar can be enlightening because it expresses a relationship to rules and exceptions, simplicity and formalism, tenses and time orientations, prepositions and space orientation, active and passive modes.
9 Etymology: looking at the origins and roots of words can also provide insights.

Finally, metalinguistic aspects, such as the use of rhetoric, silence, conversational style, overlapping, body gestures accompanying language activities, are more difficult to investigate but they are no less important. However, language proficiency is by no means a necessary condition for being able to deconstruct world views through linguistic investigation.

A practical solution for investigating world views as they are reflected by language is to interview native speakers, local collaborators and informants, observe, discuss with them, check meaning differentials and, if possible, try to speak their language even modestly. Words often have multiple meanings and it is easy to discover in dictionaries meanings which are in fact rarely used. This testifies to the fact that world views have a large degree of intersection, especially among European languages. However, the dominant usage of a word and the special way of assembling words into specific sentences does singularize what in pure dictionary terms seemed at first much alike. Glen Fisher (1988), a distinguished scholar in the field of intercultural relations, has recounted a conversation with a Latin American friend about the words used in English and Spanish for business relations. His friend first remarked that in English the word 'business' is positive. It connotes the fact of being 'busy' and emphasizes doing things. Expressions such as 'getting down to business' highlight people who have a responsible concern for their work. Fisher further explains that:

> In Spanish the word is 'negocio'. . . The key is the 'ocio' part of the word, which connotes leisure, serenity, time to enjoy and contemplate as the preferred human condition and circumstance. But when harsh reality forces one from one's 'ocio,' when it is negated, then one has to attend to 'negocio.' The subjective meaning is obviously much less positive than in English. . . It is the subjective meaning of words and expressions that needs to be captured. Time spent exploring why a given utterance does not translate well may be more productive for the one who is actually trying to communicate than concentration on technical excellence. (Fisher 1988, pp. 148–9, 172)

When Fisher uses the expression 'technical excellence' he means that a translator can be skilled enough to find the very nearest equivalent in the target language. This requires a high level of linguistic competence and a profound knowledge of both source and target language. However, the whole process may blur meaning differences because lexically equivalent words do not have exactly the same experiential meaning in the target as in the source language. If hidden, the meaning differential cannot be caught by the researcher, who loses valuable insights. Language both shapes and reflects our world views. Words and expressions reflect unique experiences and patterns of thought and action that are shared by members of a particular culture when they have a common language. The meaning of these words and expressions informs us about differences, whereas translation tries to find a similar meaning across languages, or in some way to rebuild it. When translation fails to establish meaning equivalence, we are in front of something unique, worth being understood. That is why it is worth exploring why a given utterance does not translate well and it may be dangerous to hide it by 'technical excellence'. Let us now turn to some examples.

Flexibility versus structure and rules in organizational life
A French word, *se débrouiller*, is quite often used to explain that people 'manage' as in 'you will have to manage it on your own' (Le Robert et Collins, 1993); in French, *se débrouiller* refers to a form of personal flexibility in front of organizational blocks. This emphasis on flexibility refers to quite typical situations in a high power distance and fairly bureaucratic society where people, more often than not, have to achieve while facing multiple obstacles and being given poor resources. *Se débrouiller*, and the alternative terms often used (*débrouillardise, système D, s'en sortir, faire avec*) are in general fairly positive. There is, at least, no negative value judgement. The German equivalent is a colloquial word, *sich durchwursteln*, something like to 'sausage (*wurst*) oneself through', which is negatively loaded, while the official translation (*sich zu helfen wissen*, 'to know

how to help oneself') is very rarely used (Weis/Mattutat, 1967). A detailed English–German dictionary (40,000 entries; Langenscheidt, 1970) does not even mention the word *durchwursteln* because, although both the English- and German-speaking cultures know this kind of opportunistic behaviour it is neither familiar enough nor positively valued by either culture.

In German society the rules are made for being respected, whereas in French society they are made for being explored. The French often turn slightly aside from the rule in order to test whether it is meant as serious. In a questionnaire devised by Geert Hofstede to investigate 'business goals', which I translated and administered in France, I proposed to translate 'staying within the law' by *ne pas enfreindre la loi* (that is, 'not trespass the law'). This kind of double negative expression figures out the dynamic of the respect of rules for the French much better than the simple positive expression used in the original English questionnaire.

Communication styles in intercultural business interactions
Much cross-cultural and intercultural literature mentions and some-times investigates communication misunderstandings across cultures. A popular framework for explaining these misunder-standings is that of Edward Hall (1959, 1976), contrasting high context/ implicit messages (prototypes: Japanese or Middle Eastern cultures) and low context/explicit messages cultures (prototypes: US or Northern European cultures). However, this framework is language free: *it works as if language never mattered.* A quick look at a book of Japanese grammar reveals that in Japanese there are no articles either definite or indefinite. *Hon*, for instance, means either 'the book', 'a book', 'the books' or 'books'. When the Japanese want to express their thoughts, they cannot communicate without taking cues from the context: *what is said explicitly is simply not enough.* The correspondence between high context communication and the gen-eral structure of a language is suggested by the main features of the Japanese language as they are reported by a widely used series of books for foreign learners (Association for Overseas Technical Scholarship, 1975). The general features of the Japanese language are:

1 In a sentence a predicate always comes at the end (meaning that if I say 'I study Japanese at the College of Arts of the University of Nagoya', 'study' will come at the very end of the Japanese sentence).
2 A verb has no ending to indicate person or number.
3 There is *no ar*ticle used with nouns in most cases.

4   One and the same form of a noun may mean both the singular and the plural form.
5   The grammatical case of a noun or pronoun is indicated by means of various particles occurring after the noun or pronoun.
6   Subject and object are often omitted if they are understood from the context.

If we add that there are several plain and polite styles in Japanese and that, in daily conversation, any of them may be used depending on the situation, the role of the context in Japanese appears naturally considerable. The language basically 'under-signifies' what the speakers are willing to say, that is, it provides the listener with insufficient linguistic cues to understand the message only on a digital basis.

The listener must therefore 'reconstruct' the relevant meaning by searching for additional explanatory cues such as: Who speaks? What did he say previously? How does s/he say it? Where is it said? *Watashi no hon* (my book) will be interpreted as the book authored by the speaker (if s/he has already published books) or the book that somebody has in his hands if it takes place in a library, etc. When the Japanese want to express their thoughts they refer constantly to the context to interpret the unexplicit aspect of messages. As a consequence, they are accustomed to guessing what others say in a fairly sophisticated mental process where they constantly have to search for meaning rather than find it nicely packaged in a full phrase. This high context sophistication exists to a certain extent in most languages when they are spoken in their colloquial form whereby people 'save' words and use contextual cues. This may explain also why Japanese are good 'listeners' compared to most westerners.

Specific words revealing unique concepts
A good example of such unique words is the Japanese word *ningensei*, the importance of which is emphasized by Goldman (1994). *Ningensei* literally translates into an all-encompassing and overriding concern and prioritizing of 'humanity' or *human beingness*. According to Japanese specialists of international marketing negotiations:

> The North American and U.K. negotiators failed to communicate ningensei at the first table meeting. Rushing into bottom lines and demanding quick decisions on the pending contract they also overlooked the crucial need for ningensei in developing good will . . . Hard business facts alone are not enough . . . Ningensei is critical in getting Japanese to comply or in persuading Japanese negotiating partners. (Nippon Inc. Consultation quoted in Goldman, 1994, p. 31)

Ningensei exemplifies four interrelated principles of Confucian phi-losophy: *jen, shu, i* and *li*. Based on active listening, *Jen* is a form of humanism that translates into empathetic interaction and caring for the feelings of negotiating associates, and seeking out the other's views, sentiments and true intentions. *Shu* emphasizes the impor-tance of reciprocity in establishing human relationships and the cultivation of 'like-heartedness'. According to Matsumoto (1988) it is 'belly communication', a means of coding messages within nego-tiating, social and corporate channels that is highly contingent upon affective, intuitive and nonverbal channels. The *i*, also termed *amae*, is the dimension which is concerned with the welfare of the collec-tivity, directing human relationships to the betterment of the common good. 'The *i* component of *ningensei* surfaces in Japanese negotiators' commitment to the organization, group agendas and a reciprocity (*shu*) and humanism (*jen*) that is long-term, consistent, and looks beyond personal motivation.' Finally, *li* refers to the codes, corresponding to precise and formal manners, that facilitate the outer manifestation and social expression of *jen, shu,* and *i*. The Japanese *meishi* ritual of exchanging business cards is typical of *li* coded etiquette (Goldman, 1994, pp. 32–3).

Combining qualitative and quantitative cross-cultural business research

Going beyond the stereotypical opposition between words and numbers
My third broad suggestion for becoming explorers of real meaning in the field of cross-cultural business is to stop making any false opposition between words and numbers. It is strongly ingrained in the collective and unconscious imaginary of academics that some of them deal with words, sentences and interviews and participate in 'real life stories', while others, the tribe on the other bank of the river of knowledge, deal with data in the form of numbers and statistics and spend the whole day at their computers doing number-crunching. No need to say that members of the two tribes conceive of themselves as highly different human beings. If, once again, we stop thinking in territorial terms, it is easy to recognize that both words and numbers are carriers of meaning, and to this extent com-plementary rather than competing against each other. Therefore it is highly artificial to oppose them, not only unnatural but also reduc-tionist. The opposition between words and numbers is a social contruction in academic cultures that must be constantly decon-structed. This social construction is based, however, on solid

grounds. To understand phenomena in their full complexity, some are obliged to build on words and renounce quantification which may become difficult and even meaningless in the face of human complexity. Conversely, to put reality into quantifiable categories, one needs to simplify and focus on the 'what' rather than the 'why' questions. Personal intellectual interests and abilities largely explain the choices of individual researchers. However, this divide, which may make sense in the research process, would require co-operation rather than competition; it leads to mental isolation when it is institutionalized. The very primitive aspect of academic tribes can be observed in the journal institution which testifies to high ingroup orientation in the composition of editorial boards and the choice of authors. In the words of Peng et al. (1991, p. 105): 'With the use of a combined quantitative–qualitative approach, we shall improve our capacity in revealing the holistic, naturalistic, and inductive aspects of the phenomena under investigation.'

The ways to combine quantitative and qualitative approaches of cross-cultural business research are multiple. A first avenue is to start from a qualitative approach which brings insights into the research issues, especially how the target informants see their world, and then submit these exploratory findings to other researchers who can prepare a more quantified approach but on a grounded basis. The reverse is often true: people (including me) start from a questionnaire, replicate it in a different context and, at best, discover inadequacies at the translation stage, most often ignore them, and finally produce findings which are partly uninterpretable. Their discussion generally shows that they have an intuition that something in the method went wrong and that most of the relevant meaning was lost in an inadequate process.

A second avenue is to triangulate investigation, using for this different types of data collection procedures. For instance, when researching about strategies of international banks from a cross-cultural perspective, interview bankers, investigate bank practices (for example, credit decisions) and look at international banking data (for example, corporate accounts of bank). Observation data related to meetings, reports, memos, and the like can be extremely useful to contrast ideal statements and actual behaviour, to confront conflicting interpretations or to validate self-reports made by certain actors in the case of intercultural conflicts. The research results will often be puzzling since the data sets obtained from different collection procedures are quite likely to generate different insights and possibly contradictory ones. A return to informants for checking their views or a new round of data collection will increase the depth of interpretation.

A third avenue is first to explore a problem quantitatively, that is, generate data based on concrete indicators and tangible evidence which allow assessment of whether the issue under investigation differs in some way across contexts (the 'what' question). Such an approach was used by Levine (1988) who made a field study of bank clocks in the USA and Brazil, and tried to generate data on actual time reckoners while also looking at how much time beyond schedule was considered locally as being late. The measurement of actual differences based on concrete indices is followed by two steps of investigations:

1   An account of how people interpret the actual situation within their own culture.
2   An account of how people interpret differences and similarities across cultures.

People in the various cultures are then asked to interpret the findings, that is elaborate on the 'why and how'. The initial quantitative step can be based on a multitude of actual indicators: evaluation sheets; payroll; mission statements; planners; work classifications; distribution of personnel by level of qualification; diaries of managers and time spent on particular tasks (time spent in meetings, on the phone, writing, and so on); number of days on strike; etc. The next step is to ask people to elaborate on their own reality, providing them with both the image of their own reality and the contrast images found in other cultures. This can be done in many ways, by questionnaires, in-depth interviews, or critical suggestions about the researcher's approach. Allowing local informants to express views on their own reality does not imply that the researcher takes them for granted.

The fourth step is interpretive and deals with the reciprocal projections generated by such comparative investigations. They can be particularly helpful if the cultures under study are those of individuals who are supposed to work together in joint ventures, to negotiate business, to work as expatriate managers, or for superiors of culturally alien subordinates.

Ethnographic and anthropological research in international management
Herskovits (1952) has been an early figure of economic anthroplogy, a branch of comparative economics mostly based on the study of economic behaviour among non-literate, non-industrial and non-pecuniary societies. Comparative management and its cross-cultural avenue have built little on this literature and research tradition. The

role of machines, technology and money remains largely unquestioned in the world of contemporary business which proceeds to a large extent by comparing modern societies or at least the modern aspects of contemporary societies. The underlying patterns of exchange and economic interaction are held constant: for profit transactions are made by independent individuals or organizations within a combination of markets and provisional hierarchies. However, the use of anthropological approaches is extremely useful to broaden views. For instance, in the area of consumer behaviour and market exchange, Kopytoff (1986) enlarges our perspectives about the commoditization of goods by envisaging slavery, the trade of humans and slaves as merchandise. He shows in this way how, in modern societies, human beings have been strongly drawn out of the market sphere. This critical view allows a better understanding of modern phenomena which contain in reality much primitive behaviour which is normatively hidden. Our mass market assumptions, for instance, hide the singularization of goods by their owners, the private meanings invested in them, irrespective of their market value. The 'for money' orientation hides the fact that economic rationality is very far from being the sole source of rational behaviour in business exchanges. Despite the compulsory display of prices by vendors, bargaining still exists to a large extent in modern societies and fulfils social functions that go far beyond the mere discussion of price (Allen, 1971). Thus, anthropological approaches have the immense merit of bringing about broader and more context-free interpretations which are normally the ideal of quantitative research and, often, its unverified assumption.

A typical ethnographic approach is offered in *Logique de l'honneur* (D'Iribarne, 1989), who studied work relationships, management styles and organization in three different factories of the Pechiney Group, one in France, another in the Netherlands and the third in Canada. Through an ethnographic approach, D'Iribarne was able to highlight the originality of the French system of organization and motivation, built on a deep-rooted sense of rank within the organization and an awareness of the duties attached to this rank, imposed by tradition rather than group pressure. The French, according to D'Iribarne are deeply attached to well-executed work and their intrinsic motivation factor 'is not so much what one owes to others as what one owes to oneself' (D'Iribarne, 1989, p. 59). Another typical example of an ethnographic approach in the area of management is that of Brannen (1994, 1996) who studied as a participant observer the takeover of an ailing US paper mill by a Japanese company over a four and a half year period.

One may wonder why the anthropological approach and, more generally, qualitative studies are relatively underdeveloped in cross-cultural business research. Wright (1996) notes that the interest in qualitative studies is fuelled by a relative disenchantment with the results of many quantitative studies. However, Mendenhall et al. (1993), in a study of international management articles between 1984 and 1990, find that only 14 per cent use qualitative methods and, even worse in the perspective of combining qualitative and quantitative methods, only 4 per cent use both approaches in a joint research design. A first reason why the anthropological approach is relatively underdeveloped in international business is that cultural anthropologists are often perceived as 'documenting inconsequential cultural facts about little-known peoples of the world' (Ferraro, 1990, p. 4). The unsophisticated discourse on globalization (in the style of Levitt, 1983) which is unfortunately popular in business research, has distracted researchers from in-depth and complex explanations and favoured recourse to standard explanatory grids.

A second reason is that the two broad scientific groups, the word lovers and the number crunchers, generally avoid the cross-cultural encounter between their rival professional cultures. They rarely try, and thus almost never succeed in developing joint research approaches. The differences are multiple and make joint research ventures inherently difficult. The research paradigms typically lead to quite different field research activities and the difference in intellectual focus, deep-seated meaning based on specific and local knowledge on the one hand versus general and applicable findings backed by numbers on the other, make the merger difficult. Theoretical linkage is painful since researchers do not share the same substantive paradigms, the same data collection techniques and not even the same conception of what is scientific knowledge. There are, however, some interesting exceptions such as the co-operation between Malcom Chapman (an anthroplogist by training) and Peter Buckley (an economist and specialist of international business) at the University of Leeds (see, for instance, Buckley and Chapman, 1996).

A third reason for the relative underdevelopment of qualitative methods, including ethnographic and qualitative research, is that they are often attacked for their supposed absence of criteria of scientific validity. However, a number of authors have now proved that the criteria of scientific validity found in positivistic research find their equivalents in qualitative research. For instance, in the area of marketing, the progressive recognition of qualitative research as general and applicable knowledge is evidenced by the fact that articles from this tradition are now regularly published in the *Journal of Marketing Research*, with titles such as 'Humanistic Inquiry in Marketing Research: Philosophy, Method and Criteria' (Hirschmann, 1986), or 'Market-Oriented Ethnography: Interpretation Building and Marketing Strategy Formulation' (Arnould and Wallendorf, 1994), although the *JMR* represents the mainstream tradition of marketing research, with a strong psychometric and experimental orientation, and frequent use of sophisticated statistical modelling.

What to avoid in international management research

The 'dos and don'ts' style of this section may appear a little naive. It is in fact more in the don'ts style, highlighting precautions and offering some recommendations. I must confess some ethnocentric bias. As a Frenchman I start typically on the negative side and continue on the positive, expressing positive statements as the result of double negations ('avoid doing what you shouldn't do').

Cross-cultural research as fashion and fad
Some people carry out cross-cultural business research because it is fashionable. They may underestimate the real requirements for being involved in cross-cultural research, which is demanding and thus more adapted to relatively experienced researchers. Cross-cultural research has some drawbacks for careers, namely that it may take a long time to reach findings, is lengthy to implement and is partly in opposition to the local academic culture and its hiring, evaluation and promotion criteria. It is also demanding in scientific terms. As argued in Chapter 2, culture is located everywhere, not only in the object under investigation, contexts, situations or informants, but also in the researcher and her instruments. Distancing oneself from one's own background may simply result in losing contact with firm ground and not knowing whether one is really writing something significant at least to some people. When combined with expectations for short term return, cross-cultural business research translates into direct and flat replications with a reductive two-country design, little depth and many mistaken views based on data that are purely self-reported (by the informants) and self-interpreted (by the researcher), resulting in squared ethnocentrism.

Culture over-operationalized
The most simple and frequent case of over-operationalization of culture is to take nationality as a direct proxy for culture with no

underlying rationale based on the cultures or languages of the studied national groups. A more sophisticated case occurs when the researcher tries to build some synthetic cultural indicator, for example, the cultural distance index of Kogut and Singh (1988) when they tried to assess the influence of national culture on the choice of entry mode of US companies into foreign markets. They describe their index of cultural distance in the following way: 'We hypothesize that the more culturally distant the country of the investing firm *from the United States*, the more likely the choice to set-up a joint-venture' (1988, p. 422; emphasis added). Their index is computed as follows:

$$CD_j = \frac{1}{4} \sum_{i=1}^{4} \left[(I_{ij} - I_{iu})^2 / V_i \right]$$

This composite index of cultural distance for country j (*CDj*) is based on the four cultural dimensions of Hofstede where I_{ij} is the score for the *i*th cultural dimensions and the *j*th country, I_{iu} indicates the scores of the USA on the four dimensions, and V_i is the variance of the index on the ith dimension. In Kogut and Singh's article, this index was meant only to describe cultural distance 'from the United States'. However, some researchers have further used the Kogut and Singh index of cultural distance, but in a naive and dangerous way. They have forgotten that Hofstede's study had been undertaken within an American multinational corporation and reflected world cultures in contrast to the USA, not all possible contrasts.

If, for instance, cultural distance is computed from Peru, distances range from to 0 (Peru to Peru) to a maximum of 4.65 (cultural distance from Peru to Denmark). There are a large number of 'cultural distances to Peru' which seem fairly consistent but some obviously make little sense: South Korea has 0.02 cultural distance to Peru; Arabic countries 0.56; Iran 0.59; Taiwan 0.16; Thailand 0.28; Turkey 0.18 indicating high cultural closeness. Similarly, France, as the country from where cultural distance is computed, is culturally nearer to Turkey (0.45) or to India (1.27) than to the UK (2.19), Sweden (3.17) or Denmark (3.53). Finally, Japan is nearer to France (2.37) than to South Korea (2.68). The advice here is to avoid equating nation with culture and confusing the cross-national with the cross-cultural perspective.

Ignorance of research instruments' influence on findings
Most cross-cultural researchers look for both similarities and differences, which seems at first sight to be a legitimate expectation. In fact, there are 'cross-culturally friendly' instruments: in terms of

Table 3.2 those research intruments which are nearer to phenomena and respondents, which allow differences to emerge more easily, especially when perceived by informants as enabling them freely to express contrast. On the other hand, 'cross-culturally unfriendly' research instruments are those which favour the emergence of sim-ilarities rather than differences (introducing the metaphor of friendship, I indicate very clearly here my own choice – or bias – in favour of diversity and differences). The negotiation simulation game (Kelley, 1966) is an example of such 'unfriendly' instruments because it favours the emergence of commonalities across cultures (Graham, 1993). As such, the use of instruments which favour the emergence of similarities is not good or bad, true or false. But it is puzzling to confront results from typically different research instru-ments and this may give more depth to the investigation. A typical case is described by Brannen (1996). After doing participant obser-vation and in-depth interviews which generated certain findings (emphasizing adjustment problems in the US–Japanese encounter), she undertook the administration of a questionnaire with a psy-chometric instrument on 200 subjects of the same corporate population. The findings of the survey came in flagrant contradic-tion with the observation and interviews. Re-examination of both the ethnographic and survey data sets allowed more in-depth insights.

Underestimation of cultural borrowing processes among
foreign informants
Cultural borrowing on the part of foreign researchers and infor-mants can be intense and blur the research process. Cross-cultural research can be full of magic and mystery from the point of view of informants who do not really understand what the researcher means: 'What the hell is this guy talking about?' What is socially desirable may be the foreign rather the local behavioural pattern. The reactions of informants, rather than expressing straightforward disbelief or puzzlement, are most often concerned with damage to their self-image and fear of ridicule in front of the well-mannered and highly educated foreign researcher. Informants will more often than not construct an image that is self-protective and avoids humil-iation both for themselves and for this gentle foreign scholar whose obviously sincere behaviour deserves helpfulness. Thus, imitation behaviour is likely to blur the implementation of research, espe-cially for informants in 'remote locations'. The idea of possible discrepancies between ideal patterns and actual behaviour was expressed by Linton (1945):

All cultures include a certain number of what may be called ideal patterns . . .They represent the consensus of opinion on the part of the society's members as to how should people behave in particular situations. . .comparison of narratives usually reveals the presence of a real culture pattern with a recognizable mode of variation. . . it [the ideal pattern] represents a desideratum, a value which has always been more honored in the breach than in the observance. (Linton 1945, pp. 52–4)

Management time which suffuses a lot of cross-cultural business research is quite an appropriate example of cultural borrowing. Everyday management behaviour involves appointments, schedules and meetings. Actual time behaviour of economically successful countries like the USA or those in Northern Europe has been imported by many other nations as the ideal pattern; for example, the PERT task-scheduling technique, based on graph theory with an appealing management science look and implemented mostly for its intellectual appeal rather than for actual project planning. As Deutscher states:

The peculiar relationship between what men say and how they otherwise behave is, or ought to be, a focal concern of the social sciences . . . There is no theoretical basis for assuming that what people say correlates with whatever else they may do . . . In fact sometimes they do as they say, sometimes they do not, and sometimes they do the exact opposite. (Deutscher 1973, p. 163)

These discrepancies between words and deeds (Deutscher, 1966) are a more or less universal phenomenon. Not only is economic time borrowed as an ideal pattern, but non-economic/polychronic patterns also seem to be borrowed by those who are economic time minded. I conducted some twenty in-depth interviews about business time across cultures (Usunier, 1991). Northern European (Swedish) students presented an ideal time pattern which was non-economic. They tended to develop an ideal view of time as being no money, not an economic good, and fully available to them. Other nationalities surveyed in those in-depth interviews included Chinese, Brazilian, and Moroccan. They tended to show an ideal economic time pattern, agreeing with the statement that 'time is money'. They also described their activities as rather organized, with a planner, precise appointments, and so on, showing a high level of agreement with the desired value. Ideal patterns of time and actual temporal behaviour may differ widely for negotiators who apparently use their partners' time culture rather than their own. Bista (1990), in the case of Nepal, highlights the conflict between time-based behaviour related to foreign education and the traditional influence of fatalistic beliefs on the lack of future orientation and sense of planning:

Planning involves the detailing of the connections between resources, objects and events, and the determination of an efficient course of action to attain desired results . . .Control is placed in the hands of the planner. But fatalism does not allow this kind of control, and is inherently anti-thetical to pragmatic thought . . .Over the past few decades, many Nepali students have travelled abroad to study in other countries, and have returned with advanced degrees in various professional capacities . . . Upon their return many are placed in positions of authority, as they rep-resent the cream of Nepal's manpower resources. Though they may be initially inspired by a high degree of idealism, the new values that they bring back with them immediately confront fatalism and are typically defeated by it . . .After forty years of planning and an accumulation of foreign trained graduates, Nepal, then, still has little manpower to effec-tively bridge the disparities between the culture of the foreign aid donors and that of their own. (Bista, 1990, pp. 137–8)

Cultural borrowing is extremely important for questionnaire sur-veys. When people self-report their values or behaviour, they tend to respond in the order of the ideal rather than actual behaviour (see Grunert and Muller, 1996). Some observation data help correct and possibly invalidate the questionnaire data, for instance, by looking at managers' diaries, at clocks, at the respect of time and dates for meetings, at actual delivery delays of local companies. When addressing cross-cultural issues the researcher has to check how people in the target culture react to messages, words and theories from the source culture and how their answers are consequently transformed.

Comparative results too quickly transposed to intercultural settings
Most of the settings in cross-cultural business research are compar-ative in nature, because it is easier to theorize and less costly to collect data. A co-operative venture between researchers doing the field research in their own country/culture minimizes travels and maximizes the relevance of the data collection process vis-à-vis local informants. However, it is advisable to be prudent before directly transposing data on the business behaviour or strategies of the peo-ples and countries studied in intracultural settings, to what may happen when these diverse cultures are interacting (intercultural setting). In the case of business negotiations, Japanese business people may not adopt exactly the same behaviour and strategies when they negotiate together as they do when they have to adjust to American negotiation partners. Adler and Graham (1989) have addressed the issue of whether international comparisons are fal-lacies, when and if researchers are trying, finally, to describe cross-cultural interactions accurately. They demonstrate that

negotiators tend to adapt their behaviour in intercultural negotiations and do not behave completely as predicted by observations in intracultural settings. They show that French-speaking Canadians are more problem solving orientated when negotiating with English-speaking Canadians than they normally are when working together. Therefore their behaviour as observed in intracultural negotiations can only serve as a partial basis for the prediction of their style and strategies when negotiating with people belonging to different cultures. It does not mean that every finding obtained from intracultural comparison has no implication for intercultural interactions, but one needs to put some caveats when extending intracultural findings to intercultural settings.

Hidden cultural assumptions
We are all carriers of culture and the bias-free cross-cultural researcher is not yet born. I do not argue in favour of no bias, context-free research, but more simply in favour of announcing more clearly one's own assumptions. In this sense, inexplicit cultural assumptions are worse than explicit biases. The literature on intercultural competence and the culture general assimilator (Brislin et al., 1986; Weeks et al., 1987; Cushner, 1989; Bond, 1992) is a good case in point. The learning process of intercultural competence assumes certain culture-related assumptions:

1 Task-related and doing-oriented people.
2 Subjects who can learn, at least partly, a new culture without unlearning, also partly, the previous one(s).
3 Trainees coming from low-context cultures who are used to simulation games, role playing and de-contextualized exercises, the most common type of training tools for intercultural learning.
4 Open discussion in which the teacher is a facilitator and a peer rather than a mentor, that is, low power distance and perceived equality between individuals.

Some cultures use simulated situations seriously, that is, with an educational goal. This is the case with Americans. For other nationalities this can cause real problems to participants, as noted by Weeks et al.:

> When a representative of a culture which separates game-playing from serious business like education is pressured into participation in a structured exercise, significant stresses result. Then the painful side-effects may become more intense. It is particularly difficult for a representative of a self-effacing culture like the Japanese to openly confront and oppose their group. The reaction of many Japanese students, for example, is to

> feel that it is not fair that they are forced into game playing, but because refusing to do so would be grossly impolite, they go along and suffer in silence. (Weeks et al., 1987, p. xiv)

Another basic presupposition which is necessary for the participants actively to take part in these exercises is that open-mindedness and freedom of speech contribute to mutual comprehension and have a positive social value. It is a presupposition largely shared in North America and to a lesser extent in Europe; in fact, less and less the further towards the south and east of Europe. For Far Eastern peoples, who value keeping their emotions private and even secret, a very direct mode of communication does not seem appropriate. A more indirect form of communication is preferred, whereby one relies on intuition to guess the meaning of what others want to say. Weeks et al. emphasize this in the following way:

> Many cultures rely on silence, and consider it more constructive and praiseworthy to refrain from speaking rather than to discuss the issue. When a person who *knows* that effective group work consists mainly of thinking together and picking up each other's thoughts through non-verbal cues is expected to talk his full share of time in a continuously verbal group, substantial psychic disarray is to be expected. (Weeks et al., 1987, p. xv)

The opening and the structured exercise in which each person can play any role assumes that a very strong subjective equality is felt by the participants, a low power distance as meant by Hofstede (1980a). When society is more 'verticalized', status and power are internalized by individuals. By virtue of their cultural code they know who is inferior and who is superior to them. Participants coming from high power distance cultures risk suffering a loss of identity in role playing. It is not easy to make Latin managers participate in role play as American executives would, their usual system of communication being called into question. The manner in which they are addressed in such exercises, assuming complete equality, without formality and with no reference to status or level in the hierarchy, can lead them to a complete block in communication. If they continue to communicate, they will try to recover their status and to be addressed properly according to their status within a verticalized society. If not successful, they may withdraw or antagonize the instructor. Gruère (1990) states the differences in the reactions of French students when compared with American students (my translation):

> The idea that it was possible to analyse real life experience and extract from it common lessons was received with astonishment [by the French

students] or with the desire to dodge a session of rather formal academic training after so much mutual enjoyment. It was futile to seek to validate this type of personal involvement, which did not translate into precise content, in terms of knowledge acquisition the form concealing the content: 'One cannot work like that!'. 'It's fun, but it's not serious!' . . . After a [French] group had operated with pleasure and efficiency in one session, it was generally necessary to begin again from scratch the next time so quickly had the participants' defences reconstituted themselves in the meantime . . . The American students participated more rapidly and better in my [Gruère's] view. Once a minimal consensus had been achieved, they probably wondered less. However, if they came to the view that their confidence had been misplaced or betrayed, they reacted rapidly. They were spontaneously used to the idea of a necessary consensus and a final explanation concerning their behaviour. They responded enthusiastically to the questionnaires and other introspective tools, little valued by the French. (Gruère, 1990, p. 16)

I do not argue in any way that the whole literature on intercultural competence is flawed with biases. This would be wrong and the cross-cultural training instruments have been shown to be efficient on average for the preparation of expatriates (Deshpande and Viswesvaran, 1992). However, American/modern cultural assumptions reinforced by the use of English language seem so self-evident that they become hidden and alternative cultural assumptions are literally forgotten in favour of the dominant 3A world view. Nobody in this case is ethnocentric; there is simply a need for everyone to bring into full light the gap in world views. Three strategies are feasible to make the dominant framework more explicit:

1   To present culture-based assumptions clearly at the beginning of the research; the researcher may start from somewhere provided that it is made fairly explicit.
2   To co-operate with a research colleague from a different culture by discussing differences while allowing however for consensus building.
3   To allow informants to express their views on instruments, concepts used, and so on, especially when culturally different from the researcher.

Underestimating the complexity of the data collection process
This is probably the main risk in doing cross-cultural business research. Over-ambitious researchers may add depth to width and to height (in terms of Figure 3.1) and pile up problems of cross-cultural equivalence which cannot be solved appropriately. I will not quote an example since this type of undertaking typically finishes

unpublished. Robust designs in terms of data collection can either be quantitative or qualitative. However, it is always easier to master a relatively complex design with a qualitative approach. Hoftsede's design is an example of a highly sophisticated quantitative design, involving multiple dimensions. But Hofstede's research was made possible only because a large multinational company granted the budget for such an enterprise and allowed access to its employees as interviewees (116,000 questionnaires collected in 20 language versions). Furthermore, one dimension was kept constant, that of corporate culture; a single organization was surveyed, thereby reducing the width and depth of the design.

The costs incurred with complex designs should not be underestimated: a single full translation process (including back-translation and checks) can already be costly. The complexity of cross-national research collaboration required for collecting data at relatively low cost should also not be underestimated. It includes language problems, the influence of cultural differences on communication misunderstandings within the research team, as well as problems related to authorship and property over materials to be published.

Lack of care in search for cross-cultural equivalence
The example of CCRDM above is a good case in point for the lack of rigour in the search for conceptual equivalence of the various underlying contructs (risk, hazard, peril, etc.). Furthermore, there is no comparison of underlying response patterns, and no attempt to obtain comparable samples across studies. The cross-cultural comparisons in the CCRDM literature result from the mere juxtaposition of single country studies done on the basis of comparable questionnaires but unrelated sampling and survey procedures. Basic sociodemographics are not taken into account as rival explanatory variables; age and sex may matter much more for risk perception than nationality and may even be seen as basic building stones for cross-national cultural clusters based either on gender or age classes. The lack of care in the search for cross-cultural equivalence, which is the best avenue for generating meaning differential, results in relatively poor findings that are unconvincing or intellectually bizarre. In a comparison of risk perception between Poland, the USA, Hungary and Norway, Goszczynska et al. propose the following discussion of their findings:

> The overall mean evaluation of risk shows that Poland (38.1) is closest to the United States (46.1), Norway is third (32.4), and Hungary has the lowest average (27.7) . . . It is the size of the country and not its social, economic, and cultural background, that seems to influence the degree of perceived riskiness. This influence could be caused by the availability

heuristic: the bigger the country, the more accidents and negative events occur and are reported there. When rating riskiness, people recall these instances, and thus their ratings reflect those frequencies . . . However, this simple rule of conditioning the level of perceived riskiness upon the size of the country should not be overgeneralized. (Goszczynska et al., 1991, p. 191)

Naivety about cultural convergence

Cross-cultural management has allowed important breakthroughs in the understanding of cultural differences as they pertain to managerial decisions and practices. However, certain questions are far from being completely resolved such as that of the overlap between national culture (which is somewhat overprivileged by cross-cultural research) and corporate culture (Derr and Laurent, 1989), or the conditions for successfully transposing management systems which succeeded in quite different cultural contexts. One may also wonder whether cultural convergence will not progressively reduce the managerial relevance of cross-cultural studies in management. However, the globalization process is complex and cannot be reduced to the dichotomous issue of difference and similarity, or even to its more sophisticated version, that is, looking at the magnitude of differences and their degree of impact on managerial practices to determine whether it makes sense to take into account cross-cultural differences.

The first argument is that complete convergence is certainly far in the future. Furthermore, apparent linguistic convergence produces fake perceived similarity since the language of convergence, English, is used with different underlying world views. EIL-speakers transport the world view of their native language (as I do). This gives rise to an apparently de-babelized Tower of Babel, a *Babelsturm* of its own, full of apparent understanding and real misunderstandings. The second argument is that the globalization process is achieved mostly through business and consumption activities in companies, international organizations, by some media with a worldwide reach and the Internet. In this sense globalization can be viewed critically as the 'McDonaldization of society' (Ritzer, 1993) or as different possible avenues for ordering meaning in an increasingly compressed world (Robertson, 1992). What will emerge out of this process is not simply a world culture which would be a reflection of common social adaptation to new technologies. In the globalized world, there will be a multitude of local villages with much interconnectedness, rather than a mere global village: cultural borrowing, bricolage and kaleidoscopic behaviour will be intense, in a postmodernist way.

An example of this paradoxical confrontation between local identities and global technologies is a 'dialogue' on the Internet in a discussion list between academics. The first discussant is arguing about Islam: 'See . . .the thing is . . .Moslems act violent out of their own religious teaching. There are several passages in that al Koran book, the words from their god themselves which initiated killings. Can you believe this? What kind of a religion is this?' This discussant receives the following response under the general title 'Why is the West and Hindus afraid of Islam?':

Ever since the end of cold war, demonisation of Islam in the west has hit hysterical heights. The dominant emotion in the west today is fear. Fear of what? Fear of Islam. This was evident from the march 13, '96 summit in Egypt where an attempt was made to dub Muslims as terrorists and paint them as a new plague . . . There are enough saner elements in the West who do not share this view. The media in the West and India are only echoing the fears of Muslim-bailers. This is because the media in West is controlled by Zionist which solely survive on an anti-Muslim staple diet. So much is the fear in the West that Islam has been identified as the primary threat to Western way of life itself. The ghost of Islam is haunting every White Western Christian and also Hindus in India. But what is beneath of these fears? Why the West which has produced so many eminent scholars is not answering this question? How these fears are exaggerated or invented to serve the vested interests?

Western values are crumbling. Families are breaking up. Respect for elders and the learned are vanishing. Woman has become a sex symbol. Teen age sex has killed the glory of the institution called marriage. Educational institution becoming factories. Consumer society has brought in consumerist culture. Market decides life – not the other way round. Sex, sports, drinks, dress, food, entertainment have reduced the human being into an animal. TV has killed reading habit. Religion has become a business. None commands any respect – except those with money. Moral authority is dead. This is the sum and substance of Western way of life. But the Muslim society, despite the creeping consumerist culture among its youth, is still maintaining certain values in life. Woman is respected. Elders and learned are revered. There is place for discipline, ethics, morals. Exploitation of man by man is under check. All this because Islam governs every aspect of human life in a Muslim society. Deserted Churches: in the West, hardly anybody goes to church on Sunday morning. But in Muslim Societies the Mosques are crowded at Friday prayers. This is shocking the West. How can the Muslim believe in a thing (religion) which the West has abandoned long back? The white Western Christians wanted the Muslims to forget religion just as they did. But today as the West steps up its attacks on Muslims life and values, more Muslims have started going to mosques and more Muslim women wear burqa. A Muslim nation is sprouting right in the heart of Christians Europe (e.g. Bosnia). This western hatred and racism against Islam is proving counter-productive.

Whether we progress quickly in the direction of more cross-cultural understanding is not obvious. More probably, we are facing a very slow and complex phenomenon of global cultural convergence. International interactions are driven mostly by the expanding international trade, worldwide business activities, tourism and travels, and globalized communications. They result in more active confrontation between people from different cultures and lead to an increased awareness of differences. While the primary outcome of such a process may be cultural misunderstandings, they are necessary steps towards progressive understanding of other cultures' values and behaviour. In this sense culture shock is a pre-requisite for adapation to world diversity. This process can be accelerated if we systematically search for more in-depth understanding by acknowledging frankly the clash in values, rather than by trying to dilute cultural conflicts in well-intentioned, superficial empathy.

Enlarging perspectives: strategies for cross-cultural business research

Cross-cultural research in management serves the purpose of creating unique and new insights and generating broader concepts, rather than simply comparing what is alike and what differs across contexts. For instance, the cross-national and cross-cultural literature in accounting provides unique insights on the broader meaning of concepts such as 'information disclosure' or 'goodwill', or on the link between general accounting, fiscal accounting, and cost accounting. 'Reading' the research results necessarily requires an interpretation process which also involves learning from the research process itself, as well as from the research findings. Key findings may be attained when trying to translate and transpose instruments, or by checking from voluntary comments of respondents (Knauber et al., 1993) how they have understood questions, why concepts were different, etc.

Cross-cultural research must include a strong critical component and try not to sacrifice desirability to feasibility when trade-offs are necessary; for example, if intercultural research is more desirable because it has more important implications, but intracultural comparative research is more feasible. Some topics would also deserve better coverage such as research about cross-cultural interactions, cultural intermediation and cultural mediators, intercultural competence in a broader perspective than communication and basic adjustment. In the same vein, cross-cultural research should also focus on the unlearning as well as the learning processes.

Unlearning is important because new cultural skills are not simply superimposed on previous knowledge, they largely take the place of former representations which need to be unlearned.

Cross-cultural research should also focus on extreme rather than average situations. There is a human side to culture which is typically non-average: human behaviour is a mix of programmed and non-programmed conduct. Creativity is central to real human behaviour and is generally suppressed rather than full creativity. Human aspects which suffuse culture are paradoxical, at times ambiguous, and partly unpredictable. Occasionally, the focus should be on predicting unpredictability rather than basing prediction on estimated average values. That is why a sole combination of linear models and traditional statistical approaches cannot easily describe human behaviour – especially the 'fingerprint' aspect which is not susceptible to reduction to mean values. There are other ways to use statistical methods, with less 'mean' orientation and looking more at probability density over the whole spectrum, that would allow better analysis on the fringes rather than the sole focus on central tendency. Non-linear models and continuity/discontinuity patterns are relevant to cross-cultural business research such as research on discontinuities, broken relationships and cross-cultural failures, even though academics as well as business people prefer success stories to blunders and fiascos. Analysis generally tends to be based on what has worked rather than on the reasons for failures. Research about non-average behaviour is interesting because it can tell a lot about potential behaviour: future behaviour and repressed behaviour; the central tendency may only be the result of people not daring to do what other people allow themselves.

Some advice for exploring management practices in foreign contexts
Looking at different locations apart from the standard places where research is generally conducted also appears to be a promising avenue, although a difficult one. Thomas (1996), in his call for research in forgotten locations, draws attention to the potential obstacles for publishing such research in top-tier journals:

> The methodological rigor and necessity of building on previous research inhibits the entry of research on new locations because of the lack of previously validated instruments and the scarcity of published studies on these locations. This issue is exacerbated because previously published research is a criterion defining membership on editorial boards. As a result, the scholars who decide on the acceptability of research are those who have an American or Western European perspective, perpetuating a cycle of like research. (Thomas 1996, p. 491)

Rather than systematically testing the universal hypothesis it would be useful to generate more general insights by comparing particular cases, by looking at what is different in specific organizational practices and management institutions (such as the Brazilian Jetinho described by Amado and Vinagre Brasil, 1991) as well as looking for stories which are extremely different. It may also make sense to examine how researchers, far from the western models, express exotic concepts, for example, 'blood taboo or blood prone society' in Chang (1989) about Korean management. To accomplish this, it is of the utmost importance to resist some of the latent commands of the 3A model (applicable now, doing-oriented, task-related, over-pragmatic orientation), because they taboo the exploration of remote, non directly operational, in-depth explanations. Such partial resistance is possible while retaining most of the considerable strengths of the 3A model in terms of professionalism, open-mindedness, data and facts orientation and least poor applicant for the unreachable universality.

Data collection procedures: precautions, pluralism and coherence
Data collection is a limitation for cross-cultural research which has to be considered frankly from the very start. There is no ideal method and it is probably impossible for the researcher simultaneously to reach high performance on all the criteria of Figure 3.2, that is, to describe phenomena in their full complexity, to develop pure ideas, to use sophisticated instruments and to totally respect what informants have to say. Case studies are obviously a privileged source of in-depth understanding, especially in a multiple culture perspective (see, for instance, the case of international joint venture in Parkhe, 1993, 1996). How theory can be built from case study research has been described by Eisenhardt (1989). She argues that multiples cases are a powerful means to create theory because they permit replication and extension among individual examples, while maintaining a highly rigorous approach for the identification of research questions and the design of instruments. Others such as Dyer and Wilkins (1991) argue that single-case studies, because they allow to delve into the full complexity of the materials studied, are superior for producing theoretical insights. The researcher must have this sort of choice in mind when she starts her investigation. Although the controversy about 'better stories versus better contructs' is probably false (Eisenhardt, 1991), the choice of single versus multiple case studies has an influence on the kind of value built into the findings by the research process: a unique understanding of complex patterns, involving a multiple culture

perspective in an intercultural setting (in favour of the single case study), and a better replicability and external validity of findings for multiple cases.

International business negotiations are a fascinating case because almost all data collection procedures and research styles are used by researchers who read each other and combine their results to a certain degree (see, for instance, Weiss, 1996a). However, it is an *ex-post* combination and confrontation of research findings; combining *ex ante* in the same individual research design is more difficult (such as Graham, 1985, combining negotiated simulations and direct observation of the negotiators by a video-camera).

In cross-cultural business research there is ample room for original data collection procedures, such as those which help to 're-contextualize' decisions, especially when respondents are asked to express their views on situations which they do not actually experience. 'Event management' is an example of such an approach (Smith and Peterson, 1988), whereby full segments of managerial life are presented to managers from diverse cultures. For instance, Smith et al. (1993) look at convergences and divergences across European managers by using event management. Similar methods that give some flesh and blood to hypothetical situations to which respondents are exposed are the in-basket instruments (see Tse et al., 1988) and vignette surveys (see Becker and Fritzsche, 1987). Vignettes allow re-contextualization which is extremely important for such sensitive issues as business ethics. However, wording must be very carefully prepared since the proposed situations must not bias responses. Some of these original research instruments provide surprising results such as the 'role playing executive' (Chen, 1995), an exercise used for contrasting Chinese and American preferences for reward allocations, where the Americans finally appeared as more humanistically and the Chinese more economically oriented.

The researcher must beware of a too hasty transposition of domestic research procedures to cross-cultural contexts. As emphasized in Chapter 4, transposed research techniques are sometimes not properly understood, difficult to implement because certain resources are absent (in quality or quantity), or bring about a feeling of artificiality among subjects. For instance, the speed and reliability of international mail surveys may be a problem, as well as their response rates, or the control of respondents' qualification or motivation (see Keown, 1985; Dawson and Dickinson, 1988; Jobber and Saunders, 1988). In fact, there are no 'easy' data collection procedures when applied cross-culturally: interviews, questionnaires, mail surveys or participant observation will all face the barrier of language, both as a threat and as an opportunity for improving the cross-national or cross-cultural comparability of data.

Conclusion

To a certain extent cross-cultural business research marks the historical end of the colonization process. Over two or three centuries the west has had a very profound impact on the shaping of what in the distant future could be a world culture, through the imposition of western social, political and technological models on other peoples. The violence contained in such a process is evident in the destruction of traditional cultures and the progressive elimination of their economic patterns. The globalization of business, as political and military colonization previously, has a necessary element of violence built in. However, this violence is self-contained because of the pragmatic nature of business and the free nature of markets. In the universal process of cultural homogenization, the role of language will remain intact as a key cultural differentiator, while other sources of cultural differentiation will progressively disappear. That is why doing language-free cross-cultural research is vain. It entails 'theoretical colonization' (in the words of T.K. Peng and Mark Peterson, 1998), a post-colonial enterprise doomed to failure in a world where most people will retain their native world views, even when they speak and write international English .

International management research must be the domain of openmindedness in business research. This implies methodological ecumenism, that is, the combination of qualitative and quantitative research methods, tending to promote unity among churches in a scientific world which are sometimes in quasi-religious conflict. This openmindedness implies looking at possible research options rather than engaging in readymade designs. It also bears as a consequence the renouncement of culture as a system of prejudices about the nature of reality, which could be extremely challenging and even a threat to the researcher's ego. This can be done only by confronting all sorts of biases and prejudices rather than by making language-free, prejudice-free, context-free and supposedly bias-free research.

References

Abdulla, Jasim Y.A. (1996) 'The timeliness of Bahraini annual reports', in Timothy S. Doupnik and Stephen B. Salter (eds), *Advances in International Accounting*, Greenwich, CT: JAI Press, 73–88.

Adler, Nancy J. (1983a) 'A typology of management studies involving culture', *Journal of International Business Studies*, vol. 14, 29–47.

Adler, Nancy J. (1983b) 'Cross-cultural management research: the ostrich and the trend', *Academy of Management Review*, vol. 8, no. 2, 226–32.

Adler, Nancy J. (1991) *International Dimensions of Organizational Behavior*, 2nd edn, Boston: PWS-Kent.

Adler, Nancy J. and Nigel Campbell (1989) 'From the Atlantic to the Pacific century: cross-cultural management reviewed', in Chimezie A.B. Osigweh, Yg. (ed.), *Organizational Science Abroad: Constraints and Perspectives*, New York: Plenum Press, 27–54.

Adler, Nancy J. and John L. Graham (1989) 'Cross-cultural comparison: the international comparison fallacy?', *Journal of International Business Studies*, vol. 20, no. 3, 515–37.

Adler, Nancy J., Robert Doktor and André Laurent (1989) 'In search of appropriate methodology: from outside the People's Republic of China looking in', *Journal of International Business Studies*, vol. 20, no. 1, 61–74.

Adler, Peter S. (1975) 'The transitional experience: an alternative view of culture shock', *Journal of Humanistic Psychology*, vol. 15, 13–23.

Aharoni, Yair and Richard M. Burton (1994) 'Is management science international: In search of universal rules', *Management Science*, vol. 40; no.1, 1–3.

Al-Aiban, Khalid and Jone L. Pearce (1995) 'The influence of values on management practices: a test in Saudi Arabia and the United States', *International Studies of Management and Organization*, vol. 25, no. 2, 35–52.

Albaum, Gerald (1987) 'Does source anonymity affect mail survey results?', *Journal of the Academy of Marketing Science*, vol. 15.

Albaum, Gerald, Felicitas Evangelista and Nila Medina (1995) 'The role of response behavior theory in survey research strategy of research practitioners: a study of practices and perceptions in Australia, Hong Kong and the Philippines', in Scott M. Smith, (ed.), *Proceedings of the Fifth Symposium on Cross-Cultural Consumer and Business Studies*, Provo, UT: Brigham Young University, 45–53.

Albaum, Gerald, Linda Golden, Brian Murphy and Jesper Strandskov (1987) 'Likert scale and semantic differential: issues relevant to cross-cultural research', in Charles Keown and Arch Woodside (eds), *Proceedings of the Second Symposium on Cross-Cultural Consumer and Business Studies*, Honolulu, HI: University of Hawaii, 113–16.

Alden, Dana L., Wayne D. Hoyer and Chol Lee (1993) 'Identifying global and culture-specific dimensions of humor in advertising: a multinational analysis', *Journal of Marketing*, vol. 57, 64–75.

Alexander, Cheryl S. and Henry Jay Becker (1978) 'The use of vignettes in survey research', *Public Opinion Quarterly*, vol. 42, 93–104.

Ali, Abbas J. (1993) 'Decision-making style, individualism, and attitude toward risk of Arab executives', *International Studies of Management and Organization*, vol. 23, no. 3, 53–73.

Ali, Abbas J. (1995) 'Cultural discontinuity and Arab management thought', *International Studies of Management and Organization*, vol. 25, no. 3, 7–30.

Ali, Abbas J. and Rachid Wahabi (1995) 'Managerial value systems in Morocco', *International Studies of Management and Organization*, vol. 25, no. 3, 87–96.

Allen, David Elliston (1971) 'Anthropological insights into customer behavior', *European Journal of Marketing*, vol. 5, no. 3, 45–57.

Alpert, Mark I., Judy I. Alpert and Gerald Albaum (1987) 'Response set bias and cross-cultural measures of attribute importance', in Charles Keown and Arch Woodside (eds), *Proceedings of the Second Symposium on Cross-Cultural Consumer and Business Studies*, Honolulu, HI: University of Hawaii, 121–24.

Amado, Gilles and Haroldo Vinagre Brasil (1991) 'Organizational behavior and cultural context: the Brazilian Jeitinho', *International Studies of Management and Organization*, vol. 21, no. 3, 38–61.

Amado, Gilles, Claude Faucheux and André Laurent (1991) 'Organizational change and cultural realities: Franco-American contrasts', *International Studies of Management and Organization*, vol. 21, no. 3, 62–95.

Amine, Lyn S. and S. Tamer Cavusgil (1986) 'Demand estimation in a developing country environment: difficulties, techniques and examples', *Journal of the Market Research Society*, vol. 28, no. 5, 43–65.

Angelmar, Reinhardt and Louis W. Stern (1978) 'Development of a content analysis scheme for analysis of bargaining communication in marketing', *Journal of Marketing Research*, vol. 15, 93–102.

Aoki, Masahiko (1990) 'Toward an economic model of the Japanese firm', *Journal of Economic Literature*, vol. 28, 1–27.

Arnould, Eric J. (1989) 'Toward a broadened theory of preference formation and the diffusion of innovations: cases from Zinder province, Niger Republic', *Journal of Consumer Research*, vol. 16, 239–67.

Arnould, Eric J. and Melanie Wallendorf (1994) 'Market-oriented ethnography: interpretation building and marketing strategy formulation', *Journal of Marketing Research*, vol. 31, 484–504.

Association for Overseas Technical Scholarship (1975) *Nihongo no Kiso*, [Grammatical Notes], 12–13 Honkomagome 2 chôme, Bunkyô-ku, Tokyo 113, Japan.

Aulakh, Preet S. and Masaaki Kotabe (1993) 'An assessment of theoretical and methodological development in international marketing: 1980–1990', *Journal of International Marketing*, vol. 1, no. 2, 5–28.

Bakhtari, Hassan (1995) 'Cultural effects on management style: a comparative study of American and Middle Eastern management styles', *International Studies of Management and Organization*, vol. 25, no. 3, 97–118.

Baligh, Helmy H. (1991) 'Congruence between organization and cultural setting: Islamic culture', Working Paper, Durham, NC: Duke University.

Baligh, Helmy H. (1994) 'Components of culture: nature, interconnections, and relevance to the decisions on the organization structure', *Management Science*, vol. 40, no. 1, 14–27.

Barna, L.M. (1983) 'The stress factor in intercultural relations', in D. Landis and Richard W. Brislin (eds), *Handbook of Intercultural Learning*, vol. 2, New York: Pergamon Press, 19–49.

Baydoun, Nabil (1995) 'The French approach to financial accounting and reporting', *International Journal of Accounting*, vol. 30, 222–44.

Baydoun, Nabil and Roger Willett (1995) 'Cultural relevance of western accounting systems to developing countries', *Abacus*, vol. 31, no. 1, 67–92.

Becker, Helmut and David H. Fritzsche (1987) 'A comparison of the ethical behavior of American, French and German managers', *Columbia Journal of World Business*, Winter, 87–95.

Beechler, Schon L. and Vladimir Pucik (1989) 'The diffusion of American organizational theory in postwar Japan', in Chimezie A.B. Osigweh, Yg. (ed.), *Organizational Science Abroad: Constraints and Perspectives*, New York: Plenum Press, 119–34.

Befus, Constance P. (1988) 'A multilevel treatment approach for culture shock experienced by sojouners', *International Journal of Intercultural Relations*, vol. 12, 381–400.

Belk, Russell W. (1988) 'Third world consumer culture', in E. Kumçu and A. Fuat Firat (eds), *Research in Marketing*, supplement 4, Greenwich, CT: JAI Press.

Bendixen, Mike and Bruce Burger (1995) 'Cross-cultural management philosophies', in Scott M. Smith (ed.), *Proceedings of the Fifth Symposium on Cross-Cultural Consumer and Business Studies*, Provo, UT: Brigham Young University, 1–9.

Bentler, Peter (1989) *EQS: Structural Equations Program Manual*, Los Angeles, CA: BDMP Statistical Software.

Berger, Brigitte (ed.) (1991) *The Culture of Entrepreneurship*, San Francisco, CA: ICS Press.

Berggren, Christian and Robert R. Rehder (1993) 'Uddevalla and Saturn: the global quest for more competitive and humanistic manufacturing organizations', in Gerard Albaum et al. (eds), *Proceedings of the Fourth Symposium on Cross-Cultural Consumer and Business Studies*, University of Hawaii, 193–97.

Berry, Michel (1996) ' From American standards to cross-cultural dialogues', in Betty Jane Punnett and Oded Shenkar (eds), *Handbook for International Management Research*, Cambridge, MA: Blackwell, 463–83.

Bhagat, Rabi S., Ben L. Kedia, Susan E. Crawford and Marilyn R. Kaplan (1990) 'Cross-cultural issues in organizational psychology: emergent trends and directions for research in the 1990s', in C.L. Cooper and I. Robertson (eds), *International Review of Industrial and Organizational Psychology*, New York: John Wiley, 59–99.

Bhalla, Ghaurav and Lynn Y.S. Lin (1987) 'Cross-cultural marketing research: a discussion of equivalence issues and measurement strategies', *Psychology and Marketing*, vol. 4, no. 4, 275–85.

Bista, Dor Bahadur (1990) *Fatalism and Development*, Calcutta: Orient Longman.

Black, J. Stewart (1988) 'Work role transitions: a study of American expatriate managers in Japan', *Journal of International Business Studies*, vol. 19, no. 2, 277–94.

Black, J. Stewart and Mark Mendenhall (1991) 'The U-curve adjustment hypothesis revisited: a review and theoretical framework', *Journal of International Business Studies*, vol. 22, no. 2, 225–47.

Black, J. Stewart, Mark Mendenhall and Gary Oddou (1991) 'Towards a comprehensive model of international adjustment: an integration of multiple theoretical perspectives', *Academy of Management Review*, vol. 16, no. 2, 291–317.

Bluedorn, A. C. and R. B. Denhardt (1988) 'Time and organizations', *Journal of Management*, vol. 14, no. 2, 299–320.

Boddewyn, Jean (1966) 'A construct for comparative marketing research', *Journal of Marketing Research*, vol. 3, 149–53.

Bohnet, Michael (1994) *Was Wurde in Kairo wirklich beschlossen?*, Bonn: BMZ (BundesMinisterium für Zusammenarbeit), Germany.

Bollen, Kenneth A. (1989) *Structural Equations with Latent Variables*, New York: John Wiley.

Bond, Michael Harris (1992) 'The process of enhancing cross-cultural competence in Hong Kong organizations', *International Journal of Intercultural Relations*, vol. 16, no. 4, 395–412.

Bonnacorsi, Andrea (1992) 'On the relationship between firm size and export intensity', *Journal of International Business Studies*, vol. 23, no. 4, 605–35.

Bouchet, Dominique (1995) 'Marketing and the redefinition of ethnicity', in Janeen Arnold Costa and Gary J. Bamossy (eds), *Marketing in a Multicultural World*, Thousand Oaks, CA: Sage, 68–104.

Boyacigiller, Nakiye A. and Nancy Adler (1991) 'The parochial dinosaur: organization science in a global context', *Academy of Management Review*, vol. 16, no. 2, 262–90.

Boyacigiller, Nakiye A., M. Jill Kleinberg, Margaret E. Phillips and Sonja A. Sackmann (1996) 'Conceptualizing culture', in Betty Jane Punnett and Oded Shenkar (eds), *Handbook for International Management Research*, Cambridge, MA: Blackwell, 157–208.

Brannen, Mary Yoko (1994) '"Your next boss is Japanese": negotiating cultural change at a Western Massachusetts paper plant', PhD dissertation, University of Massachusetts, Amherst.

Brannen, Mary Yoko (1996) 'Ethnographic international management research', in Betty Jane Punnett and Oded Shenkar (eds), *Handbook for International Management Research*, Cambridge, MA: Blackwell, 115–43.

Brislin, Richard W., Kenneth Cushner, Craig Cherrie and Mahealani Yong (1986) *Intercultural Interactions. A Practical Guide*, Newbury Park, CA: Sage.

Brunovs, Rudolf and Robert J. Kirsch (1991) 'Goodwill accounting in selected countries and the harmonization of international accounting standards', *Abacus*, vol. 27, no. 2, 135–61.

Buckley, Peter J. and Malcolm Chapman (1996) 'Wise before the event: the creation of corporate fulfilment', *Management International Review*, vol. 36, no. 1, 95–110.

Calder, Bobby J., Lynn W. Philips and Alice M. Tybout (1981) 'Designing research for application', *Journal of Consumer Research*, vol. 8, 197–207.

Campbell, D.T. and O. Werner (1970) 'Translating, working through interpreters and the problem of decentering', in R. Naroll and R. Cohen (eds), *A Handbook of Method in Cultural Anthropology*, New York: Natural History Press, 398–420.

Carroll, John B. (1956) *Language, Thought and Reality: Selected Writings of Benjamin Lee Whorf*, Cambridge, MA: MIT.

Cavusgil, S.Tamer and Ajay Das (1997) 'Methodology in comparative research', *Management International Review*, vol. 37, no. 1, 71–96.

Cavusgil, S.Tamer and Erdener Kaynak (1984) 'Critical issues in the cross-cultural measurement of consumer dissatisfaction: developed versus LDC practices', in Erdener Kaynak and Ronald Savitt (eds), *Comparative Marketing Systems*, New York: Praeger, 114–30.

Cavusgil, S.Tamer and Tiger Li (1992) *International Marketing: An Annotated Bibliography*. Chicago: American Marketing Association.

Chandy, P.R. and Thomas G.E. Williams, (1994) 'The impact of journals and authors on international business research: a citational analysis of *JIBS* articles', *Journal of International Business Studies*, vol. 25, no. 4, 715–28.

Chang, Chan-Sup (1989) 'Comparative analysis of management systems: Korea, Japan and the United States', in Dong Ki Kim and Lin-su Kim (eds), *Management Behind Industrialization: Readings in Korean Business*, Seoul: Korea University Press, 231–71.

Chapman, Malcolm (1992) 'Social anthropology and international business – some suggestions', paper presented at the Conference of the Academy of International Business, 20–22 November.

Chen, Chao C. (1995) 'New trends in reward allocation preferences: a Sino–U.S. comparison', *Academy of Management Review*, vol. 16, no. 3, 398–428.

Cheng, Joseph L.C. (1994) 'On the concept of universal knowledge in organizational science: implications for cross-national research', *Management Science*, vol. 40, no. 1, 162–8.

Cheng, Joseph L.C. (1996) 'Cross-national project teams: towards a task-contingency model', in Betty Jane Punnett and Oded Shenkar (eds), *Handbook for International Management Research*, Cambridge, MA: Blackwell, 507–20.

Chinese Culture Connection (1987) 'Chinese values and the search for culture-free dimensions of culture', *Journal of Cross-Cultural Psychology*, vol. 18 no. 2, 143–61.

Choi, C.J. (1994) 'Contract enforcement across cultures', *Organization Studies*, vol. 15, 673–82.

Chonko, Lawrence B., Ben M. Enis and John F. Tanner (1992) *Managing Sales People*, Boston, MA: Allyn and Bacon.

Chun, K.T., J.B. Campbell and J. Hao (1974) 'Extreme response style in cross-cultural research: a reminder', *Journal of Cross-Cultural Psychology*, vol. 5, 464–80.

Churchill, G.A. Jr (1979) 'A paradigm for developing better measures of marketing constructs', *Journal of Marketing Research*, vol. 16, 64–73.

Clark, Terry (1990) 'International marketing and national character: a review and proposal for an integrative theory', *Journal of Marketing*, October, 66–79.

Cooper, Cary L. and Charles L. Cox (1989) 'Applying American organizational sciences in Europe and the United Kingdom', in Chimezie A.B. Osigweh, Yg. (eds), *Organizational Science Abroad: Constraints and Perspectives*, New York: Plenum Press, 57–65.

Copeland, Lennie and Lewis Griggs (1985) *Going International: How to Make Friends and Deal Effectively in the Global Marketplace*, New York: Random House.

Cushner, Kenneth (1989) 'Assessing the impact of a culture-general assimilator', *International Journal of Intercultural Relations*, vol. 13, no. 2, 125–46.

Dadfar, Hossein and Peter Gustavsson (1992) 'Competition by effective management of cultural diversity: the case of international construction projects', *International Studies of Management and Organization*, vol. 22, no. 4, 81–92.

D'Andrade, Roy G. (1987) 'A folk model of the mind', in Dorothy Quinn and Naomi Holland (eds), *Cultural Models in Language and Thought*, Cambridge: Cambridge University Press, 112–48.

David, K.H. (1976) 'The use of social learning theory in preventing intercultural adjustment problems', in P. Pedersen, W.J. Lonner and J.G. Draguns (eds), *Counseling Across Cultures*, Honolulu, HI: University Press of Hawaii, 123–38.

Davis, H.L., S.P. Douglas and A.J. Silk (1981) 'Measure unreliability: a hidden threat to cross-national research?', *American Marketing Association Attitude Research Conference*, March, Carlsbad, CA, 1–40.

Dawson, Scott and Dave Dickinson (1988) 'Conducting international mail surveys:

the effect of incentives on response rates with an industry population', *Journal of International Business Studies*, vol. 19, no. 3, 491–6.

De Mente, Boye (1990) *How to Do Business with the Japanese*, Chicago, IL: NTC Books.

Denis, Jean-Emile and Jean-Claude Usunier (1995) 'Integrating the cultural dimension into international marketing', *Proceedings of the Second Conference on the Cultural Dimension of International Marketing*, Odense, 1–23.

Derr, C. Brooklyn and André Laurent (1989) 'The internal and external career: a theoretical and cross-cultural perspective', in M.B. Arthur, D.T. Hall and B.S. Lawrence (eds), *Handbook of Career Theory*, Cambridge: Cambridge University Press.

Deshpande, Satish P. and Chockalingam Viswesvaran (1992) 'Is cross-cultural training of expatriate managers effective? a meta analysis', *International Journal of Intercultural Relations*, vol. 16, no. 3, 295–310.

Deutscher, Irwin (1966) 'Words and deeds: social science and social policy', *Social Problems*, vol. 13, no. 3, 235–54.

Deutscher, I. (1973) 'Asking questions cross culturally: some problems of linguistic comparability', in Donald P. Warwick and Samuel Osherson (eds), *Comparative Research Methods*, Englewood Cliffs, NJ: Prentice-Hall, 163–86.

Dholakia, Ruby Roy, Mohammed Sharif and Labdhi Bhandari (1988) 'Consumption in the third world: challenges for marketing and economic development', in E. Kumçu and A. Fuat Firat (eds), *Marketing and Development: Toward Broader Dimensions*, Greenwich, CT: JAI Press, 129–47.

D'Iribarne Philippe (1989) *La Logique de l'Honneur*, Paris: Le Seuil.

Dorfman, Peter W. (1996) 'International and cross-cultural leadership', in Betty Jane Punnett and Oded Shenkar (eds), *Handbook for International Management Research*, Cambridge, MA: Blackwell, 267–349.

Dorfman, Peter W. and Jon P. Howell (1988) 'Dimensions of national culture and effective leadership patterns: Hofstede revisited', *Advances in International Comparative Management*, Vol. 3, Greenwich, CT: JAI Press, 127–50.

Douglas, Susan P. and C. Samuel Craig (1983) *International Marketing Research*, Englewood Cliffs, NJ: Prentice-Hall.

Douglas, Susan P. and C.S. Craig (1984) 'Establishing equivalence in comparative consumer research', in Erdener Kaynak and Ronald Savitt (eds), *Comparative Marketing Systems*, New York: Praeger, 93–113.

Douglas, Susan P. and Robert Shoemaker (1981) 'Item non-response in cross-national surveys', *European Research*, vol. 9, 124–32.

Doupnik, Timothy S. and Stephen B. Salter (1995) 'External environment, culture and accounting practice: a preliminary test of a general model of international accounting development', *The International Journal of Accounting*, vol. 30, 189–207.

Dubinsky, Alan J., Ronald E. Michaels, Masaaki Kotabe, Chaelin Lim and Hee-Chal Moon (1992) 'Influence of role stress on industrial salespeople's work outcomes in the United States, Japan and Korea', *Journal of International Business Studies*, vol. 23, no. 1, 77–99.

Dunbar, E. and Katcher, A. (1990) 'Supporting the international manager: responding to the myths of expatriation', *Training and Development Journal*, vol. 44, no. 9, 45–8.

Dunning, John H. (1980) 'Towards an eclectic theory of international production: some empirical tests', *Journal of International Business Studies*, vol. 11, no. 1, 9–31.

Dunning, John H. (1988) 'The eclectic paradigm of international production: A restatement and some possible extensions', *Journal of International Business Studies*, vol. 19, no. 1, 1–31.

Dunning, John H. (1989) 'The study of international business: a plea for a more inter-disciplinary approach', *Journal of International Business Studies*, vol. 20, no. 3, 411–36.

Durvasula, Srinivas, J. Craig Andrews, Steven Lysonsky and Richard G. Netemeyer (1995) 'Assessing the cross-national applicability of consumer behavior models: a model of attitude toward advertising in general', *Journal of Consumer Research*, vol. 19, 626–36.

Dyer, W. Gibb Jr and Alan L. Wilkins (1991) 'Better stories, not better constructs, to generate better theory: a rejoinder to Eisenhardt', *Academy of Management Review*, vol. 16, no. 3, 613–19.

Earley, P. Christopher and Harbir Singh (1995) 'International and intercultural man-agement research: what's next?', *Academy of Management Journal*, vol. 38, no. 2, 327–40.

Easterby-Smith, Mark and Danusia Malina (1997) 'International comparative research: towards a reflexive methodology', paper under review with *Academy of Management Journal*.

Eisenhardt, Kathleen M. (1989) 'Building theories from case study research', *Academy of Management Review*, vol. 14, 532–50.

Eisenhardt, Kathleen M. (1991) 'Better stories and better constructs: the case for rigor and comparative logic', *Academy of Management Review*, vol. 16, no. 3, 620–27.

El Haddad, Awad B. (1985) 'An analysis of the current status of marketing in the Middle East', in Erdener Kaynak (ed.), *International Business in the Middle East*, New York: De Gruyter, 177–97.

Englander, T., K. Farago, P. Slovic and B. Fischhoff (1986) 'A comparative analysis of risk perception in Hungary and the United States', *Social Behavior*, vol. 1, 55–66.

Erikson, Erik (1950) *Childhood and Society*, New York: Norton.

Farley, John U. and Donald R. Lehmann (1994) 'Cross-national "laws" and differ-ences in market response', *Management Science*, vol. 40, no. 1, 111–22.

Farmer R.N. and B.M. Richman (1965) *Comparative Management and Economic Progress*, Homewood, IL: Irwin.

Faucheux, Claude (1976) 'Cross-cultural research in experimental social psychol-ogy', *European Journal of Social Psychology*, vol. 6, no. 3, 269–322.

Faucheux, Claude and Jacques Rojot (1978) 'Social psychology and industrial rela-tions: a cross-cultural perspective', in G.M. Stephenson and C.J. Brotherton (eds), *Industrial Relations: A Social-Psychological Approach*, New York: John Wiley, 33–49.

Fayol, Henri (1970 [1916]) *Administration Industrielle et Générale*, Paris: Dunod.

Ferraro, Gary P. (1990) *The Cultural Dimension of International Business*, Englewood Cliffs, NJ: Prentice-Hall.

Firat, A. Fuat (1995) 'Consumer culture or culture consumed,' in Janeen Arnold Costa and Gary J. Bamossy (eds), *Marketing in a Multicultural World*, Thousand Oaks, CA: Sage, 105–25.

Fischer, George W., M. Granger Morgan, Baruch Fischhoff, Indira Nair and Lester B. Lave (1991) 'What risks are people concerned about?', *Risk Analysis*, vol. 11, no. 2, 303–14.

Fisher, Glen (1980) *International Negotiation: A Cross-Cultural Perspective*, Yarmouth, ME: Intercultural Press.

Fisher, Glen (1988) *Mindsets*, Yarmouth, ME: Intercultural Press.

Foo, Check-Teck (1992) 'Culture, productivity and structure. A Singapore study', *Organization Studies*, vol. 13, no. 4, 589–609.

Frijda, N. and G. Jahoda (1966) 'On the scope and methods of cross-cultural research', *International Journal of Psychology*, vol. 1, no. 2, 109–27.

Furnham, Adrian, Bruce D. Kirkcaldy and Richard Lynn (1994) 'National attitudes to competitiveness, money, and work among young people: first, second, and third world differences', *Human Relations*, vol. 47, no. 1, 119–32.

Galtung, Johan (1981) 'Structure, culture and intellectual style: an essay comparing Saxonic, Teutonic, Gallic and Nipponic approaches', *Social Science Information*, vol. 20, no. 6, 817–56.

Galtung, Johan (1990) 'Cultural violence', *Journal of Peace Research*, vol. 27, no. 3, 291–305.

Gans, Herbert (1962) *The Urban Villagers*, New York: Free Press.

Gauthey, Franck and Dominique Xardel (1990) *Le Management Intercuturel*, PUF, Collection 'Que Sais-Je?': Paris.

Geertz, Clifford (1983) *Local Knowledge*, New York: Basic Books.

Ghauri, Pervez N. and Jean-Claude Usunier (1996) *International Business Negotiations*, Oxford: Pergamon/Elsevier Science.

Glenn, E. (1981) *Man and Mankind: Conflict and Communication Between Cultures*, Norwood, NJ: Ablex.

Goffman, Erving (1974) *Relations in Public*, New York: Harper & Row.

Goldman, Alan (1994) 'The centrality of "Ningensei" to Japanese negotiating and interpersonal relationships: implications for US–Japanese communication', *International Journal of Intercultural Relations*, vol. 18, no. 1, 29–54.

Goodenough, Ward H. (1971) *Culture, Language and Society*, Reading, MA: Addison-Wesley.

Goodyear, Mary (1982) 'Qualitative research in developing countries', *Journal of The Market Research Society*, vol. 24, no. 2, 86–96.

Goszczynska, Maryla, Tadeusz Ryszka and Paul Slovic (1991) 'Risk perception in Poland: a comparison with three other countries', *Journal of Behavioral Decision Making*, vol. 4, 179–93.

Graham, John L. (1985) 'Cross-cultural marketing negotiations: a laboratory experiment', *Marketing Science*, vol. 4, no. 2, 130–46.

Graham, John L. (1993) 'Business negotiations: generalisations about Latin America and East Asia are dangerous', *UCINSIGHT*, 6–23.

Graham, John L. (1996) 'Vis-à-vis international business negotiations', in Pervez Ghauri and Jean-Claude Usunier (eds), *International Business Negotiations*, Oxford: Pergamon/Elsevier Science, 69–90.

Graham, J.L., A.T. Mintu and W. Rodgers (1994) 'Explorations of negotiation behaviours in ten foreign cultures using a model developed in the United States', *Management Science*, vol. 40, no. 1, 72–95.

Gray, S.J. (1988) 'Towards a theory of cultural influence on the development of accounting systems internationally', *Abacus*, vol. 3, 1–15.

Gruère, Jean-Pierre (1990) 'Réflexions d'un Français sur l'application de méthodes pédagogiques américaines dans un contexte latin', *Intercultures*, no. 10, 13–20.

Grunert, Suzanne C. and Thomas E. Muller (1996) 'Measuring values in international settings: are respondents thinking "real" life or "ideal" life?', *Journal of International Consumer Marketing*, vol. 8, no. 3/4, 169–85.

Grunert, Suzanne C., Klaus G. Grunert and Kai Kristensen (1993) 'Une méthode d'estimation de la validité interculturelle des instruments de mesure: le cas de la mesure des valeurs des consommateurs par la liste des valeurs LOV', *Recherche et Applications en Marketing*, vol. 8, no. 4, 5–28.

Ha, Francis Inki (1995) 'Shame in Asian and Western cultures', *American, Behavioral Scientist*, vol. 38, no. 8, 1114–31.

Haire M., E.E. Ghiselli and L.W. Porter (1966) *Managerial Thinking: An International Study*, New York: John Wiley.

Hall, Edward T. (1959) *The Silent Language*, New York: Doubleday.

Hall, Edward T. (1960) 'The silent language in overseas business', *Harvard Business Review*, 87–96.

Hall, Edward T. (1966) *The Hidden Dimension*, New-York: Doubleday.

Hall, Edward T. (1976) *Beyond Culture*, New York: Doubleday.

Hall, Edward T. (1983) *The Dance of Life*, New York: Anchor Press/Doubleday.

Hampden-Turner, Charles (1991) *Charting the Corporate Mind*, Oxford: Blackwell.

Han, C. Min (1988), 'The role of consumer patriotism in the choice of domestic versus foreign products', *Journal of Advertising Research*, June–July, 25–32.

Harbison, F. and C.A. Myers (1959) *Management in the Industrial World*, New York: McGraw-Hill.

Harnett, Donald L. and L.L. Cummings (1980) *Bargaining Behavior: An International Study*, Houston, TX: Dame Publications.

Hay, Michael and Jean-Claude Usunier (1993) 'Time and strategic action: a cross-cultural view', *Time & Society*, vol. 2, no. 3, 313–33.

Hayashi, Shuji (1988) *Culture and Management in Japan*, Tokyo: University of Tokyo Press.

Hayek, F.A. (1978) *The Pretence of Knowledge*, Chicago: University of Chicago Press.

Herskovits, Melville J. (1952) *Economic Anthropology*, New York: Alfred A. Knopf.

Hill, John S., Richard R. Still and Ünal O. Boya (1991) 'Managing the multinational sales force', *International Marketing Review*, vol. 8, no. 1, 19–31.

Hirschmann, Elisabeth C. (1985) 'Primitive aspects of consumption in modern American society', *Journal of Consumer Research*, vol. 12, 142–54.

Hirschmann, Elisabeth C. (1986) 'Humanistic inquiry in marketing research: philosophy, method and criteria', *Journal of Marketing Research*, vol. 13, 237–49.

Hofstede, Geert (1968) *The Game of Budget Control*, London: Tavistock .

Hofstede Geert (1980a) *Culture's Consequences: International Differences in Work Related Values*, Beverly Hills, CA: Sage.

Hofstede, Geert (1980b) 'Motivation, leadership and organization: do American theories apply abroad?', *Organizational Dynamics*, Summer, 42–63.

Hofstede, Geert (1983) 'National cultures in four dimensions: a research-based theory of cultural differences among nations', *International Studies of Management and Organization*, vol. 12, nos. 1–2, 46–74.

Hofstede, Geert (1991) *Culture and Organizations: Software of the Mind*, Maidenhead: McGraw-Hill.

Hofstede, Geert (1994a) 'Management scientists are human', *Management Science*, vol. 40, no. 1, 4–13.

Hofstede, Geert (1994b) 'The business of international business is culture', *International Business Review*, vol. 3, no. 1, 1–14.

Hofstede, Geert (1995) 'Multilevel research of human systems: flowers, bouquets and gardens', *Human Systems Management*, vol. 14, 207–17.

Hoftsede, Geert and Michael Harris Bond (1984) 'Hoftsede's cultural dimensions: an independent validation using Rokeach's value survey', *Journal of Cross-Cultural Psychology*, vol. 15, no. 4, 417–33.

Hoftsede, Geert and Michael Harris Bond (1988) 'The Confucius connection: from cultural roots to economic growth', *Organizational Dynamics*, vol. 16, no. 4, 4–21.

Holtgrave, David R. and Elke U. Weber (1993) 'Dimensions of risk perception for financial and health risks', *Risk Analysis*, vol. 13, no. 5, 553–8.

Hovden, Jan and Tore J. Larsson (1987) 'Risk: culture and concepts', in W.T. Singleton and J. Hovden (eds), *Risks and Decisions*, New York: John Wiley, 47–59.

Hubbard, Raymond and J. Scott Armstrong (1994) 'Replications and extensions in marketing: rarely published but quite contrary', *International Journal of Research in Marketing*, vol. 11, no. 3, 233–48.

Ichikawa, Akira (1993) 'Leadership as a form of culture: its present and future states in Japan', *International Review of Strategic Management*, vol. 4, 155–70.

Inkeles, Alex and Daniel J. Levinson (1969) 'National character: the study of modal personality and sociocultural systems', in Gardner Lindzey and Elliot Aronson (eds), *Handbook of Social Psychology*, Vol. 4, Reading, MA: Addison-Wesley, 418–506.

Inkpen, Andrew and Paul Beamish (1994) 'An analysis of twenty five years of research in the Journal of International Business Studies', *Journal of International Business Studies*, vol. 25, no. 4, 703–14.

Jaeger, Alfred M. (1983) 'The transfer of organizational culture overseas: an approach to control in the multinational corporation', *Journal of International Business Studies*, vol. 14, 91–114.

Jobber, David and John Saunders (1988) 'An experimental investigation into cross-national mail survey response rates', *Journal of International Business Studies*, vol. 19, no. 3, 483–9.

Johanson, J. and J.E. Vahlne (1977) 'The internationalisation process of the firm: a model of knowledge development and increased market commitments', *Journal of International Business Studies*, vol. 8, no. 1, 23–32.

Johansson, Johny K. and Ikujiro Nonaka (1987) 'Market research the Japanese way', *Harvard Business Review*, 16–22.

Johansson, Johny K. and Ikujiro Nonaka (1996) *Relentless: The Japanese Way of Marketing*, New York: HarperCollins.

Jones, Michael John and Yusuf Karbhari (1996) 'Auditors' reports: a six country comparison', in Timothy S. Doupnik and Stephen B. Salter (eds), *Advances in International Accounting*, Greenwich, CT: JAI Press, 129–155.

Jöreskog, Karl G. and Dag Sörbom (1993) *Lisrel 8, User's Guide*, Chicago, IL, Scientific Software International.

Kahle, Lynn R., Sharon E. Beatty and Pamela Homer (1986) 'Alternative measurement approaches to consumer values: the list of values (LOV) and values and lifestyles (VALS), *Journal of Consumer Research*, vol. 13, 405–9.

Kale, Sudhir H. and Roger P. McIntyre (1991) 'Distribution channel relationships in diverse cultures', *International Marketing Review*, vol. 8, no. 3, 31–45.

Kantor, Jeffrey, Clare B. Roberts and Stephen B. Salter (1995) 'Financial reporting practices in selected Arab countries: an empirical study of Egypt, Saudi Arabia and the United Arab Emirates', *International Studies of Management and Organization*, vol. 25, no. 3, 31–50.

Kanungo, Rabindra N. and Richard W. Wright (1983) 'A cross-cultural comparative study of managerial job attitudes', *Journal of International Business Studies*, vol. 14, 115–29.

Karpowicz-Lazreg, C. and E. Mullet (1993) 'Societal risk as seen by the French public', *Risk Analysis*, vol. 13, no. 3, 253–8.

Kawabuko, Michiko (1987) 'Organizational control and commitment: a study of Japanese employees in retail industry', in Charles F. Keown and Arch G. Woodside (eds), *Proceedings of the Second Symposium on Cross-Cultural Consumer and Business Studies*, University of Hawaii, 104–7.

Kelley, Harold H. (1966) 'A classroom study of the dilemmas in interpersonal negotiations', in K. Archibald (ed.), *Strategic Interaction and Conflict*, Berkeley, CA:
Institute of International Studies, University of California.

Kelley, Lane and Reginald Worthley (1981) 'The role of culture in comparative management: a cross-cultural perspective', *Academy of Management Review*, vol. 24, no.
1, 164–73.

Kelley, Lane, Arthur Whatley and Reginald Worthley (1987) 'Assessing the effect of
culture on managerial attitudes: a three culture test', *Journal of International
Business Studies*, vol. 18, no. 2, 17–31.

Keown, Charles F. (1985) 'Foreign mail surveys: response rates using monetary incentives', *Journal of International Business Studies*, vol. 16, 151–3.

Kleinhesselink, Randall R. and Eugene A. Rosa (1991) 'Cognitive representations of
risk perceptions: a comparison of Japan and the United States', *Journal of Cross-
Cultural Psychology*, vol. 22, no. 1, 11–28.

Kluckhohn, Florence R. and Frederick L. Strodtbeck (1961) *Variations in Value
Orientations*, Westport, CT: Greenwood Press.

Knauber, Ines, Barbara C. Garland and John C. Crawford (1993) 'Factors influencing
the questionnaire design of cross-cultural studies: a content analysis of voluntary
comments', in Kenneth D. Bahn and M. Joseph Sirgy (eds), *World Marketing
Congress*, Blacksburg, VA: Academy of Marketing Science, 112–14.

Kogut, Bruce and Harbir Singh (1988) 'The effect of national culture on the choice of
entry mode', *Journal of International Business Studies*, vol. 19, no. 3, 411–32.

Kopytoff, Igor (1986) 'The cultural biography of things: commoditization as process',
in Arjun Appadurai (ed.), *The Social Life of Things, Commodities in Cultural
Perspective*, Cambridge: Cambridge University Press, 64–91.

Kotler, Philip (1994) *Marketing Management*, 8th edn, Englewood Cliffs, NJ: Prentice-
Hall.

Koza, Mitchell P. and Jean-Claude Thoenig (1995) 'Organizational theory at the cross-
roads: some reflections on European and United States approaches to
organizational research', *Organization Science*, vol. 6, no. 1, 1–8.

Kozan, M. Kamil (1993) 'Culture and industrialization level influences on leadership
attitudes for Turkish managers', *International Studies of Management and
Organization*, vol. 23, no. 3, 7–17.

Kracmar, J.Z. (1971) *Marketing Research in Developing Countries: A Handbook*, New
York: Praeger.

Kushner, J.M. (1982) 'Market research in a non-western context: the Asian example',
Journal of the Market Research Society, vol. 24, no. 2, 116–22.

Lachman, Ran, Albert Nedd and Bob Hinings (1994) 'Analyzing cross-national management and organization: a theoretical framework', *Management Science*, vol. 40,
no. 1, 40–55.

Langenscheidt (1989) *German–English/English–German Dictionary*, New York: Pocket
Books.

Laurent, André (1983) 'The cultural diversity of western conceptions of management', *International Studies of Management and Organization*, vol. 12, nos. 1–2,
75–96.

Lawler, E.E. (1973) *Motivation in Work Organizations*, Belmont, CA: Wadsworth.

Lazer, William, Shoji Murata and Hiroshi Kosaka (1985) 'Japanese marketing:
towards a better understanding', *Journal of Marketing*, vol. 49,69–81.

Lee, James A. (1966) 'Cultural analysis in overseas operations', *Harvard Business
Review*, March–April, 106–11.

Le Robert et Collins (1993) *Dictionnaire Français–Anglais/Anglais–Français*, Glasgow: HarperCollins.

Lessem, Ronnie and Fred Neubauer (1994) *European Management Systems*, Maidenhead: McGraw-Hill.

Leung, Kenneth (1989) 'Cross-cultural differences: individual level vs culture-level analysis', *International Journal of Psychology*, vol. 24, 703–19.

Leung, Kenneth and Michael Harris Bond (1989) 'On the empirical identification of dimensions for cross-cultural comparison', *Journal of Cross-Cultural Psychology*, vol. 20, 133–51.

Levine, Robert A. and Donald T. Campbell (1972) *Ethnocentrism: Theories of Conflicts, Ethnic Attitudes, and Group Behavior*, New York: John Wiley.

Levine, Robert V. (1988) 'The pace of life across cultures', in Joseph E. McGrath (ed.), *The Social Psychology of Time*, Newbury Park, CA: Sage, 39–60.

Levi-Strauss, Claude (1974) *Anthropologie Structurale*, Paris: Plon.

Levitt, Theodore (1983) 'The globalization of markets', *Harvard Business Review*, vol. 61, 92–102.

Lincoln, James R. and Arne L. Kalleberg (1985) 'Work organization and workforce commitment: a study of plants and employees in the U.S. and Japan', *American Sociological Review*, vol. 50, 738–60.

Lincoln, Yvonna S. and Egon G. Guba (1986) *Naturalistic Inquiry*, London: Sage.

Linton, Ralph (1945) *The Cultural Background of Personality*, New York: Appleton-Century.

Loss, M. (1983) *Culture Shock: Dealing with Stress in Cross-Cultural Living*, Winona Lake, IN: Light and Life Press.

McCracken, Grant (1991) 'Culture and consumer behaviour: an anthropological perspective', *Journal of the Market Research Society*, vol. 32, no. 1, 3–11.

McDaniels, Timothy L. and Robin S. Gregory (1991) 'A framework for structuring cross-cultural research in risk and decision making', *Journal of Cross-Cultural Psychology*, vol. 22, no. 1, 103–28.

McGrath, Rita Gunther and Ian MacMillan (1992) 'More like each other than anyone else? A cross-cultural study of entrepreneurial perceptions', *Journal of Business Venturing*, vol. 7, 419–29.

McGregor, D. (1960) *The Human Side of Enterprise*, New York: McGraw-Hill.

Marchand, Olivier (1993) 'An international comparison of working times', *Futures*, June, 502–10.

Marshall, Roger, Jane Xin Mao and Christine Kwai Choi Lee (1995) 'A cross-cultural, between-gender study differences in the consumption and appreciation of late 19th century art', in Scott M. Smith, (ed.), *Proceedings of the Fifth Symposium on Cross-Cultural Consumer and Business Studies*, Provo, UT: Brigham Young University, 221–30.

Maruyama, Magoroh (1990) 'International meta-marketing: strategic judo, foreign user habits and interactive invention', *Human Systems Management*, vol. 9, 29–42.

Maslow, Abraham H. (1954) *Motivation and Personality*, New York: Harper and Row.

Matsumoto, M. (1988) *The Unspoken Way: Haragei – Silence in Japanese Business and Society*, New York: Kodansha International.

Mattson, Melvin R., Esmail Salehi-Sangari and Hooshang M. Beheshti (1993) 'A comparative study of decision making in the business acquisition process', in Gerard Albaum et al. (eds), *Proceedings of the Fourth Symposium on Cross-Cultural Consumer and Business Studies*, University of Hawaii, 267–71.

Mayer, C.S. (1978) 'Multinational marketing research: the magnifying glass of methodological problems', *European Research*, March, 77–84.

M'biti, John (1968) 'African concept of time', *Africa Theological Journal*, vol. 1, 8–20.

Mead, Margaret (1948) *Male and Female*, New York: William Morrow.

Mendenhall, Mark E., Edward Dunbar and Gary R. Oddou (1987) 'Expatriate selection, training and career-pathing', *Human Resource Management*, vol. 26, no. 3, 331–45.

Mendenhall, Mark E., D. Beaty and Gary R. Oddou (1993) 'Where have all the theories gone? An archival review of the international management literature', *International Journal of Management*, vol. 10, no. 2, 146–53.

Misumi, J. and Mark F. Peterson (1985) 'The performance–maintenance (PM) theory of leadership: review of a Japanese research program', *Administrative Science Quarterly*, vol. 30, 196–223.

Montesquieu, Charles de (1721) *Persian Letters*, Penguin Classics edn 1973, London: Penguin.

Morris, Tom and Cynthia Pavett (1993) 'Do cultural differences affect management and productivity?', in Vitor Corado-Simoes (ed.), *Proceedings of the 19th Annual EIBA Conference*, Lisbon December, vol. 1, 215–32.

Moscovici, Serge (1976) *Social Influence and Social Change*, London: Academic Press.

Mullen, Michael R. (1995) 'Diagnosing measurement equivalence in cross-national research', *Journal of International Business Studies*, vol. 26, no. 3, 573–96.

Myrdal, Gunnar (1968) *Asian Drama, an Enquiry into the Poverty of Nations*, New York: Pantheon.

Nakane, Chie (1973) *Japanese Society*, New York: Penguin.

Nath, Raghu (1968) 'A methodological review of cross-cultural management research', *International Social Science Journal*, vol. 20, no. 1, 35–62.

Nath, Raghu (1988) *Comparative Management*, Cambridge: Ballinger.

Neghandi, Anant R. (1983) 'Cross-national management research: trends and future directions', *Journal of International Business Studies*, vol. 14, 17–28.

Neghandi, Anant, R. and S. Benjamin Prasad (1971) *Comparative Management*, New York: Appleton-Century-Crofts.

Nehrt, Lee C., J. Frederick Truitt and Richard W. Wright (1970) *International Business Research: Past, Present and Future*, Bloomington, IN: Indiana University Bureau of Business Research.

Netemeyer, Richard G., Srinivas Durvasula and Donald R. Lichtenstein (1991) 'A cross-national assessment of the reliability and validity of the CETSCALE', *Journal of Marketing Research*, vol. 28, 320–7.

Nunnally, Jum (1978) *Psychometric Theory*, New York: McGraw-Hill.

Oberg, K. (1972) 'Culture shock and the problem of adjustment to new cultural environments', in D. Hoopes (ed.), *Readings in Intercultural Communications*, Pittsburgh, PA: Pittsburgh Intercultural Communications Network of the Regional Council for International Education.

Ogilvie, Robert and Celeste Wilderom (1993) 'Management made in Germany', paper presented at the Conference on Intercultural Cooperation in Europe marking the retirement of Geert Hofstede, Maastricht, October.

Okazali-Luff, Kazuko (1991) 'On the adjustment of Japanese sojourners: beliefs, contentions and empirical findings', *International Journal of Intercultural Relations*, vol. 15, 85–102.

Osigweh, Chimezie A.B., Yg. (1989) 'The myth of universality in transnational organizational science', in Chimezie A.B. Osigweh, Yg. (ed.), *Organizational Science Abroad: Constraints and Perspectives*, New York: Plenum Press, 2–26.

Ouchi, William G. (1981) *Theory Z*, New York: Addison Wesley/Avon Books.

Parameswaran, Ravi and Attila Yaprak (1987) 'A cross-national comparison of consumer research measures', *Journal of International Business Studies*, Spring, 35–49.

Parkhe, Arvind (1993) '"Messy research", methodological predispositions, and theory development in international joint ventures', *Academy of Management Review*, vol. 18, no. 2, 227–68.

Parkhe, Arvind (1996) 'International joint ventures', in Betty Jane Punnett and Oded Shenkar (eds), *Handbook for International Management Research*, Cambridge, MA: Blackwell, 429–59.

Pascale, R.T. and R. Athos (1981) *The Art of Japanese Management*, New York: Simon and Schuster.

Peng, T.K., Mark F. Peterson and Yuh-Ping Shyi (1991) 'Quantitative methods in cross-national management research: trends and equivalence issues', *Journal of Organizational Behavior*, vol. 12, 87–107.

Peng, T.K. and Mark F. Peterson (1998) 'Contingent and noncontingent social rewards and punishments from leaders: do US and Japanese subordinates make comparable distinctions?', *International Business Review*, vol. 8, no. 1.

Peterson, Mark F., Peter B. Smith and collaborators (1995) 'Role conflict, ambiguity, and overload: a 21–nation study', *Academy of Management Journal*, vol. 38, no. 2, 429–52.

Peterson, Robert A., Dana L. Alden, Mustapha O. Attir and Alain J.P. Jolibert (1988) 'Husband–wife report disagreement', *International Journal of Research in Marketing*, vol. 5, no. 2, 125–36.

Peterson, Robert A. and Alain Jolibert (1976) 'A cross-national investigation of price and brand as determinants of perceived product quality', *Journal of Applied Psychology*, vol. 61, 533–6.

Petit, Karl (1960) *Dictionnaire des Citations*, Verviers: Marabout.

Pike, K. (1966) *Language in Relation To a Unified Theory of the Structure of Human Behavior*, The Hague: Mouton.

Polonky, Michael Jay, Sören Askegaard, Pandora L. Patton, David K. Tse and Ryh-Song Yeh (1995) 'Cross-cultural data analysis: some issues and potential solutions', in Scott M. Smith (ed.), *Proceedings of the Fifth Symposium on Cross-Cultural Consumer and Business Studies*, Provo, UT: Brigham Young University, 106–13.

Poortinga, Ype H. (1989) 'Equivalence in cross-cultural data: an overview of basic issues', *International Journal of Psychology*, vol. 24, 737–56.

Pras, B. and R. Angelmar (1978) 'Verbal rating scales for multinational research', *European Research*, March, 62–7.

Prasad, S. Benjamin and David A. Sprague (1996) 'Is TQM a global paradigm?', in S. Benjamin Prasad (ed.), *Advances in International Comparative Management*, Vol. 11, Greenwich, CT: JAI Press, 69–85.

Punnett, Betty Jane and Oded Shenkar (1996) *Handbook for International Management Research*, Cambridge, MA: Blackwell.

Pye, Lucian (1986) 'The China trade: making the deal', *Harvard Business Review*, vol. 46, no. 4, 74–84.

Raimbault, Michel, Jean-Michel Saussois and Jean-Claude Usunier (1988) *Analyse des Systèmes d'Action Collective de Soutien à l'Exportation: Comparaison Internationale*, Paris: FNEGE-ESCP.

Rajan, Raghuram G. and Luigi Zingales (1995) 'What do we know about capital structure? Some evidence from international data', *The Journal of Finance*, vol. L, no. 5, 1421–60.

Razzouk, Nabil Y. and Lance A. Masters (1985) 'Cultural marginality in the Arab world: implications for western marketers', in Erdener Kaynak (ed.), *International Business in the Middle East*, Berlin, New York: De Gruyter, 151–9.

Reitsperger, Wolf D. and Shirley J. Daniel (1990) 'Japan vs. Silicon Valley: quality-cost trade-off philosophies', *Journal of International Business Studies*, vol. 21, no. 2, 289–300.

Richins, M. (1983) 'Negative word-of-mouth by dissatisfied consumers: a pilot study', *Journal of Marketing*, vol. 47, 68–78.

Richins, M. and B. Verhage (1985) 'Cross-cultural differences in consumer attitudes and their implications for complaint management', *International Journal of Research in Marketing*, vol. 2, 197–205.

Ritzer, George (1993) *The McDonaldization of Society*, Thousand Oaks: CA, Pine Forge Press.

Robertson, Roland (1992) *Globalization*, London: Sage.

Rodriguez, Carlos M. (1995) 'Relevancy, measurement and modeling of religiosity in consumer behavior: the case of Peru', in Gerard Albaum et al. (eds), *Proceedings of the Fourth Symposium on Cross-Cultural Consumer and Business Studies*, University of Hawaii, 279–85.

Rosenzweig, Philip M. (1994) 'When can management science research be generalized internationally?', *Management Science*, vol. 40, no. 1, 28–39.

Sakade, Florence (ed.) (1982) *A Guide to Reading and Writing Japanese*, Tokyo: Charles E. Tuttle.

Sapir, Edward (1929) 'The status of linguistics as a science', *Language*, vol. 5, 207–14.

Schneider-Lenné, E. (1993) 'The governance of good business', *Business Strategy Review*, vol. 4, no. 1, 75–85.

Sechrest, L., T. Fay and S.M. Zaidi (1972) 'Problems of translation in cross-cultural research', *Journal of Cross-Cultural Psychology*, vol. 3, no. 1, 41–56.

Sekaran, Uma (1983) 'Methodological and theoretical issues and advancements in cross-cultural research', *Journal of International Business Studies*, vol. 14, 61–73.

Seringhaus, F.H., Rolf and Guenther Botschen (1991) 'Cross-national comparison of export promotion services: the views of Canadian and Austrian companies', *Journal of International Business Studies*, vol. 22, no. 1, 115–33.

Shaari, Hamid, Russell Craig and Frank Clarke (1993) 'Religion a confounding cultural element in the international harmonization of accounting', *Abacus*, vol. 29, no. 2, 131–48.

Shenkar, Oded and Mary Ann Von Glinow (1994) 'Paradoxes of organizational theory and research: using the case of China to illustrate national contingency', *Management Science*, vol. 40, no. 1, 56–71.

Shimp, T.A. and S. Sharma (1987) 'Consumer ethnocentrism: construction and validation of the CETSCALE', *Journal of Marketing Research*, vol. 26, 280–9.

Simon, Paul (1980) *The Tongue Tied American* New York: Continuum Press.

Singelis, Theodore M., Harry C. Triandis, Dharml P.S. Bhawuk and Michele J. Gelfand (1995) 'Horizontal and vertical dimensions of individualism and collectivism: a theoretical and measurement refinement', *Cross-Cultural Research*, vol. 29, no. 3, 240–75.

Singh, Jagdip (1988) 'Consumer complaint intentions and behavior: definitions and taxonomical issues', *Journal of Marketing*, vol. 52, 93–107.

Singh, Jagdip (1995) 'Measurement issues in cross-national research', *Journal of International Business Studies*, vol. 26, no. 3, 597–620.

Slovic, Paul (1987) 'Perception of risk', *Science*, 236, 280–5.

Slovic, P., B. Fischhoff and S. Lichtenstein (1984) 'Behavioral decision theory perspectives on risks and safety', *Acta Psychologica*, vol. 56, 183–203.

Slovic, P., B. Fischhoff and S. Lichtenstein (1985) 'Characterizing perceived risk', in R.W. Kates, C. Hohenemser and J.X. Kasperson (eds), *Perilous Progress: Technology as Hazard*, Boulder, CO: Westview, 91–123.

Smith, Peter B. and Mark F. Peterson (1988) *Leadership, Organizations and Cultures: An Event Management Model*, London: Sage.

Smith, Peter B., Mark F. Peterson, Pierre-Henri François, Jorge Jesuino, Klarens Hofmann, Paul Koopman and Arja Ropo (1993) 'In search of the "Euro-Manager": convergences and divergences in event management', paper presented at the Conference on Intercultural Cooperation in Europe marking the retirement of Geert Hofstede, Maastricht, 30 September–1 October, CRICCOM Papers no. 8.

Smith, Peter B., Fons Trompenaars and Shaun Dugan (1995) 'The Rotter locus of control scale in 43 countries: a test of cultural relativity', *Journal of Cross-Cultural Psychology*, December, 377–400.

Snyder, Leslie B., Bartjan Willenborg and James Watt (1991) 'Advertising and cross-cultural convergence in Europe, 1953–1989', *European Journal of Communication*, vol. 6, 441–68.

Sondergaard, Michael (1994) 'Hofstede's consequences: a study of reviews, citations and replications', *Organization Studies*, vol. 15, 447–56.

Sood, James H. (1990) 'Equivalent measurement in international market research: is it really a problem?', *Journal of International Consumer Marketing*, vol. 2, no. 2, 25–41.

Stanton, J.L., R. Chandran and S. Hernandez (1982) 'Marketing research problems in Latin America', *Journal of the Market Research Society*, vol. 24, no. 2, 124–39.

Sullivan, Jeremiah and Ikujiro Nonaka (1988) 'Culture and strategic issue categorization theory', *Management International Review*, vol. 28, no. 3, 6–10.

Sullivan, Jeremiah and Richard B. Peterson (1981) 'The relationship between conflict resolution approaches and trust: a cross-cultural study', *Academy of Management Journal*, vol. 24, no. 4, 803–15.

Sullivan, Jeremiah and Richard B. Peterson (1988) 'Factors associated with trust in Japanese–American joint ventures', *Management International Review*, vol. 22, no. 2, 30–40.

Sumner, G.A. (1906) *Folk Ways*, New York: Ginn Custom Publishing.

Szpiro, Georges G. (1986) 'Relative risk aversion around the world', *Economic Letters*, vol. 20, 19–21.

Szpiro, Georges G. and Jean-François Outreville (1988) 'Relative risk aversion around the world: further results', *Studies in Banking and Finance*, vol. 6, 127–8.

Tangney, June Price (1995) 'Recent advances in the empirical study of shame and guilt', *American, Behavioral Scientist*, vol. 38, no. 8, 1132–45.

Teigen, K.H., W. Brun and P. Slovic (1988) 'Societal risks as seen by a Norwegian public', *Journal of Behavioral Decision Making*, vol. 1, 111–30.

Thomas, Anisya S. (1996) 'A call for research in forgotten locations', in Betty Jane Punnett and Oded Shenkar (eds), *Handbook for International Management Research*, Cambridge, MA: Blackwell, 485–506.

Thomas, Anisya, Oded Shenkar and Linda Clarke (1994) 'The globalization of our mental maps: evaluating the geographic scope of *JIBS* coverage', *Journal of International Business Studies*, vol. 25, no. 4, 675–86.

Triandis, Harry C. (1983) 'Dimensions of cultural variation as parameters of organizational theories', *International Studies of Management and Organization*, vol. 12, no. 4, 139–69.

Triandis, Harry C. (1994) *Culture and Social Behavior*, New York: McGraw-Hill.

Trompenaars, Fons (1981) 'The organization of meaning and the meaning of organi-zation', unpublished doctoral thesis, Wharton School, University of Pennsylvania.

Trompenaars, Fons (1993) *Riding the Waves of Culture*, London: Nicholas Brealey.

Tse, David K., Kam-hon Lee, Ilan Vertinsky and Donald A. Wehrung (1988) 'Does culture matter? A cross-cultural study of executives' choice, decisiveness, and risk adjustment in international marketing', *Journal of Marketing*, vol. 52, no. 4, 81–95.

Tuncalp, S. (1988) 'The marketing research scene in Saudi Arabia', *European Journal of Marketing*, vol. 22, no. 5, 15–22.

Tung, Rosalie L. (1981) 'Selection and training of personnel for overseas assign-ments', *Columbia Journal of World Business*, vol. 16, no. 1, 68–78.

Tung, Rosalie L. (1984a) 'Strategic management of human resources in the multina-tional enterprise', *Human Resource Management*, Summer, 129–43.

Tung, Rosalie L. (1984b) 'How to negotiate with the Japanese', *California Management Review*, vol. 26, no. 4, 62–77.

Tung, Rosalie L. (1996) 'Negotiating with East Asians', in Pervez N. Ghauri and Jean-Claude Usunier (eds), *International Business Negotiations*, Oxford: Pergamon/ Elsevier Science, 369–81.

Usunier, Jean-Claude (1991) 'Business time perceptions and national cultures: a com-parative survey', *Management International Review*, vol. 31, no. 3, 197–217.

Usunier, Jean-Claude (1996) *Marketing Across Cultures*, Hemel Hempstead: Prentice-Hall.

Van Herk, Hester and Theo M. Verhallen (1995) 'Equivalence in empirical interna-tional research in the food area', *Proceedings of the Second Conference on the Cultural Dimension of International Marketing*, Odense, 392–402.

Van Maanen, John and André Laurent (1992) 'The flow of culture: some notes on globalization and the multinational corporation', in S. Ghoshal and E. Westney (eds), *Organization Theory and the Multinational Corporation*, New York: St Martin's Press, 275–312.

Van Raaij, W.F. (1978) 'Cross-cultural methodology as a case of construct validity', in M.K. Hunt (ed.), *Advances in Consumer Research*, Ann Arbor, MI: Association for Consumer Research, 693–701.

Vernon, Raymond P. (1966) 'International investment and international trade in the product life cycle', *Quarterly Journal of Economics*, vol. 80, no. 2, 191–207.

Weber, Max (1958) *The Protestant Ethic and the Spirit of Capitalism*, New York: Charles Scribner's Sons.

Weber, Max (1970) *Essays in Sociology*, edited by H.H. Geerth and C.W. Mills. London: Routledge and Kegan Paul (original edition 1948).

Weeks, William H., Paul B. Pedersen and Richard W. Brislin (1987) *A Manual of Structured Experiences for Cross-Cultural Learning*, Yarmouth, ME: Intercultural Press.

Weis/Mattutat (1967) *Deutsch–Französisch/Französisch–Deutsch Wörterbuch*, Stuttgart: Ernst Klett Verlag.

Weiss, Stephen E. (1987) 'Creating the GM–Toyota joint venture: a case in complex negotiation', *Columbia Journal of World Business*, vol. 22, no. 2, 23–37.

Weiss, Stephen E. (1993) 'Analysis of complex negotiations in international busi-ness – the RBC perspective', *Organization Science*, vol. 4, no. 2, 269–300.

Weiss, Stephen E., (1996a) 'International negotiations: bricks, mortar, and prospects', in Betty Jane Punnett and Oded Shenkar (eds), *Handbook for International Management Research*, Cambridge, MA: Blackwell, 209–65.

Weiss, Stephen E. (1996b) 'The IBM–Mexico microcomputer investment negotiations', in Pervez N. Ghauri and Jean-Claude Usunier (eds), *International Business Negotiations*, Oxford: Pergamon/Elsevier Science, 305–34.

Whitehill, Arthur M. (1991) *Japanese Management: Tradition and Transition*, London: Routledge.

Wilk, Richard (1995) 'Real Belizean food: building local identity in the transnational Caribbean', *Proceedings of the Second Conference on the Cultural Dimension of International Marketing*, Odense, 372–91.

Wong, Nancy and Aaron Yahuvia (1995) 'From tofu to caviar: conspicuous consumption, materialism and self-concepts in east-Asian and western cultures', *Proceedings of the Second Conference on the Cultural Dimension of International Marketing*, Odense, 68–89.

Wright, Lorna L. (1996) 'Quantitative international management research', in Betty Jane Punnett and Oded Shenkar (eds), *Handbook for International Management Research*, Cambridge, MA: Blackwell, 63–81.

Wright, Richard W. and David A. Ricks (1994) 'Trends in international business research: twenty five years later', *Journal of International Business Studies*, vol. 25, no. 4, 687–702.

Yau, Oliver H.M. (1988) 'Chinese cultural values: their dimensions and marketing implications', *European Journal of Marketing*, vol. 22, no. 5, 44–57.

Yavas, Burhan F. and George A. Marcoulides (1996) 'An examination of cross-cultural quality management practices in American and Asian firms', in S. Benjamin Prasad (ed.), *Advances in International Comparative Management*, Vol. 11, Greenwich, CT: JAI Press, 51–67.

Zaharna, R.S. (1989) 'Self shock: the double-binding challenge of identity', *International Journal of Intercultural Relations*, vol. 13, no. 4, 501–26.

Zax, M. and S. Takashi (1967) 'Cultural influences on response style: comparison of Japanese and American college students', *Journal of Social Psychology*, vol. 71, 3–10.

Author Index

Subject Index